DISCARD

S0-CBF-108

709

④
11/92

THE
ONCE AND FUTURE
SUPERPOWER

THE
ONCE AND FUTURE
SUPERPOWER

How to Restore America's

Economic, Energy, and

Environmental Security

JOSEPH J. ROMM

William Morrow and Company, Inc.
New York

Copyright © 1992 by Joseph J. Romm

All rights reserved. No part of this book may be reproduced or utilized in any form or by any means, electronic or mechanical, including photocopying, recording, or by any information storage or retrieval system, without permission in writing from the Publisher. Inquiries should be addressed to Permissions Department, William Morrow and Company, Inc., 1350 Avenue of the Americas, New York, N.Y. 10019.

It is the policy of William Morrow and Company, Inc., and its imprints and affiliates, recognizing the importance of preserving what has been written, to print the books we publish on acid-free paper, and we exert our best efforts to that end.

Library of Congress Cataloging-in-Publication Data

Romm, Joseph J.
    The once and future superpower : how to restore America's economic, energy, and environmental security / Joseph J. Romm.
        p.   cm.
    ISBN 0-688-11868-2
    1. United States—Economic policy—1981   2. United States—Military policy.
    3. Environmental policy—United States.   4. Competition, International.
    5. United States—Foreign economic relations—Japan.   6. Japan—Foreign economic relations—United States.   I. Title.
    HC106.8.R64   1992
    338.973—dc20   92-7757
                                                                       CIP

Printed in the United States of America

First Edition

1   2   3   4   5   6   7   8   9   10

BOOK DESIGN BY PATRICE FODERO

To Colonel John Boyd

Acknowledgments

If this work presents a coherent worldview, it is in large part because I was fortunate enough to hear Colonel John Boyd deliver a brilliant series of lectures, "A Discourse on Winning and Losing." In a world of analysts, he is that rare breed—a synthesist. I had long hoped to write a book explaining the power of a "systems" approach to solving America's problems, and Colonel Boyd gave me an orientation, a paradigm for integrating information from several fields.

I first began thinking about environmental, energy, and economic security at the Rockefeller Foundation, as the president's assistant on International Security. I am grateful to Peter Goldmark for giving me the freedom to explore such nontraditional thinking.

This book derives in large part from the class, Rethinking National Security, which I taught in 1990 and 1991 at Columbia University's School of International and Public Affairs. I am indebted to Deans Robin Lewis and Steve Cohen for making the class possible, and to my students for challenging my views.

Special thanks go to the Council on Foreign Relations' "Project on America's Task in a Changed World" for supporting my work on new thinking about national security. I am particularly grateful to Gregory

Treverton and Pat Ramsay for their insightful comments on my writing, and to Paul Kennedy for chairing a workshop on my report for the Council, *Defining National Security*. I also thank the Greek Institute for International and Strategic Studies for sponsoring my work.

The innovative ideas emanating from Rocky Mountain Institute have inspired my thinking on energy issues for some time. My being surrounded by so many keen minds during the final stages of writing this book has made it better in countless ways. I am grateful to Amory Lovins, John Barnett, and Jennifer McCulloch for many stimulating discussions about nonmilitary security, and to Michael Shepard and David Houghton for their critiques of the energy analysis.

Subrata Chakravarty and James Michaels did remarkable editorial work in shortening an early version of the Introduction for *Forbes* magazine, which in turn inspired significant improvements in my final draft.

I am grateful to Dean Grodzins for helping me with the historical treatment of national security; to Tad Smith for sharing his knowledge of business and economics; to Hadi Dowlatabadi for bringing his energy and environmental expertise to bear; to Peter Gleick and Ralph De Gennaro for their comments on the environmental analysis; and to Bill Kaufmann, Franklin Spinney, and Stephen Alexis Cain for reviewing an early draft of my defense spending analysis.

Joseph Cirincione has—well beyond the call of duty—read and reread my work and shared his insights on a spectrum of defense and security topics. Matthew Bunn provided his usual incisive comments on the manuscript. Cirincione and Bunn provided particularly invaluable contributions to the Appendix, which originally appeared in the October 1989 issue of *Arms Control Today*.

My mother, Ethel Grodzins Romm, improved the book immeasurably by applying her remarkable language skills to innumerable drafts. I cannot adequately thank my father, Al Romm, for repeatedly focusing his world-class editorial skills on the book. I am obliged to Anne Lipow and give special thanks to Stephanie Lipow for their extraordinary reference skills, I am grateful to Samuel M. Silvers for his useful comments; to Gary Ferdman for his advice throughout the writing process; to Clay Fong, Kate-Louise Gottfried, Amy Marsh, and Bob Shuman for their help; and to my editor, Lisa Drew, for believing in this book.

Finally, I owe much to my agent, Peter Matson, whose unflagging support and wise counsel helped ensure timely publication.

Contents

Preface

The Once and Future Superpower: How to Restore America's Economic, Energy, and Environmental Security

The nineteenth-century English poet Matthew Arnold wrote of "wandering between two worlds, one dead, the other powerless to be born." So we wander today. Our current national security paradigm is a legacy of the dead world of the cold war. The need for expensive military forces and a military-oriented industrial policy has vanished. The economic, energy, and environmental security that we had taken for granted since World War II has also vanished.

Everyone seems to agree on the need to revitalize America, but few offer a detailed national agenda, in part because the profound changes of the past few years have left us with obsolete solutions and in part because any worthwhile agenda is seen as both costly and difficult.

By updating our definition of security and reorienting priorities, we can make the necessary changes with wiser, rather than greater, government spending. We can transfer money from four deep pockets:

- from military security to economic security (research and development, diffusion of manufacturing technology, new infrastructure)

- from military intelligence to civilian intelligence (worker training, Head Start, education)
- from military-oriented foreign aid to aid emphasizing civilian needs
- from traditional, polluting sources of energy (such as fossil fuels and nuclear power) to cleaner, more affordable sources (energy efficiency and renewable power)

Many of these changes will save the federal government money by replacing policies that encourage waste with policies that encourage efficiency. The goal must be a resource-efficient national and global economy that increases everyone's living standard without harming the environment.

Chapter 1 covers the history of the American idea of national security. The old military-security paradigm, a relatively recent phenomenon, still exerts a pervasive influence on the nation's policies, even as it grows less and less adequate for addressing the nation's problems.

Chapter 2 discusses how and why the standard of living of most Americans has stagnated or declined since the mid-1970s. I will then suggest a manufacturing industrial policy to restore America's economic competitiveness and bring back high-paying jobs. The necessary investment in technology, education, worker training, and advanced manufacturing can be paid for without increasing taxes, if we demilitarize our industrial policy.

Chapter 3 focuses on how Japan—a small, resource-poor island— has become an economic superpower; on how the Japanese doctrine of comprehensive security has helped Japan promote its economic strength systematically; and on how Japan has expanded its national industrial policy into a vast regional industrial policy encompassing much of Asia.

Chapter 4 explains how America's post-1980 energy industrial policy has undermined our nation's vitality. It details how we can eliminate energy policies that encourage waste and instead harness market forces on behalf of more efficient, cleaner, and cheaper forms of energy. Such an approach would reduce air pollution and the trade deficit, as well as our dependence on Persian Gulf oil, while creating tremendous savings for businesses, consumers, the government, and schools.

Chapter 5 deals with global environmental problems, such as global warming and regional water scarcity, that threaten the security of Americans and the entire planet. The danger of global warming can be significantly reduced at no net cost to the nation if we adopt the energy policies detailed in Chapter 4. Furthermore, an industrial ecosystem—manufacturing that minimizes resource use and pollution—could make businesses more profitable and boost foreign trade while preserving the environment. The federal government can help ensure that American companies become the leaders in this optimally competitive type of manufacturing.

Chapters 6 and 7 discuss how the end of the cold war and the victory in the Persian Gulf War make it possible to cut the defense budget in half, freeing up resources to restore America's economic vitality without sacrificing our military strength. In addition, an updated foreign aid policy can promote sustainable development and global demilitarization, decrease the prospect for conflict with the Third World, and perhaps make possible even deeper cuts in United States military spending—all without increasing the foreign aid budget. The Appendix explains why the Strategic Defense Initiative, or Star Wars, remains a deeply flawed program of little benefit to our national security.

America no longer provides a rising standard of living for most of its people. One in five of our children lives in poverty. We are the only major industrialized nation whose manufacturing workers experienced a drop in hourly compensation between 1978 and 1988. Our economic insecurity restricts our ability to solve both our own problems and those of other nations, and if our anemic growth rate continues, by the year 2010 Japan's economy may well be larger than ours. At the same time, we are the world's single largest source of most pollutants; we are one of the world's most wasteful users of scarce resources, particularly of energy; and we give short shrift to international programs that would help get to the root of many of the world's troubles.

We are the preeminent superpower in the military sense alone. Economically and environmentally, we have abandoned the position of world leader.

The domestic and foreign policies put forward in this book are designed to overcome all of the problems described above—without requiring increased taxes. Such a remarkable outcome is achievable because these policies are systematic in nature. Piecemeal, halfhearted, and underfunded attempts would have little impact. America's economic, environmental, energy, and military problems are all interconnected and therefore must be addressed comprehensively and simultaneously.

The Introduction discusses the essence and the power of the systematic approach using two recent examples: the Allies' overwhelming victory in the Persian Gulf War, and Japan's remarkable success in the manufacturing trade war.

Introduction

Why America Beat Iraq
but Loses to Japan

*[A] neuron's fibers can change significantly in a few
days or weeks, presumably in response to changing
demands on the nervous system. . . . neurons
continually rewire their own circuitry, sprouting new
fibers that reach out to make contact with new groups
of other neurons and withdrawing old fibers from
previous contacts. . . . This rewiring process may
account for how the brain improves one's ability, such
as becoming proficient in a sport or learning to play a
musical instrument.*

—*The Washington Post*, 1985[1]

The ability to sever old intellectual connections and sprout new ones as
circumstances change is as necessary for a successful nation as it is for
a successful brain. For forty-five years the United States pursued a national security strategy focused on one goal: containing the Soviet Union.
This single-minded strategy drove our military and foreign policies, and
dominated our economic, industrial, energy, and environmental policies.

In the last few years, America has been bombarded by changing
demands, not only arising from the collapse of the Soviet Union and
Warsaw Pact as the military threat on which we had narrowly focused,
but also from the domestic budget and trade deficits, the stagnation of
American wages in the face of global economic competition, and mounting environmental traumas. Yet our national strategy has hardly changed.
Decades of single-mindedness have left us poorly equipped to respond
to nonmilitary security threats. This book will show how we can redesign

our military-oriented national security policy to embrace everything a nation requires to be truly secure.

Our energy policy, for example, highlights the need for replacing old connections with new ones. American dependence on Persian Gulf oil grew 500 percent from 1985 to 1989, dramatically increasing our vulnerability to the vagaries of the region's politics. Yet, at the end of the Persian Gulf War, the Bush administration proposed a continuation of the supply-side energy policy of the 1980s, favoring subsidies of fossil fuels and nuclear power. If the United States were to adopt such a plan, America's reliance on Middle East oil would increase, the trade deficit would increase, and emissions of carbon dioxide (the primary cause of global warming) would increase 25 percent over the next quarter century.

A comprehensive energy policy, on the other hand, would not simply consider how to increase energy supply but would attempt to reduce both energy demand and energy-generated pollution. Such a systematic approach, making use of the remarkable advances in energy technologies of the 1980s, would be cheap and pro-growth, reducing the trade deficit and reducing global warming, while enhancing our energy independence and international competitiveness.

America already has demonstrated the power of a systematic approach—and its success astonished the critics. The strategy America needs in order to revitalize itself is closely related to the one we applied in the Persian Gulf War. America won the military war against Iraq the same way the Japanese are winning the high-technology trade and manufacturing war against us: by using a fast-cycle competitive strategy. Saddam Hussein's entrenched Iraqi forces were dug in, anticipating our usual head-on attack. We flanked them instead. This is almost precisely what the Japanese are doing to us in industry. American industry still uses the traditional mass production techniques that built this nation over the past century. The Japanese have flanked us with fast-cycle flexible manufacturing operations.

The Advantages of Time-Based Competition in Warfare and Business

The idea that time is an essential component of military strategy is hardly new. Almost two hundred years ago, Napoleon said: "Strategy is

16

the art of making use of time and space. I am less chary of the latter than the former. Space we can recover, time never. . . . I may lose a battle, but I shall never lose a minute." The World War II German General Gunther von Blumentritt described the German blitzkrieg this way: "The entire operational and tactical leadership method hinged upon . . . *rapid,* concise assessment of situations . . . *quick* decisions and *quick* execution, on the principle: 'each minute ahead of the enemy is an advantage' " (emphasis in original).[2]

That was the way the United States fought the Gulf war, but it is not the way in which the United States has historically fought its wars. General David Jones, former chairman of the Joint Chiefs of Staff, has candidly acknowledged: "Although most history books glorify our military accomplishments, a closer examination reveals a disconcerting pattern: unpreparedness at the start of a war; initial failures; reorganizing while fighting; cranking up our industrial base; and ultimately prevailing by wearing down the enemy—by being bigger, not smarter."[3]

Abandoning this traditional, muddling-through, warfare-by-attrition approach, the United States fought smarter in the Gulf war. The new time-based military strategy used a theoretical framework developed by now-retired U.S. Air Force Colonel John Boyd, a renowned pilot in the Korean War. Boyd was puzzled by the fact that in Korea the American F-86 Sabre jet consistently beat the Soviet-built MiG-15 in aerial dogfights even though the MiG was a "superior" plane by traditional standards: It could accelerate more rapidly, climb faster, and generally turn tighter than the F-86.[4]

But Colonel Boyd discovered that the F-86 had two crucial advantages. First, the jet's glass-domed bubble canopy enabled the pilot to observe enemy activity more easily than did the MiG cockpit, with its more restricted view. Second, the F-86 could change from one maneuver to another much more quickly—decelerating and diving while turning or switching directions.

Thus better intelligence and faster maneuvering canceled the superiority of the MiGs. As each plane danced around the other in a classic dogfight, the F-86 would gain a larger and larger positional advantage, rapidly changing from potential victim to predator. At Nellis Air Force base after the war, Boyd acquired the nickname Forty-Second Boyd for his open challenge to pay any fighter pilot forty dollars if Boyd could not outmaneuver the pilot in forty seconds. Boyd never lost.

17

Over the next two decades, Boyd studied engineering and military history to learn how to generalize his Korean War experience into a coherent theory of warfare. His theory evolved into a series of briefings, totaling nine hours, entitled "A Discourse on Winning and Losing." The key to winning, Boyd preached, is to operate at a faster tempo than an adversary, to get inside what he called their "O-O-D-A loop."

The O-O-D-A Loop

The loop consists of observing (O) the competition's actions, orienting (O) oneself to the unfolding situation, deciding (D) what to do, and then acting (A). The action (and any response it evokes) then alters the situation, necessitating new observations and a repetition of the cycle. When one side's O-O-D-A loop is faster, shorter, or more efficient than its opponent's, the faster side will run circles around the slower. The slower side will be constantly reacting to its adversary's previous moves, unable to take the initiative.

This is exactly how the Japanese use flexible manufacturing to out-compete us: They get inside our time-cycle loop. In the manufacture of such products as automobiles, air conditioners, and projection televisions, they can cycle through the entire production system—marketing, research, development, production, and sales—in one half to one third the time of any other nation, usually with a comparable reduction in cost and personnel.

Take automobiles. The establishment of Honda's Acura division and of GM's Saturn were announced at roughly the same time, but by the time the Saturn arrived, Honda had already completed three major Acura model changes. Moreover, in the time it took General Motors to bring Saturn to market, Honda had been able to incorporate into its Civic CRX "almost all of the innovative aspects of the Saturn design that have been made public so far."[5]

The flexible manufacturing strategy that bestows such time-based advantage was originally developed for Toyota Motor Company by Taiichi Ohno. By the early 1980s, his strategy had spread to a variety of Japanese manufacturing companies (and some American ones). The rapid manufacturing capability in turn led to Ohno's "just-in-time" supply system, based on the notion that new parts should be made only to fill an immediate need. Just-in-time allows Toyota assembly lines to stock

18

only about two hours' worth of parts inventory, compared with two weeks' worth of expensive inventory for a typical General Motors plant.

At double or triple speed, Japanese companies achieve an enormous advantage with quick innovation through a process of steady incremental improvements that keep them at least a step ahead of their competitors. For example, every year between 1979 and 1988, Melco (the Mitsubishi Electric Company) added a new feature or made a major design change in its three-horsepower heat pump, including the introduction of integrated circuits to control the pump cycle (1980), microprocessors (1981), and "learning circuitry," which allows the unit to learn when to defrost itself and how best to respond to each consumer's particular temperature environment (1988). Not until the mid-1980s did the leading American company even consider the use of integrated circuits in its residential heat pump. It would have taken four to five years to bring the product to market, and even then the United States firm would only have had in 1990 a product comparable to the 1980 Melco heat pump. The American company threw in the towel, purchasing its advanced air conditioners, heat pumps, and components from the Japanese competition. The Japanese had gotten so far inside its competitor's time-cycle loop that the American company had had to surrender.[6]

Reducing Friction

How can an organization develop a system that gets ahead and keeps ahead of the competition? Any organizational system, to be as efficient as possible, must minimize the friction in each of its four loop phases. Friction is usually thought of in mechanical terms: the lack of smooth operation of moving parts, which generates waste heat. The great nineteenth-century military strategist Carl von Clausewitz first made the analogy to war. "Friction," he said, "is the only concept that more or less corresponds to the factors that distinguish real war from war on paper." "Friction . . . is the force that makes the apparently easy so difficult." Friction in war could be bad weather, mistaken intelligence, equipment that fails, orders that are never received. He also called it the "fog of war."[7] Friction in business can come from parts that are not available, defects that have to be repaired after production, inventory pile-up, or changes in consumer tastes that occur after the product is

19

designed—whatever delays the adding of value. We could call it the fog of business.

Applying Clausewitz's reasoning to modern warfare, Boyd concluded that since we want to compress our own cycle time, we must eliminate friction wherever we can in the cycle. Consider the first O of the O-O-D-A loop: observation. To get the best observations, we must be as directly connected to our environment as possible. In Operation Desert Storm, we could assess the effectiveness of our actions not only with satellite images, but also with reconnaissance planes, because of our rapidly achieved air superiority. The central idea is to gather and disperse the information as quickly as possible.[8]

Superior observation and communication are crucial in most businesses. Alone among the networks, the Cable News Network, CNN, was able to keep its Baghdad correspondents, Peter Arnett and Bernard Shaw, on the air during the first night of Allied bombing in large part because of an expensive dedicated voice circuit. All of the other networks had relied on regular phone lines, which stopped working. CNN had avoided the classic wartime friction: missed communications. The coverage of the Gulf war attracted the largest audience in CNN history. Although only eleven years old, CNN has now surpassed the networks in providing instantaneous global coverage of fast-breaking news stories. It is not surprising that the best coverage of a fast-cycle war was done by such a fast-cycle news organization.[9]

In manufacturing, observations are made most directly by the retail salespeople, who learn day by day what sells and what does not. Speed requires continual upgrading of customer information, instant transmission to the home office, and analysis on computer. To reduce the friction in the development cycle of its new cars, Toyota lends sales staff to development teams. Such direct interaction provides the design crews with the latest observations: information on ever-changing customer needs, desires, and attitudes.

The ability to decide and act quickly depends on having as few layers of management and bureaucracy as possible, which reduces organizational friction. Decision-making should be delegated to those in the field wherever possible. In business, as in warfare, there is usually no time to refer decisions all the way up the chain of command. Local responsibility and decentralized scheduling, together with the elimination of of the many layers of indirect workers and middle management who add only friction but no value, is the essence of flexible manufacturing, the method for producing the same goods with fewer people in less time. The biggest United States manufacturer of automobile suspension components uses 107 direct laborers and 135 indirect ones to produce 10 million units per year (at $100 per unit). A smooth-running Japanese competitor who produces one third as many units—3.5 million per year (at $49 per unit)—uses 50 direct laborers, but only 7 indirect ones.[10]

What is the opposite of delegation? What is maximum friction in an organization? America carried the notion of a centralized chain of command to its extreme during the Vietnam War, in which bombing targets were often selected by President Johnson and his advisers inside the White House. In the Gulf war, President Bush fully delegated the conduct of the war to General H. Norman Schwarzkopf, sitting in Saudi Arabia, the theater of operations.

Unfortunately most American companies remain mired in high-friction bureaucracy, with an alarmingly topheavy management system. Here is how many major companies tipped the scales in 1990: At General Motors, the quintessential American manufacturer, 77.5 percent of the work force is white-collar and salaried, 22.5 percent are hourly blue-collar workers; Mobil Oil is 61.5 percent white-collar; General Electric 60 percent; Du pont, 57.1 percent; Chrysler, 44.4 percent; Exxon, 43 percent; AT&T, 42 percent; Ford, 37 percent. At IBM, which does much of its manufacturing overseas, a stunning 91.5 percent of the staff is white-collar. As UCLA professor Richard Rosecrance noted: "More than half of the modern American corporation consists of workers uninvolved in operations or production work, an astounding fact. . . . The ratio in typical corporations in Japan is about one-sixth of the American figure."[11]

For an organization to think and move quickly and independently, it must be specially trained. That requires, in the words of blitzkrieg master General Blumentritt, "an officers training institution which allows the subordinate a very great measure of freedom of action and freedom in the matter of executing orders and which primarily calls for independent daring, initiative, and sense of responsibility."[12]

The Need for a Common Orientation

A fast tempo by independent groups within the same organization requires that all group leaders head in the same direction. For Blumentritt, this is a "body of officers to whom all tactical conceptions were fully clear." For Boyd, their common outlook will "simultaneously encourage subordinate initiative yet realize superior intent."[13] This is the orientation—the second O—of the O-O-D-A loop. Orientation clarifies or distorts how one interprets information. It is the lens through which one views the world. (The terms "orientation," "worldview," and "paradigm" are synonymous here.)

Orientation is crucial because no matter how efficiently an organization observes, decides, and acts—no matter how fast its cycle time— it is doomed to fail when it is headed in the wrong direction, whether building cars no one wants or attacking in the wrong place. Each organization needs a coherent paradigm to shape and adapt to unfolding events, to head in the right direction. Since the world is constantly changing, successful adaptation requires constant reeducation, followed by reorientation.

This concept is the first crucial element of flexible manufacturing: a highly educated work force, highly trained, yet continually being retrained. The common orientation can be promoted by such techniques as lifetime employment guarantees, companywide commitment to quality, or the decision to become a fast-cycle operation itself. As a *Harvard Business Review* article put it: "Fast cycle time is a management paradigm, a way of thinking about how to organize and lead a company."[14] The common orientation helps achieve internal harmony, which is necessary to respond coherently to changing circumstances. Without it, different groups within an organization will respond differently. New external threats will lead to confusion and disorder, even internal paralysis. For example, after introducing a new car design, American auto companies typically require eleven months to return to their previous level of quality, while Japanese lean-production auto plants take but six weeks, even though they start with a higher level of quality.[15] To compete, United States companies must avoid compartmentalization, rigidity, disconnection, and alienation from the environment. Surviving external competition requires achieving internal cooperation—less friction.

In the Gulf war, internal harmony was in large part achieved because most of Schwarzkopf's key planning officers were graduates of the School of Advanced Military Studies (SAMS) at Fort Leavenworth, Kansas. The school was established in 1983 by Brigadier General Huba Wass de Czege to teach top Army officers the operational art of war. Each year 150 students take intensive seminars on military history and war theory. The strategy taught focuses on maneuverability, agility, and speed, rather than the Army's traditional tactics of superior firepower and frontal assaults. Colonel Boyd regularly gave his briefing on how the history of warfare—from the battles of Alexander the Great, Hannibal, Genghis Khan, Frederick the Great, and Napoleon, to the blitzkrieg and the Vietnam War—demonstrated the importance of fast-cycle, maneuver-based warfare.

The school tried to foster a "bond of common knowledge and common interest" among the students, according to Colonel Richard Sinnreich, SAMS director between 1985 and 1987. "Huba's view, and mine, was that *common orientation was not only valuable, but essential*" (emphasis added). This bonding "facilitated within the Army an ability to communicate tactical and operational constructs concisely and clearly," according to Lieutenant Colonel Hal Winton, a former deputy director. General Schwarzkopf relied heavily on SAMS graduates for strategic planning during the war with Iraq. In Saudi Arabia, every level, from division and corps command up to U.S. Central Command in Riyadh, had a planning group of three to five officers, most of whom were SAMS graduates.[16] In harmony, they succeeded beyond everyone's wildest hopes.

The internal coherence that brought quick victory in Desert Storm has not been the norm in most recent United States military operations. More typical is the failed 1980 Desert One Iranian hostage rescue mission. Desert One should have been a small, tightly knit operation. Daring commando raids require a high degree of cohesion and split-second timing. Instead, all four services—Army, Navy, Air Force, and Marines—took part. Confusion between Marine helicopter pilots and Air Force refueling tankers apparently caused a collision in which eight died, helping to doom the mission.[17]

Similarly, in United States manufacturing, too often there is competition between labor and management, between the financial division and the design engineers, and so on throughout the organization. In the 1960s and 1970s, this friction slowed innovation and the adoption of the latest technology in many of our major manufacturing companies. It helped delay the introduction of cars with front-wheel drive at Ford Motor Company for more than a decade. To reverse the trend, Ford had to eliminate a great deal of this friction by reorienting some of its operations. In developing the Taurus, Ford abandoned its rigidly hierarchical pyramid organization and chose a hub-rim approach, with the overall car program management in the center connected to all elements of the team, from manufacturing to service. Such a management structure increases flexibility and adaptability and decreases internal friction. The result has been one of the best—and one of the safest—cars built in America, an outstanding success in an American industry that has had too few successes of late.

The Japanese, and some American companies, have established a close, cooperative relationship not just between management and labor and the various internal divisions of a company, but also between major companies and their component suppliers, and, most important, between the company and the customer. Once a strong bond is formed between a company and a customer, achieved with quality products and superb customer service, it can be difficult to break. It was to a great extent the high quality of Japanese manufactured goods (coupled with initially lower costs) that broke the weak bonds of customer loyalty between American consumers and manufacturers, bonds weakened from long years of corporate inattention to both quality and customer service.

Maximizing the Enemy's Friction

Destroying a competitor's interconnections became a key element of Boyd's military theory. In providing the military framework for the new United States approach to fighting wars, Colonel Boyd went beyond Clausewitz's idea of minimizing one's own friction to the idea of maximizing friction for the enemy at the same time. One could do it by clouding an adversary's observations. With deceptive or ambiguous pictures of reality, he is disoriented and ultimately his worldview is destroyed. This idea came from Sun Tzu, the brilliant Chinese military strategist of the fourth century B.C. Sun Tzu's teachings, *The Art of War,* have been widely used for more than two thousand years by military commanders, including Mao Tse-tung. The book is a favorite among Japanese businessmen.

The Wisdom of Sun Tzu

"All warfare is based on deception."

"Offer the enemy a bait to lure him; feign disorder and strike him."

"In war, numbers alone confer no advantage. Do not advance relying on sheer military power."

"The enemy must not know where I intend to give battle. For if he does not know where I intend to give battle he must prepare in a great many places. And when he prepares in a great many places, those I have to fight in any one place will be few."

"To win one hundred victories in one hundred battles is not the acme of skill. To subdue the enemy without fighting is the acme of skill.

"Thus, what is of supreme importance in war is to attack the enemy's strategy."[18]

In the fast-cycle framework, it is of supreme importance to upset the enemy's strategy by attacking his orientation, his worldview. The strategy of Saddam Hussein, no Sun Tzu fan, was to dig in, stand fast, withstand our blows, and try to force us to fight the kind of war he had fought so long with the Iranians—direct frontal assault against fortified positions. General Schwarzkopf did not oblige him. Schwarzkopf attacked and destroyed Hussein's strategy by first creating a false impression that the United States-led coalition intended to do just what Hussein expected and by then rapidly flanking the fortified positions. The very name Desert Storm implied that the aim of the United States attack was to multiply enemy confusion and friction, to maximize Iraq's "fog of war."

Mass Production and Trench Warfare

In manufacturing, America's traditional, successful strategy has been mass production. For a generation, the Japanese have been attacking this strategy using flexible manufacturing. As one manufacturing analyst wrote of traditional, slow-cycle production: "What distorts the system is time: lengthy delays inevitably create an inaccurate view of the market."[19] By exploiting time-based competition to accelerate the pace of innovation

25

and production, by developing product cycles two to three times faster than are possible under mass production, the Japanese make their competitors' inaccurate view of the market an even greater liability.

According to management guru Peter Drucker, "Detroit still operates on the assumption that the U.S. car market is segregated into four or five 'socioeconomic' groups. But this theory became obsolete 15 years ago." The Japanese, on the other hand, not only understand the many more "life-style" segments of the American market, but the flexible manufacturing system allows more different models to be generated, and at a faster pace, which in turn allows the Japanese to adjust their cars more rapidly to changes in consumer tastes. Nissan in particular has developed a manufacturing factory so advanced that it can be retooled simply by changing its computer software, rather than by changing the machine tools themselves. This "intelligent" assembly line may be able to reduce new-model changeover times from over nine months to under three months, giving Nissan a tremendous advantage in the growing niche markets of cars and trucks that sell fewer than two hundred thousand units a year.[20]

The fossilization of American industry during the 1960s and 1970s and what happened to the American military are analogous. Here is how Colonel Boyd describes the old way of thinking, as epitomized by World War I trench warfare: "The aristocratic tradition, the top-down command and control system, the slavish addiction to the 'Principle of Concentration,' and the drill regulation mind-set, all taken together, reveal an 'obsession for control' by high-level superiors over low-level subordinates that restricts any imagination, initiative, and adaptability needed by a system to evolve the indistinct-irregular-mobile tactics that could counter the increase in weapons lethality."[21] Substitute "foreign competition" for "weapons lethality" and this is an uncanny indictment of many large United States companies.

The rigid, head-on, attrition-based strategy was a common one for America in most wars. It is how the Marines fought the Japanese at Iwo Jima. It was the basis for the "body count" mentality of the Vietnam War. As noted earlier, General David Jones acknowledged that America ultimately prevailed in its wars "by wearing down the enemy—by being bigger, not smarter." Before the Army's field manual was rewritten by Brigadier General Wass de Czege in the 1980s to reflect more maneuver-oriented warfare, it instructed the commanders at the battlefront: "The chief mission of these forces must be to fight with sufficient strength and tenacity to force the enemy to disclose the size and direction of his main attack, and to buy time while defending forces concentrated *in front of the main thrust*. . . . In mounted warfare, armored and mechanized elements must be set in motion toward the battle positions *in the path* of the enemy thrust" (emphasis added).[22]

Taking the enemy head-on requires large forces and ensures high casualties. Because virtually all of the nation's military experts expected the military to fight the traditional way, they significantly overestimated the American casualty rate in the Gulf war.

Winning the Gulf War the Fast-Cycle Way

The first clue that the Gulf war might be different came with news reports in early January 1991 that the commandant of the Marine Corps, General Alfred Gray, had sat through, and paid attention to, the briefings of a Colonel John Boyd, an officer not known to the general public. When Gray took command of the Marines in the late 1980s, he had had their basic fighting manual rewritten according to the principles developed by Colonel Boyd. He mailed Sun Tzu's book to every officer and in 1990 designated it the "Book of the Year"—required reading for all Marines.[23]

Sun Tzu's axioms—such as "In war, numbers alone confer no advantage. Do not advance relying on sheer military power"—are the antithesis of attrition warfare. Discussing how to deal with the entrenched Iraqi forces shortly before the air war began, Brigadier General Russel Sutton, head of Marine Corps planning, said, "The last thing we want to do is try to meet him [Hussein] head-on. This is simply pure Sun Tzu."

The next, and clearest, evidence that this was a time-based, fast-cycle operation came just before the ground war began. In a mid-February briefing, Marine Brigadier General Richard Neal, U.S. Central Command's deputy director of operations, said, "We're inside his decision-making cycle. . . . We're kind of out-thinking him. . . . We can see what he's been doing, we can kind of anticipate what his next move is going to do, and we can adapt our tactics accordingly."[24]

Compare this with Boyd's central message: "Mentally we can isolate our adversaries by presenting them with ambiguous, deceptive, or novel situations, as well as by operating at a tempo they can neither make out nor keep up with. Operating inside their O-O-D-A loops will accomplish

27

this by disorienting or twisting their mental images so that they can neither appreciate nor cope with what's really going on."[25]

Isolating the Iraqis in all possible ways was a primary goal. We used the UN to isolate them politically and economically. Then, our military plan for the Iraqi Army was, in the words of Colin Powell, chairman of the Joint Chiefs of Staff: "First we are going to cut it off. And then we're going to kill it."[26]

The final sign that the Gulf war was a John Boyd war came from the February 27 news conference in which General Schwarzkopf spelled out the war strategy of the United States-led coalition. First, we had destroyed the Iraqi ability to observe our actions. In Schwarzkopf's words: "We knew that he had very, very limited reconnaissance means. And therefore, when we took out his air force, for all intents and purposes, we took out his ability to see what we were doing down here in Saudi Arabia. . . . We had taken out his eyes."[27] At the same time, we destroyed Iraqi communication facilities, command and control bunkers, and bridges, degrading the army's ability to decide and act quickly and to maintain internal coherence. These disorienting attacks, coupled with the initial feinting buildup along the Kuwait-Saudi border, froze Iraq's strategic plans and guaranteed that any response to a changing Allied strategy would be very slow.

Once Iraq's eyes and ears were taken out, Allied troops and supply bases were rapidly shifted west, in one of the most sophisticated, high-speed logistical operations in history. About three hundred thousand troops, together with thousands of tons of fuel, ammunition, spare parts, and food were moved in a few weeks. When the ground war began, the Marines and the Saudis launched two thrusts directly across the Kuwaiti border to convince the Iraqis we were going to take them head-on into their most heavily defended area. At the same time, amphibious feints were launched to freeze Iraqi forces deployed along the coast.

A sweeping flanking attack was then launched from the west, to encircle and cut off the Iraqi Army. As many of the smaller direct assaults penetrated the Iraqi lines, the Iraqis became completely surrounded and disoriented, making the ultimate defeat of their once-feared Republican Guard surprisingly simple.[28] This is Boyd's strategy: "Present many (fast-breaking) simultaneous and sequential happenings to generate confusion and disorder—thereby stretching out time for adversary to respond in a directed fashion."[29]

A 1988 *Harvard Business Review* article on the impact of flexible manufacturing remarkably foretold the United States military strategy against the large, entrenched Iraqi Army: "Indirect attack requires surprise. Competitors either do not understand the strategies being used against them or they do understand but cannot respond—sometimes because of the speed of the attack, sometimes because of their inability to mount a response. . . . Time-based strategy offers a powerful new approach for successful indirect attacks against larger, established competitors."[30]

Success through surprise requires variety, rapidity, and novelty. Mastering a variety of rapid responses has three advantages. First, it increases adaptability; an organization can quickly try many approaches for responding to changing circumstances. Second, it accelerates the learning process; the more approaches that are tried, the more opportunities there are "to learn from the feedback of experience."[31] Third, it allows the organization to keep the initiative, while competitors can do little more than react to the multiple attacks. Novelty further slows down adversaries by confronting them with unfamiliar events, ones that have not been experienced before. The Iraqis were familiar with the head-on, human-wave attacks of the Iranians, not the rapid, flanking maneuvers of the Allies.

Similarly, a key advantage of flexible manufacturing is that it can quickly generate a large variety of novel products to overwhelm a competitor. Consider the Honda-Yamaha "variety war," in which one Japanese company defeated a rival Japanese company by getting inside its time-cycle loop. The two companies started with 60 models of motorcycles. In eighteen months, Honda introduced or replaced 113 models, turning over its production line twice. Yamaha managed only 37 changes. Honda introduced novelty—four-valve engines, composites—which customers began to expect. But Yamaha could not deliver and it was crushed. At one point it had more than twelve months of inventories in its dealers' showrooms. Its cycle time had been stretched out; its friction (that expensive inventory) had been maximized. Honda had been able to "turn manufacturing into a marketing weapon."[32]

The Allies had a variety of options—continuing the air campaign to starve out the Iraqi Army, a frontal blitzkrieg assault using multiple pincer attacks, an amphibious assault, or, the one they chose, a sweeping attack around the Iraqi right flank. Yet the specific ground war plan the

Allies used to achieve victory was less important than their ability to achieve a much faster cycle time than the Iraqis. After all, the Iraqis might have guessed what we would do and changed their tactics, but even if they had, we would have seen the Iraqi movements, and changed our tactics, perhaps by destroying the moving forces from the air, or by driving through whatever hole was opened up by the Iraqi movement. Since we had more options and a faster response time, we could be assured of ultimately outmaneuvering them. A fast-cycle strategy reduces the risk of being caught off guard by enemy actions.

Fast-Cycle Manufacturing Brings Jobs Home

Is American business slower than the American military to recognize the need for a new strategy? Yes, but more United States companies appear to be beginning to understand the importance of speeding up their cycle times. A 1992 newspaper advertisement touts Chrysler's new multifunctional teams of "product engineers and manufacturing engineers, planners and buyers, marketers, designers and finance analysts" as achieving "better quality, lower cost and a reduction in the time it takes to get a product to market."[33]

A fast-cycle business strategy reduces risk as efficiently as a fast-cycle military strategy. For instance, the danger posed to Honda's market share by GM's Saturn has been reduced by Honda's ability to incorporate Saturn designs into its Civic CRX before Saturn was even introduced. Risk reduction can be even more dramatic in volatile businesses such as women's fashion. New clothing orders from the Far East can require a nine-month lead time, but demand can be as much as 40 percent above or below such long-range forecasts.[34]

In recent years, United States domestic textile and clothing manufacturers have cut the lead time from months to weeks, which reduces the inaccuracy of forecasts to a manageable plus or minus 10 percent. The American textile manufacturer Milliken and Company can deliver fabric to customers in a week or less, and has been working with American apparel manufacturers to reduce their production-cycle times and to put in place just-in-time inventory controls.

According to Bud Konheim, president of Nicole Miller, a maker of women's clothing: "Everybody contracting in Hong Kong is projecting three and four months ahead of time, which means they're almost always

30

doomed to overbuying." The company started moving manufacturing back to the United States in 1986, and almost all of its dresses and suits are now made here. Since 1989, Euro-American Textile Corporation has increased its volume of American-made fabric from $3 million to $25 million, while European manufacturing dropped to 78 percent. Fast-cycle manufacturing is a way to bring jobs back home.[35]

The nation would benefit greatly if flexible manufacturing were widely used by United States companies. Lean manufacturing achieves higher efficiency, quality, and flexibility the closer each element of the system is to the other elements, from design to assembly to marketing and sales. As competition between foreign and domestic lean producers intensifies, the advantage will accrue to the company that does most of its manufacturing in the United States. Therefore, the more that American companies adopt flexible manufacturing, the more high-paying jobs will be created, both by the American companies and by competitors increasingly forced to manufacture components as well as final products in the United States. It is not merely blue-collar manufacturing jobs that would increase, but also the countless others that are directly related to a successful manufacturing system—in the areas of research and development, construction, finance, accounting, and so on—and indirectly connected through the multiplier effect of increased domestic wages.[36]

Revitalizing America Systematically

America triumphed in the Persian Gulf War because we had heavily invested in a highly trained force and advanced technology, and we applied John Boyd's time-based systems approach to our Gulf strategy. America is having trouble competing economically because we do too few of these things: We fail to invest in a highly trained work force; we devote inadequate resources to advanced civilian technology; and we lack a systematic approach to our economic strategy, such as a fast-cycle production system or a manufacturing industrial policy.[37]

We all know what is needed to support sophisticated manufacturing— a great deal of research and development (R&D) into advanced manufacturing technology, rapid diffusion of that know-how to American companies, and heavy investment in worker training and infrastructure. Success in manufacturing at a micro level requires a company to adopt

31

a common orientation that integrates research, development, design, and production. Similarly, success in manufacturing at a macro level requires a nation to adopt a common orientation—an industrial policy—that integrates R&D, worker training, infrastructure, and a host of other programs. In that industrial policy, the government does not pick winners and losers, but rather it creates an economic climate that benefits all industries, helping them adapt rapidly to changing circumstances. Chapter 2 will cover the details of this policy.

Boyd's fast-cycle theory is based on the idea of enhancing one's security by increasing connections, both internal and external. His is called a "systems-oriented" approach. In business, for example, instead of viewing research and development in isolation from manufacturing, a systems approach views R&D as part of an entire production cycle where products are actually designed to be easy to manufacture. The goal is to maximize efficiency and minimize waste. Flexible manufacturing minimizes wasted time and effort. But wasted time is not the only inefficiency in America. Indeed, the federal government has strong reasons to reduce two other inefficiencies: energy use and pollution.

Reorienting Energy Policy

As will be discussed in Chapter 4, overuse of energy by industry, by households, by the government—by everyone—has many damaging side effects. It makes our economy overly reliant on unstable regions such as the Middle East; it increases the trade deficit, half of which is now due to oil imports; it makes us the single largest source of atmospheric pollution, which causes environmental damage to both our nation and the world; and it soaks up money from businesses and from people, money that would otherwise be spent far more productively.

For the past decade, our federal energy policy, both foreign and domestic, has been extremely inefficient. The United States spends tens of billions of dollars each year on military forces to help maintain access to the billions of dollars' worth of oil we import from the Middle East. We spend tens of billions of dollars every year on domestic policies that support nuclear power and fossil fuels. This centrally planned energy industrial policy has subsidized the most polluting forms of energy.

Those who argue that America should continue a supply-side, or laissez-faire, or so-called "market-driven" energy policy need to see the market as an imperfect barometer—an inefficient system. We delude ourselves: The price we pay at the pump for oil does not take into account its full cost to society, which includes the money the Defense Department spends to safeguard the oil supplies in the Persian Gulf (in peacetime and war), the federal government's subsidies to the oil industry, the health costs and environmental damage caused by petroleum combustion, and the employment lost owing to the outflow of capital to pay for imported oil. This true cost has been estimated at more than $100 per barrel *above* the actual cost. By underpricing oil, we overuse it, which is economically and environmentally disastrous.

In the best energy policy, the federal government removes the barriers obstructing the wider use of less expensive, less environmentally harmful energy sources. Those sources include renewable energy, such as wind and solar, and energy-efficient products, such as compact fluorescent light bulbs. Because these sources cost the least, the energy industrial policy needed to promote their use requires far less government spending than the current policies, which favor more inefficient and polluting forms of energy. Such a policy will also cut federal and state government energy bills in their own office buildings, in the low-income housing that they subsidize, and in the school systems they support.

Ultimately, we must make the transition to an industrial ecosystem— where all resource inputs, such as water and materials, are minimized, and all harmful outputs, such as water pollution and solid waste, are minimized. To achieve this end, businesses can no longer view pollution as isolated from manufacturing and the other elements of making a marketable product. When they adopt a systems approach, lean production will be joined by "clean production," where industrial waste is seen as one part of an entire production system, and products are actually designed to reduce waste in the production process, to reduce pollution when they are used, and to be as recyclable as possible. The federal government has a role to play in harnessing the market forces needed to speed the transition to the industrial ecosystem (as will be examined in Chapter 5).

Reorienting Industrial Policy

The agenda for action detailed in this book proposes a fundamental shift in American policy. It will require a reconnection or realignment of neurons in our national brain, so to speak, in the face of changing circumstances. I do not doubt we can do it. Our policies are obsolete and need reorienting. For instance, our expensive energy industrial policy is, in theory, aimed at securing adequate supplies of energy. Unfortunately, our energy policics no longer provide us energy security; we can ill afford a Department of Energy that directs most of its budget to military-related programs.

Similarly, since World War II we have devoted many of our economic policies to winning the cold war. It is outrageous, as well as foolish, for the federal government to spend more than one hundred times as much money on defense research and development as on industrial development. A key assumption—that defense R&D has spin-offs for civilian technology—worked well in the 1950s and 1960s when we had undisputed world preeminence in technology. But for the past two decades, that policy has been increasingly ineffective and has now been completely undercut by the success of flexible manufacturing. Originating technology is meaningless when a nation cannot develop, manufacture, and market it quickly enough, as we have learned with VCRs, televisions, and a humbling array of other American inventions. The Japanese innovate too rapidly, and they market those innovations even more rapidly. Defense research, usually shrouded in secrecy, diffuses too slowly to produce high-paying civilian manufacturing jobs.

As a result, the United States is losing a manufacturing war with Japan that threatens to leave us with a reduced standard of living relative to other nations and even threatens to leave us critically dependent on the Japanese for key technologies crucial in military as well as civilian production. It is not merely at the micro level of flexible manufacturing that individual Japanese companies beat individual United States companies. As we will see in Chapter 3, the Japanese government has itself adopted a systematic approach to ensure that Japan will be producing the very highest value-added products in the world for the foreseeable future.

The Japanese have improved the idea of government intervention in the marketplace, turning it into an art form that might best be labeled "geo-economics." The goal of geo-economics is "to provide the best possible employment for the largest proportion of the population."[38] The Japanese pour resources into all aspects of economic competition—creating what might be called their economic security system—from R&D policy to low-cost capital, from trade policy to foreign aid. They have one goal in mind: maximizing the industrial vitality of their country. In part this stems naturally from the Japanese national security doctrine, aptly called comprehensive security, which has always had a strong economic component. For example, to attain energy security they spend a massive 22 percent of their federal R&D on energy while we spend a shameful 4 percent. Unless we change course swiftly, Japan will attain preeminence in the international market for new energy technologies in the twenty-first century.

The most important element of Colonel Boyd's theory is the *orientation,* for no organization—no nation—no matter how good its people or how abundant its resources, can succeed if it is headed in the wrong direction or if its people are headed in different directions. Japan understands this. Its companies have made flexible manufacturing the primary industrial goal and its government has made economic security the primary national goal. A nation's orientation, its direction, is set by its national security policies; those are the policies that take precedence over and drive all others.

Updating the definition of national security is, therefore, not an academic exercise. I believe that one explanation for America's strategic rigidity in the face of mounting troubles is that there is no coherent alternative national security paradigm available. You can't beat a horse with no horse. Or, as Thomas Kuhn put it in his classic book, *The Structure of Scientific Revolutions,* the act of judgment that leads one "to reject a previously accepted theory is always based upon more than a comparison of that theory with the world. The decision to reject one paradigm is always simultaneously the decision to accept another, and the judgment leading to that decision involves the comparison of both paradigms with . . . each other."[39]

America has won the cold war but is losing the economic war. Yet we remain mired in industrial policies that are legacies of the cold war. The federal government heavily supports nuclear power, but not solar energy; it promotes aerospace technology, but not advanced manufacturing. Many Americans deny that we have an industrial policy, perhaps because they do not use that label for programs designed to achieve national security goals, such as the development of traditional energy supplies or superior military technology. Since that is so, a redefinition of security is required if we are to change our industrial policies, as discussed in Chapter 2.

Industrial policy can run into trouble when it focuses on saving specific companies, rather than on achieving long-term goals. The ideal industrial policy identifies the most desirable end state for the nation and then assists the free market in achieving that state. The nation's new goals should be to maximize domestic high-paying jobs, while minimizing energy use and pollution. In other words, the nation's goals are economic security, energy security, and environmental security.

These three goals must be achieved in an integrated or systematic fashion.[40] We cannot achieve one without the other two. We cannot achieve real security without all three—just as no manufacturing company can long succeed if it fails to integrate *all* elements of the production cycle (research, development, design, and manufacturing). If a company fails in one area today, it fails in all areas.

Military security is decidedly not eliminated in this new national security paradigm, but it is no longer placed above economic, energy, and environmental security. I will propose an action agenda in each of these areas, as well as a program for a scaled-down but strong military. These new proposals would not require higher federal expenditures, in part because they would achieve levels of efficiency higher than the policies they replace, and in part because the new security model reallocates resources. These proposals would also increase our military security, since our defense and foreign aid budgets now tend to be focused on inefficient military solutions to world problems, rather than on the root causes of conflict and the conditions that lead to weapons proliferation.

Before the discussion of the new model, a little history. The old military-security paradigm that sometimes seems carved in stone is a relatively recent phenomenon. It has become increasingly inadequate for addressing the nation's problems, but it continues to exert a pervasive influence on the nation's policies.

THE
ONCE AND FUTURE
SUPERPOWER

1

National Security, an Evolving Idea

Does the National Security depend on fostering
Domestic Industries?

—Yale undergraduate debate question, 1790s[1]

Since 1945 the United States has conducted its affairs under a national security doctrine aimed almost exclusively at winning the cold war with the Soviet Union. To that end we directed not only our military policy, but also our industrial policy, foreign policy, and trade policy, at the expense of economic strength, energy independence, and environmental health. With the cold war over and won, the fairly new idea that national security means only military security can be replaced by a more expansive one in which economic security—providing the best possible jobs for the greatest number of people—is at least an equal priority. To Americans raised under the post-World War II security paradigm, such a change of national goals may seem novel, but it has its roots in discussions that date from the earliest days of the republic.

In January 1790, Congress instructed Alexander Hamilton to write a report on "the encouragement and promotion of such manufactures as will tend to render the United States independent of other nations for essential, particularly for military supplies."[2] Hamilton responded with his *Report on Manufactures* of 1791, which concluded that "not only the wealth but the independence and security of a country appear to be

39

materially connected with the prosperity of manufactures."[3] The connection between America's security and our manufacturing is well established.

For much of America's history, presidents have followed the advice given by George Washington in his 1796 farewell address: "The great rule of conduct for us, in regard to foreign Nations, is in extending our commercial relations, to have with them as little political connections as possible."[4] Not that the United States national security and foreign policies lacked a military component. They were never without one, but economic security and trade have long been present and often been preeminent. This was in large part because, as the historian C. Vann Woodward has written, between the War of 1812 and World War II, "the United States was blessed with a security so complete and so free that it was able virtually to do without an army and for the greater part without a navy as well." This "free security" was based on America's abundant natural resources, the foundation of its economic independence, and on "nature's gift of three vast bodies of water interposed between this country and any other power that might constitute a serious menace to its safety"—the Atlantic and Pacific Oceans and "a third body of water, considered so impenetrable as to make us virtually unaware of its importance, the Arctic Ocean and its great ice cap to the north."[5]

Our free military security was truly free. In the nineteenth century, annual military spending rarely reached 1 percent of GNP, except during war years. In 1861, the United States had the second largest merchant marine fleet in the world but no battle fleet, and the U.S. Navy had one tenth the number of men the British Navy had. In the 1880s, military expenditures never exceeded four tenths of 1 percent.

By the late nineteenth century, America's emerging foreign policy had a strong economic focus. "Roosevelt, Taft, Wilson, and their primary advisers all acknowledged a close interconnection between imperial politics and imperial financing, and each administration provided whatever diplomatic support it felt it could for the bankers' ambitions, not merely because they were United States citizens but because they were citizens who trafficked in a power indispensable to United States policy."[6] President Taft's secretary of state, Philander C. Knox, a corporate lawyer, was so aggressive in promoting American business interests overseas and extending American investment into underdeveloped regions that his policies were labeled "dollar diplomacy."[7]

40

On the eve of World War I, the United States was spending only 0.8 percent of its GNP on the military. Even Germany, a country that spent a considerably larger sum of money on defense, engaged in aggressive economic security tactics. Consider the following features of German trade that "attracted most attention in the days before the First World War," as described in 1945 by economist Albert Hirschman:

1. The rapid expansion of German exports, both absolutely and relatively, to other countries;

2. The scientific methods by which this expansion was achieved— in particular, the systematic study of the needs and habits of foreign consumers;

3. Unfair competition and, in particular, the dumping of some German exports . . . ;

4. The attempt by Germany, in connection with the dumping . . . to destroy competitive industries which had already been established;

5. The export of German capital, business enterprises, and of managerial and scientific personnel;

6. German methods of financial control over foreign enterprises.[8]

The list should sound familiar. These are the identical features of Japanese trade that have attracted the most attention in the 1980s and 1990s.

During the 1930s, Hoover's and Roosevelt's foreign policies were based more on the nation's immediate economic needs than on issues of war and peace.[9] Increasing foreign trade with the Soviet Union and Latin America were high on Roosevelt's diplomatic agenda. His Good Neighbor policy did not mean abandoning attempts to influence Latin America, but rather emphasized economic influence over military force. As late as 1937, America's military appropriations came to only 1.5 percent of GNP, compared with 6 percent for Great Britain, 9 percent for France, 24 percent for Germany, 26 percent for the Soviet Union, and 28 percent for Japan. Even after World War II began in 1939, one of the arguments advanced during the next two years for going to war with Germany and Japan was that doing so would help maintain access to foreign markets for American goods, thus avoiding industrial strangulation.[10]

The Era of National Security As Solely Military Security

The attack on Pearl Harbor quashed whatever illusions Americans might still have had about our invulnerability, our free military security. At the end of the war, the United States would assume a new role in world affairs—the global military superpower. "Our national security can only be assured on a very broad and comprehensive front," Navy Secretary James Forrestal told the Senate in August 1945. "I am using the word 'security' here consistently and continuously rather than 'defense.'" Replied Senator Edwin Johnson, "I like your words 'national security.'"[11]

The phrase had not been widely used before, and it needed explanation.[12] Very soon, however, both the term "national security" and the idea that it referred almost exclusively to military security became commonplace, primarily because the principal "external" threats to the American way of life—that is, to our security—quickly came to be seen as the spread of communism and the growing military capability of communist countries. By 1947, the phrase had become so widely used that the National Security Act, which established among other things the National Security Council, did not bother to define the term, but left open an expansive (i.e., not purely military) interpretation by stating: "The function of the Council shall be to advise the President with respect to the integration of domestic, foreign, and military policies relating to the national security."

Secretary Forrestal himself apparently had a broader conception of the phrase than his defining comment suggested, since in the same Senate hearing he said, "The question of national security is not merely a question of the Army and Navy. We have to take into account our whole potential for war, our mines, industry, manpower, research, and all the activities that go into normal civilian life."[13] In 1947, Secretary of State Dean Acheson described the broad and systematic nature of the burden America would bear in the cold war:

We are in a period now I think of the formulation of a mood. The country is getting serious. It is getting impressed by the fact that the business of dealing with the Russians is a long, long job. People . . . now see it as a long, long pull, and that it can only be done by the United States getting itself together, determining that we cannot maintain a counter-balance to the communistic power without strengthening all those other parts of the world which belong in the system with us. That takes money, imagination, American skill and American technical help and many, many years.[14]

Acheson's formulation of national security policy reached into every corner of United States policy. It meant that although the goal of the policy might be military in nature—containing the Soviet Union—the means could include a host of nonmilitary measures. And in the late 1940s, economic measures would be the main instrument of containment,[15] particularly the Marshall Plan, a massive foreign aid program for rebuilding Europe in large part to help thwart the spread of communism. Since 1949 and the establishment of NATO (North Atlantic Treaty Organization), the United States has also used export policy to help contain the Soviet Union, through the *ad hoc* Coordinating Committee on Multilateral Export Controls, known as CoCom. Working through CoCom, the United States and its NATO allies (except Iceland) restricted exports of sensitive technology to the Soviet Union and its Warsaw Pact allies. In the long run, these export policies hurt the competitiveness of United States industries by denying American commercial manufacturers access to important foreign markets, but through the 1950s and 1960s, the United States was undeniably the world's technological leader. Our economic security was taken for granted. Only our policy of containment mattered.[16]

The first formal and comprehensive statement of what United States cold war policy should be was NSC 68, a joint State-Defense Department review and reassessment of American foreign and defense policy, delivered to the National Security Council in April 1950. According to NSC 68: "The Kremlin seeks to bring the free world under its dominion by the methods of the cold war."[17] Failing to respond strongly and quickly to the growing Soviet threat, the report argued, would progressively isolate

43

the United States, since "the Soviet Union would quickly dominate most of Eurasia, probably without meeting armed resistance." Ultimately, the only options left to the United States would be "to capitulate or to fight alone and on the defensive, with drastically limited offensive and retaliatory capabilities in comparison with the Soviet Union." Avoiding this fate will require "a large measure of sacrifice and discipline" by the American people: "They will be asked to give up some of the benefits which they have come to associate with their freedoms." NSC 68 recognized the importance of economic strength in winning the cold war, but made clear that in this aspect of strength the United States was far ahead of the Soviet Union. Stopping the Kremlin, however, would necessitate:

A substantial increase in expenditures for military purposes. . . .

A substantial increase in military assistance programs. . . .

Reduction of federal expenditures for purposes other than defense and foreign assistance, if necessary by the deferment of certain desirable programs.

Increased taxes.[18]

Achieving public support for these policies was made easier by the North Korean invasion of South Korea on June 25, 1950. The Korean War became the first major military containment operation, and resulted in a rapid buildup of the defense budget, from $9.5 billion in 1948 (the equivalent of $85 billion today) to $67.5 billion in 1952 (the equivalent of $451 billion today). The defense budget never again dropped below $200 billion (in today's dollars). The aim of the ensuing rearmament effort was not merely to fight and win the Korean War, but also to create forces strong enough to balance Soviet power and deter Soviet aggression.[19]

More than any other postwar president, Dwight D. Eisenhower saw the economic dimension of security. For instance, he defended his trade program by saying, "If we fail in our trade policy, we may fail in all. Our domestic employment, our standard of living, our security, and the solidarity of the free world—are all involved."[20] Eisenhower understood the dangers of overspending on defense, the delicate balance between military security and economic security. As he said in 1957: "Beyond a wise and reasonable level, which is always changing . . . money spent on arms may be money wasted. . . . National security requires far more than military power. Economic and moral factors play indispensable roles. Any program that endangers our economy could defeat us."[21]

Economic security does not mean using economic means to achieve military-oriented national security ends. Economic security means regarding economic strength as an end in itself. For Eisenhower, the defense budget was the centerpiece of his overall deficit-reduction strategy. He believed "the economy was the pillar of U.S. strength and security, and unbalanced budgets threatened that pillar," in the words of one analyst of his defense policies.[22] For this reason, Eisenhower was committed to reducing the defense budget and getting the overall budget in balance. By 1955, the Korean War long over, he had reduced the defense budget to $33 billion (the equivalent of $228 billion today).

The 1950s would see a host of nonmilitary programs justified in the name of national security, defense, and the cold war, many with the word "Defense" in their titles. Congress in part justified a major infrastructure bill, the National Defense Highway Act, establishing a forty-thousand-mile national highway system, as a means of rapidly spreading armaments throughout the country in the event of war. After the 1957 launch by the Soviet Union of *Sputnik*, the first satellite to orbit the earth, a previously languishing education bill became the National Defense Education Act, whose purpose was to create a generation of American scientists and engineers able to compete with the Russians.[23]

DARPA and Industrial Policy

The same post-*Sputnik* frenzy saw the establishment of the Defense Department's Advanced Research Projects Agency (DARPA), "to help maintain U.S. technological superiority over, and to prevent unforeseen technological advances by, its potential adversaries." DARPA support was crucial in the development of key advanced military technology, such as stealth, lasers, and military aircraft design. Nevertheless, DARPA interpreted its mission broadly and spent nearly half its budget on "dual-use" technologies, those with both military and civilian applications, sometimes with stunning success. One business publication has called DARPA "the biggest venture capital fund in the world."[24]

DARPA grants led to the first computer time-sharing system, the first local area computer network, the idea of the personal computer, as well as the menu- and icon-driven software used in the first Apple Macintosh. As the Harvard Business School case study on DARPA explains:

> [DARPA] supplied grants and, later, the venture capital, to fund development of artificial intelligence and parallel processing computers. In fact, in the late 1960s it designated four research institutions— Stanford, Berkeley, Carnegie-Mellon, and MIT—as academic centers for the study of computers and computing; using agency seed money, DARPA virtually single-handedly created the United States' position of world leadership in computer sciences. (The four DARPA-funded centers would train, directly or indirectly, nearly every computer sciences expert in the nation.)[25]

DARPA owes much of its success to its being a classic fast-cycle organization. It is streamlined, with only three administrative levels and few rigid rules governing day-to-day operations. As the Harvard case study notes, "Decisions were made quickly and the organization could adapt rapidly to the needs of the moment." And like any fast-cycle company, it had one unifying mission that guided its efforts. Former director Craig Fields explained, "All DARPA can do is generate zero-cost intellectual property. Someone else out there has to market, manufacture, export, license, gain access to markets, and protect their rights. All that is outside of DARPA's immediate area of responsibility."[26]

Thus, throughout the 1940s and 1950s, foreign aid, export policy, infrastructure policy, education policy, industrial policy, and, of course, military spending increases were all justified in part or in whole as a means to contain the Soviet Union and strengthen United States military security. Containment, of course, meant isolation, and in this sense our strategy against the Soviet Union was the same one we used against Iraq in Operation Desert Storm, the same one Colonel Boyd's fast-cycle theory emphasized: isolating the enemy. Moreover, we adopted a systems-oriented approach; all relevant aspects of United States economic and military policy were applied to the same end. These are among the main reasons America won the cold war.

New Elements of Security

The early 1970s put an end to any simple or specific meaning the term "national security" might have had. The Vietnam War was one turning point. Was America's national security at stake in Vietnam? Early on in America's growing involvement in the conflict, the answer, for many, seemed a clear yes. During the wrenching process of disentangling America from the conflict, however, President Lyndon Johnson and his successors said that independence for Vietnam was not crucial to American security.[27]

At the same time that America's failure in Vietnam was challenging traditional notions of the military aspect of national security, America's economic vitality was sapped by rising inflation, the growing economic strength of Europe and Japan, and the first oil shock. In a 1974 essay, "The Legitimate Claims of National Security," Maxwell Taylor wrote that "the most formidable threats to this nation are in the nonmilitary field," including "retarded economic growth, higher costs of industrial production, new deficits in international payments, and increased inflation." Taylor worried that the National Security Council paid "only incidental attention to relevant domestic matters and almost none to environmental factors of such critical importance to our security as the population explosion." His essay followed the Arab oil embargo of 1973 and a steep rise in the price of oil. He wrote: "One could hardly hope to find a better example of the seriousness of nonmilitary threats to national security than the present energy crisis."[28] Energy security, like the other elements of an updated definition of national security, has both nonmilitary and military components.

Energy insecurity came in the 1970s as a brand new phenomenon for the United States; we had always had our tremendous native production capability. In the mid-1950s, America still produced roughly half of all of the world's oil—twice as much oil as the Middle Eastern and North African oil states combined. By the late 1960s, the United States surplus production had vanished. Between 1967 and 1973, oil imports rose from 19 percent to 36 percent of total United States oil consumption. In 1972, before the first oil price shock, the then-chairman of the Atomic Energy Commission, James Schlesinger, urged the promotion of energy conservation for reasons of national security, foreign economic policy, and environmental improvement, but few shared his view.[29] Within two

47

years, however, Congress would proclaim that "the urgency of the Nation's energy challenge will require commitments similar to those undertaken in the Manhattan and Apollo projects."[30] In 1975, fuel efficiency standards and the strategic petroleum reserve were established. In April 1977, President Jimmy Carter called America's actions on energy "the moral equivalent of war." Carter, together with Schlesinger (first, his energy "czar" and later secretary of energy), implemented a broad "nonmilitary" energy program aimed at reducing United States oil imports— by eliminating price controls on American domestic oil, promoting energy conservation, and supporting the development of alternative fuels (including synthetic fuels) and renewable energy, like solar.

But there would be a strong military emphasis in Carter's energy policy as well. The December 1979 Soviet invasion of Afghanistan jumpstarted the President's military energy policy, known as the Carter Doctrine. Within a month of the invasion, Carter announced, "An attempt by any outside force to gain control of the Persian Gulf region will be regarded as an assault on the vital interests of the United States of America and such an assault will be repelled by any means necessary, including military force."[31] In 1980, Carter established the Rapid Deployment Joint Task Force to make possible a quick response to any Soviet incursion. The military contribution to energy security—keeping the shipping lanes open—was laid out in the annual Defense Department report for fiscal year 1981:

> Clearly the independence and territorial integrity of the United States is a necessary condition of security. But it no longer is, if it ever was, a sufficient condition. . . . The particular manner in which our economy has expanded means that we have come to depend to no small degree on imports, exports, and the earnings from overseas investments for our material well-being. In 1978, our imports of goods and services amounted to $229 billion. Exports were $225 billion, or around 10 percent of the Gross National Product. . . .
>
> With time and a reduction in our standard of living, we could forgo or substitute for much of what we import. But any major interruption of this flow of goods and services could have the most serious nearterm effects on the U.S. economy. In no respect is that more evident than in the case of oil. A large-scale disruption in the supply of foreign oil could have as damaging consequences for the United States as the loss of an important military campaign, or indeed a war. Such a

48

disruption could be almost fatal to some of our allies. It is little wonder, in the circumstances, *that access to foreign oil*—in the Middle East, North and West Africa, the North Sea, Latin America, and Southeast Asia—*constitutes a critical condition of U.S. security.* More generally, our economic well-being and security depend on expanding world trade, freedom of the arteries of commerce at sea and in the air, and increasingly on the peaceful unhindered uses of space [emphasis added].

The Carter energy policies, coupled with rising oil prices, accomplished a great deal. From 1973 to 1986, the nation's GNP growth averaged 2.5 percent a year, but our energy use did not grow at all, saving America about $150 billion a year in energy costs (compared to the case where energy use and GNP grow in tandem). By the mid-1980s, we were able to save the equivalent of thirteen million barrels of oil a day compared with 1973 levels, making energy efficiency the largest new source of oil for the United States by far—a new energy source two-fifths bigger than the domestic oil industry. Oil imports, which had reached 46 percent of consumption in 1977, had dipped to 28 percent by 1982. Projects to boost energy efficiency funded by the Department of Energy (DOE) during the Carter years have paid off remarkably. Analysis by the Lawrence Berkeley Laboratory showed that for three projects the DOE funded in the 1970s, federal investment totaling $6 million will eventually generate savings of $82 billion—a return on taxpayer investment of 14,000 to 1. (Not all of Carter's energy policies were successful. The Synthetic Fuels Corporation, for example, never produced a single barrel of oil substitutes, despite an investment of several billion.[32])

Unfortunately, Ronald Reagan's administration largely reversed Carter's nonmilitary energy program. The efficiency standards for new cars were rolled back, federal funding for energy conservation was cut by 70 percent, and funding for solar and other renewable forms of energy was cut by 85 percent. (In contrast, Japan's funding for such R&D doubled during the 1980s; the Japanese now spend more money on solar energy than we do, as do the Germans.) These reversals, coupled with the 1986 collapse of oil prices (mainly caused by the glut created by energy efficiency), brought back rising energy use. Oil imports, which had dipped to 28% of overall consumption in 1985, began to rise steadily, reaching 50 percent for the first seven months of 1990 (prior to the Iraqi invasion of Kuwait), the highest level ever. Our reliance on Persian Gulf oil soared more than 500 percent in the four years from 1985 to 1989. In 1990, oil accounted for more than half of our $100 billion trade deficit. The Reagan administration's energy policy was almost wholly a military approach, guaranteeing that the United States would spend tens of billions of dollars each year safeguarding the flow of oil, ultimately reflagging eleven Kuwaiti oil tankers and providing a naval presence for support.[33]

President Bush went to war with Iraq at least in part to maintain access to the region's oil supply, yet his 1991 National Energy Strategy rejected a nonmilitary energy program based on demand reduction. Having largely ignored potential solutions to the problem, the report is forced to conclude: "The National Energy Strategy review . . . revealed that our Nation and the world are likely to depend *more* on Middle East oil suppliers under any realistic scenario for the foreseeable future."[34] The Bush energy strategy will be examined at greater length in Chapter 4.

Access to foreign oil was not the only new national security issue. Access to all resources and resource scarcity in general, together with related problems of environmental degradation and overpopulation, joined the list of national security issues in the 1970s and 1980s. In 1976, Franklin P. Huddle, the director of the congressional study, *Science, Technology and American Diplomacy,* wrote: "National security requires a stable economy with assured supplies of materials for industry. In this sense, frugality and conservation of materials are essential to our national security. Security means more than safety from hostile attack; it includes the preservation of a system of civilization."[35]

In a 1977 paper, *Rethinking National Security,* Lester Brown, the president of the Worldwatch Institute, discussed at length a variety of resource and environmental problems he called national security threats, including deforestation; soil erosion of croplands; "the threat of climate modification," in particular, the greenhouse effect; and food scarcity, agricultural mismanagement, and starvation. Brown wrote: "Non-military threats to a nation's security are much less clearly defined than military ones. They are often the result of cumulative processes that ultimately lead to the collapse of biological systems or to the depletion of a country's oil reserves. These processes in themselves are seldom given much thought until they pass a critical threshold and disaster strikes."[36]

Brown was not worrying over abstract, theoretical relationships between the environment and security. Disasters were all too evident around the globe. The tiny island nation of Haiti provides an example close to home. The Haitian exodus to the United States in the late 1970s, 1980s, and 1990s has been at least partly due to environmental degradation. Peasant landholders had cut most of the Haitian forests, causing erosion so severe that half the bedrock is exposed in some areas. As one environmental analyst has written: "Soil erosion in Haiti is so rapid that some farmers believe stones grow in their fields, while bulldozers are needed to clear the streets of Port-au-Prince of topsoil that flows down from the mountains in the rainy season."[37] A 1980 report to the United States Agency for International Development (USAID) concluded: "The general prognosis for Haiti's future is apocalyptic, with little or no indication from current trends and conditions that the country will be much more than an ecological wasteland by the year 2000."[38] Today, only 2 percent of the land is still forested. Only 11 percent of the land is able to sustain farming, and the farmable land continues to shrink.[39]

Similarly, a 1982 draft report prepared for USAID on the environment of El Salvador said: "The fundamental causes of the present conflict are as much environmental as political, stemming from problems of resource distribution in an overcrowded land."[40] El Salvador has a population density that exceeds India's. A still-classified 1984 CIA study, *Population, Resources, and Politics in the Third World: The Long View*, is reported to anticipate conflict because of tensions over water, extreme population pressure, immigration, and resource depletion. The study foresees more authoritarian governments and expects conflicts to become more frequent, particularly in the Third World.[41]

The fact that American experts were labeling economic, resource, and environmental problems as national security problems did not move the government or the nation to recognize them as such, or to devote to them "money, imagination, American skill and American technical help and many, many years," as Dean Acheson had said the cold war would require. Quite the reverse was true with the advent of the Reagan administration in 1981. Spending on military security jumped 50 percent between 1980 and 1985. This shopping spree did not begin with the new Republican administration; defense spending began to rise in the last year of the Carter administration. But Carter at least maintained a balance between military and nonmilitary security policy, stressing, for example, a comprehensive energy strategy. Reagan dropped the nonmilitary energy policy; further, Reagan eliminated, weakened, or ignored environmental regulations, and cut funding for federal R&D in civilian technology. The decline in America's competitive position in a host of industries accelerated. Our budget and trade deficits exploded. Our energy security diminished as our dependence on foreign oil increased. Our environmental problems generally worsened, and the military became the largest source of toxic and nuclear waste as well as key ozone-destroying chemicals. Our economic, energy, and environmental security have all suffered at the expense of military security.

With the ending of the cold war, the debate over the meaning of national security has begun anew. For instance, in the Winter 1990/91 issue of *Foreign Affairs*, Theodore Moran, director of the Program in International Business Diplomacy at Georgetown University's School of Foreign Service, listed six "primary areas" for "U.S. national security policy in the 1990s." They are "encouraging stability and reform in the Soviet Union, maintaining a cooperative U.S.-Japanese relationship, and avoiding vulnerabilities from the globalization of America's defense industrial base," and "reducing dependence on oil from the Persian Gulf, moderating the impact on the Third World of the prolonged debt crisis, and limiting the damage from the narcotics trade."[42] On the other hand, in the Spring 1989 issue of *Foreign Affairs*, Jessica Tuchman Mathews, vice president of the World Resources Institute, wrote that global developments suggested the need for broadening the definition of national security "to include resource, environmental and demographic issues."[43]

The new debate over national security may seem fuzzy; the debate has in fact always been fuzzy.

National Security, an Ambiguous Concept

"National security" was and is a widely invoked phrase. But any term that encompasses tools as diverse as nuclear bombs and educational policy—any goal that can be seen by one as requiring higher defense budgets but by another as justifying lower defense budgets—begs for a better definition.

The definitional problem and its dangers have not been lost on either the scholarly or the political community. In a 1950 essay, "The Meaning of National Security Policy," political scientist Harold Lasswell wrote:

> All measures which are proposed in the name of national security do not necessarily contribute to the avowed end. In particular, caution is needed against conceiving of national security policy in terms of foreign divorced from domestic policy; and so far as foreign policy is concerned, against confounding defense policy with armament. Our greatest security lies in the best balance of all instruments of foreign policy, and hence in the coordinated handling of arms, diplomacy, information, and economics; and in the proper correlation of all measures of foreign and domestic policy.[44]

Political scientist Arnold Wolfers, in his 1962 essay, "National Security as an Ambiguous Symbol," wrote of the phrases "national security" and "national interest":

> They may not mean the same things to different people. They may not have any precise meaning at all. Thus, while appearing to offer guidance and a basis for broad consensus, they may be permitting everyone to label whatever policy he favors with an attractive and possibly deceptive name.[45]

The British scholar Barry Buzan has argued that one reason national security remains a "weakly conceptualized, ambiguously defined, but politically powerful concept" is that "for the practitioners of state policy, compelling reasons exist for maintaining its symbolic ambiguity. . . . An undefined notion of national security offers scope for power-maximizing strategies to political and military elites, because of the considerable leverage over domestic affairs which can be obtained by invoking it."[46]

In theory, a good definition of national security is critical, since courts often have had to determine whether material could be kept classified for "national security" reasons. Yet, as the author of a *Yale Law Journal* article wrote: " 'National security' has long been recognized by courts . . . as a notoriously ambiguous and ill-defined phrase." The chairman of the House subcommittee that considered the original 1967 Freedom of Information Act stated, "National security [is] such an ill-defined phrase, that no one can give you a definition. . . . In 16 years of chairing the committee prior to Mr. Moorhead, I could never find anyone who could give me a definition." William Blair, deputy assistant secretary of state for public affairs, who helped draft the 1972 Executive Order No. 11,652, "Classification and Declassification of National Security Material," told Congress, "Our national security today depends on things like balance of payments, economic affairs, foreign assistance."[47]

Various definitions offered for "national security" serve only to underscore its ambiguous nature:

A nation has security when it does not have to sacrifice its legitimate interests to avoid war, and is able, if challenged, to maintain them by war. —*Walter Lippmann* (1943)

. . . to preserve the United States as a free nation with our fundamental institutions and values intact. —*National Security Council* (1950s)

Security, in an objective sense, measures the absence of threats to acquired values, in a subjective sense, the absence of fear that such values will be attacked. —*Arnold Wolfers* (1962)

. . . the ability of a nation to protect its internal values from external threats. —*International Encyclopedia of the Social Sciences* (1968)

Security itself is a relative freedom from war, coupled with a relatively high expectation that defeat will not be a consequence of any war that should occur. —*Ian Bellany* (1981)

National security, however, has a more extensive meaning than protection from physical harm; it also implies protection, through a variety of means, of vital economic and political interests, the loss of which could threaten fundamental values and the vitality of the state. —*Amos Jordan and William Taylor* (1981)

National security . . . is best defined as *the capacity to control those domestic and foreign conditions that the public opinion of a given community believes necessary to enjoy its own self-determination or autonomy, prosperity, and well-being.* [Emphasis in original] — *Charles Maier* (1990)[48]

The problem with the narrower, more traditional definitions is that America did not have the classic national security burden—ensuring the territorial inviolability of the country—as its principal concern. Even after World War II, the possibility of an external conventional military invasion of the United States was remote. Even if the entire nuclear weapons budget were allotted to ensuring the territorial integrity of the United States, it rarely accounted for more than 15 percent of the overall military budget. So, by the narrower definitions, such as Bellany's, the United States has had very little insecurity, and should not have sacrificed significant resources in the name of "national security."

The problem with the broader definitions, such as Maier's, is that virtually anything could be construed as a national security threat. Defining national security in terms of protecting "fundamental values" or "national interests" substitutes one undefined term for another; moreover, those terms include economic strength and so immediately suggest a broader formulation than military security.

As Richard Ullman, among others, has argued, the threat posed by the Soviet Union was not put forth principally as one of direct attack on America with drastic degradation in our quality of life (except in the case of nuclear war).[49] Rather, the threat was more that the Soviets would assert domination over Western Europe or other countries that shared our values, substantially closing those societies to us. That is also how the threat to the United States from Nazi Germany was discussed in the years before our entry into World War II.

The result of Soviet domination of Europe would have been, in Ullman's words, "fewer opportunities for American traders and investors . . . [and] for unfettered intellectual, cultural, and scientific exchange." The subordination of civil and political liberties in those countries "would have made it more difficult to assure their preservation in an isolated and even besieged United States." Therefore, in a variety of ways, "the range of options open to the United States government, and to persons and groups within American society, would have been importantly diminished."[50] Security requires maintaining interconnections and preserving choices.

Ullman offers the following definition, to which I will return later: "A threat to national security is an action or sequence of events that (1) threatens drastically and over a relatively brief span of time to degrade the quality of life for the inhabitants of a state, or (2) threatens significantly to narrow the range of policy choices available to the government of a state or to private, nongovernmental entities (persons, groups, corporations) within the state."[51]

*   *   *

Every problem facing the nation is not a national security threat. Historically, labeling a problem a "national security threat" has implied that it takes precedence over other problems and therefore dealing with it may entail some sacrifice for the nation. Moreover, the idea of national security has served as a unifying theme, a common orientation, by which political leaders have marshaled the full capabilities of the American system. For most of the nation's history, trade and economic strength have been vital components of America's security. The narrow concept of national security as solely military security was born in the ashes of World War II, when winning the cold war was identified as our principal postwar national security task—and the entire American system was devoted to containing the Soviet Union and the spread of communism. Some Presidents, such as Eisenhower and Carter, sought a balance between military and nonmilitary security, but winning the cold war remained the constant goal.

America's triumph in the cold war should lead to a complete reorientation of our security paradigm, refocusing on nonmilitary problems. While such a reorientation seems inevitable, it has been slow in developing. America remains without a comprehensive energy, environmental, or economic (i.e., industrial) policy, while it persists in an unwarranted, and indeed counterproductive, military policy. Without a new orientation, we cannot make the new decisions and actions necessary to solve our problems. Rigidity is particularly dangerous in a time of budget deficits and constrained resources. We cannot afford to do everything we would like. We need a new worldview, for ranking priorities, for making trade-offs.

The first cornerstone of such a worldview must be economic security. Echoing Eisenhower's words of thirty-five years ago, Robert Hormats, an economic adviser during the Reagan administration, has recently written: "If America's economy does falter, so will the underlying source of its international power. Thus this nation's central foreign policy priority in coming years and its central domestic priority must be the same: strengthening the American economy."[52]

The tragic spring 1992 riots in Los Angeles suggest the continuing relevance of words Harold Lasswell wrote more than forty years ago:

Two of the chief points of attack against the United States in foreign countries, for instance, are the alleged inherent instability of our economic system and the prevalence of discrimination against colored peoples. Whatever measures are taken at home to maintain high levels of productive employment and to reduce discrimination also strengthen our position abroad. Security policies are thus being made whenever any decision influences the stability of our economic life or the degree to which opportunity is made to depend upon individual merit.[53]

Nations we have accused of human rights violations—China, Libya, Iraq—piously accuse of hypocrisy. But even our allies increasingly see us as a nation that either cannot or will not solve its problems. If we are not a model for other nations, if we do not restore our economic security, our position of world leadership will be jeopardized.

The broad elements of an economic security program were discussed in the Introduction: To compete economically in the manufacturing trade war and sustain high-paying jobs, we must invest in technology and worker training, and promote fast-cycle manufacturing. The next chapter will discuss the specific policies needed to achieve economic security. Such policies can be paid for without increasing taxes, if we change from our current military-oriented industrial policy to one with a civilian focus. Our current economic policies are failing. We need a reorientation.

2

Restoring Economic Security

The opportunity to work, without interruption and for good wages, is the most valuable form of security for most Americans.

—Final Report of the American Assembly,
Economic Security for Americans, 1953[1]

The United States no longer provides economic security for most of its people. That is, since the mid-1970s, the standard of living for most Americans has stagnated or declined. In this chapter, I will discuss some of the long-term economic problems facing this country and detail a program for fixing them.

Declining real wages are a clear sign of America's economic insecurity: For roughly two thirds of all wage earners, real wages dropped 12 percent in the decade and a half before 1991. Wages slid back to 1960s levels, adjusted for inflation.[2]

Family income is equally disappointing. According to a 1992 report by the Federal Reserve Board, "real median pre-tax income for families was virtually unchanged between 1983 and 1989." By 1990, the median income of American families was lower than it was in 1973. Since the late 1970s, only the upper class—the richest 20 percent of Americans— experienced significant real income growth after taxes (more than 10 percent); the richest 1 percent of American families saw their family income leap 74 percent—an average rise of $233,000 per family. The income of the upper-middle class (the next richest 20 percent) grew a few percent. The actual middle class—the middle 20 percent—saw its income stagnate.[3]

The unlucky bottom 40 percent of American families experienced shrinking incomes, which is particularly tragic because they were making so little to begin with. *In 1990, more than 13 million children, one fifth of all children under the age of 18, lived in poverty, and one quarter of all children under age 3 were poor.*[4]

Family income has not fallen as fast as wages have, in large part because wage earners have been working longer hours. In her 1991 book, *The Overworked American,* economist Juliet Schor explains that for the production and nonsupervisory employees who make up 80 percent of the labor force, *"just to reach their 1973 standard of living, they must work 245 more hours, or 6-plus extra weeks a year"* (emphasis in original). Many families sent a second wage earner into the work force to help make ends meet. The Economic Policy Institute reported in 1991 that "all of the increase in incomes of married couples with children since 1979 has been contributed by working mothers."[5] In many cases, two paychecks provide little increase in a family's net wealth, because of added expenses such as day care and taxes on the second income. A 1992 study of working families concluded that after adjusting for increased hours of work and work expenses, "the standard of living for the bottom 80 percent of families declined or showed no improvement" from 1979 to 1989.[6]

A startling sign of how difficult the struggle has been for most Americans was revealed in a December 1990 Census Bureau report on household net worth (assets minus debt): Only the richest 20 percent of American families became wealthier between 1984 and 1988—a period of growth widely touted as benefiting the entire populace.[7] Everyone but the top fifth declined in net worth (see page 61). And an April 1992 survey by researchers at the Federal Reserve Board and the Internal Revenue Service revealed that by 1989, the top 1 percent of American families was worth more than the bottom 90 percent and that their share of total net worth had risen from 31 percent in 1983 to 37 percent in 1989.[8]

Median NET WORTH by Income Quintile: 1988 and 1984

	1988	1984 (in 1988 dollars)
Upper class (top 20%)	$111,770	$98,411
Upper-middle class	46,253	49,947
Middle class	28,044	29,459
Lower-middle class	19,694	21,248
Lowest class (bottom 20%)	4,324	5,130

The "trickle-down" theory of the 1980s failed, and failed badly. Even during the mid-1980s, a period of steady economic growth, only the rich got richer; the money neither flooded down nor trickled down.

Moreover, most famlies increased their debt in the 1980s because the costs of the American dream outpaced income. According to a 1991 Census Bureau report, 57 percent of all American families cannot buy a median-priced home in the region where they live. More alarming, 90 percent of all families now renting their homes are unable to buy a median-priced house. Similarly, the cost of keeping one student at a university or private college rose from 22 percent of the average income of a family with children in 1979 to 31 percent of that income in 1987. If you have two children, ages four and ten, and started saving for their private college tuition today, *Newsweek* columnist Jane Bryant Quinn estimates, you must put away $1,500 *every month—$18,000 every year.*[9]

Who can know the toll, as more and more Americans see their hopes fade for a better future for themselves and their children?

While the cost may be unknowable, the cause is not. The Congressional Office of Technology Assessment explained it in a 1990 report:

The weaknesses in U.S. manufacturing technology must be cured if the Nation is to enjoy rising living standards together with a strong, stable position in international trade. Most of the U.S. trade deficit is in manufactured goods. . . . Manufacturing also supports most of this country's commercial research and development. . . .

For industrial nations, technology is the key to competitive success. Nations that rely on low wages to sell their goods in the world market are, by definition, poor, whereas superior technology raises productivity and thus supports rising standards of living.[10]

In 1988, the average weekly American wage for retail trade was $184; for services, $290; for finance, insurance, and real estate, $326; and for manufacturing, $418.[11] The high-paying jobs are in manufacturing. Unfortunately, while manufacturing productivity grew somewhat in the 1980s, data released by the Commerce Department in 1992 revealed that contrary to previous calculations, *manufacturing's share of United States GNP did not rebound in the 1980s.* Instead, manufacturing's share of GNP apparently continued a slow but steady decline throughout the decade. At the same time, manufacturing suffered decreased employment and declining wages. The manufacturing sector lost three million jobs from 1979 to 1991, according to the Bureau of Labor Statistics and the vast majority of those jobs were lost in the very high-paying durable goods sector, which makes cars and other long-lasting products. There are now fewer manufacturing jobs than there were in 1967. In the late 1960s, manufacturing workers made up more than 25 percent of the labor force, a figure that dropped to 20 percent by the late 1970s and then plunged to roughly 15 percent by the early 1990s. Equally dismaying, given the economic growth of the mid-1980s, real hourly compensation for manufacturing workers (including benefits) declined in 1987, 1988, 1989, and 1990—the first such four-year decline since World War II. Real hourly compensation today is lower than it was in 1976.[12]

The United States was the only major industrialized nation whose manufacturing production workers experienced a drop in hourly compensation between 1978 and 1988. During that decade, the hourly compensation of American production workers dropped 0.41 percent per year. In contrast, the wages of production workers in Japan, France, and West Germany grew every year by 0.92 percent, 2.15 percent, and 1.89 percent respectively.[13]

The much-acclaimed job boom of the 1980s came from the relatively low-paying service sector, where productivity growth has been terrible. Half the jobs created between 1979 and 1987 paid wages below the poverty level for a family of four. Many of those jobs did not provide adequate health coverage or adequate pensions.[14]

62

*   *   *

America's economic insecurity is likely to worsen in the 1990s. Real family earnings fell by about 5 percent in 1989, and dropped again in 1990. The recession that began in 1990 has started wiping away what meager gains had been made in the mid-1980s. *In 1990, the real net worth of American households suffered its largest decline since 1946.* In 1991, Americans' per-capita income shrank (adjusted for inflation) for the first time in nine years.[15]

By 1990, the declining wages of the bottom 60 percent of Americans were being experienced by the upper-middle class—that 20 percent below the top quintile. As *The Economist* stated in February 1991: "The recession is cutting a swath through America's managerial and professional elite—accountants, lawyers, engineers, bankers, advertising men, property agents and, especially, middle managers. . . . Companies are eliminating entire layers of middle management."[16] A 1990 *Fortune* magazine survey of 1,005 corporations revealed that 90 percent of all companies with more than five thousand employees have reduced white-collar workers since 1985; 59 percent have done so in 1990 alone. And 41 percent of the top personnel executives polled expected further managerial reductions in the next five years.[17]

The job cuts are expected to continue long after the recession ends. While Japanese fast-cycle corporations are exceedingly lean, with a relatively low proportion of white-collar workers, American companies are exceedingly fat. In most American corporations, as noted in the Introduction, more than half the workers take no part in operations or production work. In companies such as General Motors, Mobil Oil, General Electric, and IBM, 60 percent or more of the work force is white-collar.[18] With so many top-heavy companies now on an Ultra-Slim Fast program to trim their highly paid white-collar work force, those middle managers are competing for fewer and fewer well-paying jobs. The gap between the upper class and the remaining 80 percent of Americans will continue to grow.

Other factors will tend to widen that gap further. First, what economic success America did have in the 1980s was achieved in large part by borrowing tremendous sums from foreigners and by selling companies and real estate to them; the Japanese in particular have been snapping up high-tech companies. This squandering of national wealth can only make Americans poorer in the long run; a significant portion of the nation's future earnings will now go to foreigners who hold our debt and own our companies.[19]

Second, the government deficits run up in the 1980s have guaranteed us higher state and federal taxes—and therefore a bigger bite out of take-home pay. Funding for essential state services, such as education and infrastructure (roads, bridges, sewer systems), is being scaled back, which will hamper long-term growth.

Third, the manufacturing sector is highly unlikely to create many new jobs, since America lags in the area of fast-cycle manufacturing, which is crucial to national competitiveness. A 1991 study found that the United States was behind or falling behind in a depressingly long list of critical areas: flexible manufacturing; design of the manufacturing process; integration of research, design, and manufacturing; high-speed machining; precision machining and forming; and total quality management.[20] In robotics and automated equipment, the United States is no longer even a player. Such disadvantages are the very reasons America cannot commercialize so many of the products it invents.

These deficiencies are certain to grow; the other major industrialized countries continue to invest in capital goods at a higher proportion of their gross domestic product (GDP) than we do. In 1990, the Japanese invested more than 23 percent of its GDP in new factories, machinery, and other capital goods. The United States investment came to a paltry 12.6 percent. America is stuck in a vicious circle. Our relatively low rate of capital investment is in part due to our notoriously poor personal savings rate, which in turn cannot be expected to rise much if most American families are unable to maintain their standard of living. Yet how can living standards grow, if the strategy of American manufacturers for remaining globally competitive is to eliminate high-paying jobs, reduce wages, manufacture abroad, and hope the United States dollar remains weak? Being the low-cost producer is not the path to economic security.[21]

Fourth, as will be discussed in the next chapter, Japan's Asian industrial policy will bring tens of millions of Asian laborers into a sophisticated manufacturing network that will squeeze American wages *and* salaries even further. It is the stated purpose of Japan's policy to pull up the living standards of all Asia through a systematic export-driven manufacturing strategy. To a significant, but lesser extent, America will face growing competition from Europe, as a result of the unification of Germany, the elimination of trade barriers in the European Community in 1992, and the slow assimilation of the rest of Eastern Europe into a united market.

A *Business Week* special report on competitiveness concluded gloomily in December 1990, *"Without changes, much of the decline in living standards is yet to come."*[22] The United States labor force is expected to increase by only 1 percent a year in this decade, and we are doing nothing to increase productivity beyond its current dismal growth rate of 1 percent a year. Unless something changes fundamentally—systematically—this almost guarantees that America's economy cannot grow more than 2 percent a year—the same growth rate achieved during the Great Depression of the 1930s! If Japan is able to maintain a 4-percent annual growth rate, its economy will surpass ours in size in about twenty years.[23]

None of this is preordained, but changing our future—and achieving economic security—will require a major reorientation of our national priorities.

Defining Economic Security

The primary goal of economic security must be to reverse the decline in the living standard of the majority of Americans. Equity, or ensuring that the poorest Americans are not left behind as the country grows richer, is part of that goal.[24] America's recent record on equity has not been acceptable. The poor have become poorer since the 1970s, income inequality has grown steadily in the 1980s, and children in particular have swelled the ranks of the poor. Who can doubt that the growing disparity between haves and have-nots contributed to the April 1992 riots in south central Los Angeles? America's income distribution does not compare favorably with that of other industrialized nations.[25] In America, the income of the richest fifth of the population is 8.9 times the income of the poorest fifth. In France, that ratio is 6.5, in Germany it is 5.7, and in Japan it is 4.3.

Finally, economic security will not long endure if it is achieved in an environmentally unsustainable fashion, such as by using up nonrenewable resources or by destroying our ecosystem. Chapters 4 and 5 will discuss how economic vitality can be sustainably attained.

65

First a definition: *Economic security measures a nation's ability to improve the living standards of its citizens in an equitable and sustainable fashion.*[26]

Two related questions arise. First, should we now see economic security as equal to or even more important than military security in our conception of national security? Second, should we adopt a technology or industrial policy for economic reasons (because we are worried about our manufacturing competitiveness) and/or for military reasons (because the United States military is becoming increasingly dependent on foreign suppliers, particularly Japanese high technology)? This entire book is dedicated to demonstrating that the answer to the first question is yes. This chapter will focus on United States industrial policy.

The first question, economic security versus military security, grows out of a long-standing debate[27] rekindled in the late 1980s by Paul Kennedy's best-seller, *The Rise and Fall of the Great Powers,* which argued that the United States was suffering from strategic overstretch: too many military commitments that were undermining the American economy. Joseph Nye, Jr., in his 1990 book, *Bound to Lead,* wrote one of the many "antideclinist" responses to Kennedy. Nye does argue for a broader definition of security: "National security has become more complicated as threats have shifted from military ones (that is, threats against territorial integrity) to economic and ecological ones." But in Nye's formulation, Japan's economic strength is not a greater challenge than Soviet military power, the United States is clearly still the world's hegemonic power, and "leadership means pointing out that the U.S. economy can afford both domestic and international security if Americans are willing to pay for them."[28]

There is no need to rehash the declinist debate for it has been rendered largely moot by events. Communism's collapse (as well as America's success in the Gulf war) seems to support the position of those who see the United States as the major superpower for the near future. But the principal result of those events has been to raise the importance of economic issues and underscore United States weaknesses. In his 1990 essay, "The World Economy After the Cold War," C. Fred Bergsten, former assistant secretary of the treasury, argues:

America may soon be the only military superpower. Such status, however, will be of decreased utility as global military tensions are substantially reduced and international competition becomes largely economic.

Moreover the United States is in relative economic decline, caught in a scissors movement between increasing dependence on external economic forces and a shrinking capacity to influence those forces. . . .

In the short to medium term, America's international economic position is likely to decline further.[29]

The end of the cold war has caused an early reassessment in the thinking of the conservative analyst Samuel Huntington, director of Harvard University's Institute for Strategic Studies. At the end of 1988, he wrote an article taking exception with the "declinists" and arguing that "American hegemony looks quite secure":

Currently, the popular choice—and the choice of the declinists—for the country that will supersede the United States is, of course, Japan. "The American Century is over," a former U.S. official has said. "The big development in the latter part of the century is the emergence of Japan as a major superpower." With all due respect to Clyde Prestowitz, this proposition will not hold up. Japan has neither the size, natural resources, military strength, diplomatic affiliates nor, most important, the ideological appeal to be a twentieth-century superpower. . . .

Mr. Prestowitz's prediction as to which century belongs to which country is likely to be less accurate than that of Seizaburo Sato: "The twentieth century was the American century. The twenty-first century will be the American century."[30]

Two years later, with the Berlin Wall down and the Warsaw Pact in tatters, Huntington recast his position:

The issue for the United States is whether it can meet the economic challenge from Japan as successfully as it did the political and military challenges from the Soviet Union. If it cannot, at some future time the United States could find itself in a position relative to Japan that is comparable to the position the Soviet Union is now in relative to the United States. Having lost its economic supremacy, the United States would no longer be the world's only superpower and would be simply a major power like all others.

67

In this later article, Huntington argues that America is rightly "obsessed with Japan for the same reasons that it was once obsessed with the Soviet Union. It sees that country as a major threat to its primacy in a crucial arena of power."[31]

The key question today is *not*, Has America's spending on military security already led to relative economic decline? The key question is, Does America now have more important ways to spend its defense dollars? The answer is yes, because military security is no longer the preeminent component of national security.

There are two economic components to national security. The first is economic security, defined previously—a nation's ability to provide a rising living standard for its people, equitably and sustainably. How can America consider itself secure if it fails to provide all its people good jobs, increasing wealth, home ownership, and opportunities for higher education?[32]

The second component is economic independence or flexibility. It is our ability to influence world events favorably, our capacity to mount a Marshall Plan when needed. The notion of "economic independence" is a traditional definition of security. As political scientist Harold Lasswell wrote in 1950: "The distinctive meaning of national security is *freedom from foreign dictation*."[33] It was, for instance, the principal concern of most of those who raised the energy security issue after the oil shock of 1973.

The need for both economic competitiveness *and* economic independence leads to a definition of national security with two parallel elements: "A threat to national security is whatever threatens to significantly (1) degrade the quality of life of the people, or (2) narrow the range of policy choices available to their government."[34]

The economic threats to United States national security are interconnected and severe. Although I have separated the two components, competitiveness and independence, we could not achieve one for very long without the other. The erosion of American manufacturing is degrading the quality of life of Americans because sustaining high real incomes requires maintaining high value-added jobs—those jobs that can be very high paying, such as advanced manufacturing, because they involve adding a high value to whatever good or service is being produced. Fear of narrowed policy choices is the concern of those who worry that as the United States declines economically relative to other countries, we may lose our power to influence world events. The erosion of the American semiconductor and high-technology manufacturing base not only threatens our economic security, but it also affects our capacity to make and use our own sophisticated weaponry independently.

Semiconductors and Security

A food chain exists in electronics. At the high end are computers and electronics, which "feed on" semiconductor chips, which in turn feed on a host of devices that are crucial to their manufacture. As America loses market share at the high end, we lose market share in the middle and bottom ranges, especially since Japanese cartels (keiretsu) invariably buy components from their own suppliers. Open up an Apple Macintosh or another name-brand American computer and you will find an array of Japanese and Asian components, chips, transformers, and display screens. Americans will buy from anyone.

From 1984 to 1989, United States world market share in computers and office equipment fell from 51 percent to 32 percent, while Japan's share jumped from 14 percent to 32 percent. From 1985 to 1989, the United States share of the world electronics market fell from 65 percent to 51 percent; Japan's share rose from 22 percent to 31 percent. From 1980 to 1989, the United States share of the world semiconductor market fell from 57 percent to 35 percent; Japan's share climbed from 27 percent to 52 percent. In the dynamic random access memory chips crucial to all computers, Japan's share of the world market catapulted to 70 percent from 40 percent during the 1980s, while America's share collapsed to 15 percent from 55 percent. At the bottom end of the electronic food chain, Japan's share of the worldwide market for stepping aligners needed to manufacture chips soared from under 10 percent in 1979 to more than 70 percent in 1988, while America's share plummeted from over 90 percent to 20 percent. Other semiconductor equipment showed similar declines. In 1982, none of the world's top three semiconductor equipment suppliers was Japanese; in 1988, they all were (and *each* of those three Japanese companies had world sales larger than the *combined* sales of the three top suppliers in 1982).[35]

Semiconductors are an economically strategic industry. They are the foundation of the information age and an essential element in consumer electronics and a growing number of other products. Semiconductors are also a militarily strategic industry.

In the Gulf war, more than twenty weapons systems, including the F-15, F-16, and F-18 fighters, relied on components not made in America, such as transistors and microchips. Many, such as the M-1 tank, could not be manufactured without Japanese machine tools. Allied officers had to go to Japan for urgently needed battery packs used in command and control computers, for video display terminals needed to analyze real-time data from reconnaissance planes, and for semiconductors and other key components. In all, the Bush administration made nearly thirty requests to foreign governments during the course of the war for key parts.[36] Moreover, most of the weapons we used in the Gulf war were based on American technology developed in the 1970s. The next generation of our weapons systems increasingly relies on advanced technologies that America does not control.

In his book, *The Japan That Can* Really *Say No,* the Japanese politician and author, Shintaro Ishihara, writes: "What made [the Americans'] pinpoint bombing so effective was PTV, a high-quality semiconductor used in the brain part of the computers that control most modern weapons. There were 93 foreign-made semiconductors in the weapons used by the United States. Among them, 92 were made in Japan." America "should wake up from this illusion" of superpower status because it "had to ask other countries to contribute money so it could fight, and it depended on foreign technology to carry out its war strategy."[37]

Ishihara carries the rhetorical flourish too far—America remains *the* military superpower. Yet as America's technological weakness imperils our status as the preeminent *economic* superpower, our military strength, too, will begin to suffer. A fast-cycle military strategy cannot succeed if it is based on foreign parts for important weapons. In the Gulf war, America had the luxury of more than five months to prepare our weapons, test them in the desert, and see what spare parts were needed and what components needed fixing. In a future war, we may not be so lucky, and we might not have such cooperative allies as were assembled for the coalition. The United States military is renowned for its ability to quickly jury-rig troubled systems. But as foreign components make up larger and more integral parts of increasingly complex weapons, such rigging will become harder and harder to do.

*   *   *

A civilian industrial policy would bring back a rising living standard for most Americans and bolster the defense industrial base. There are two more good reasons to adopt an industrial policy: It has worked for America in the past, and it is working for Europe and Japan today.

Why a New Industrial Policy?

In the movie *Casablanca*, the local French chief of police (played by Claude Rains) announces he is going to close down Rick's American Café. Rick (Humphrey Bogart) demands to know why, and Rains says, "I'm shocked, shocked to find that gambling is going on in here." At that moment, one of Rick's employees hands Rains some money, saying, "Your winnings, sir."

So it is with America's industrial policy. The shocked "opponents" of industrial policy protest, "It is not government's role to pick winners and losers in industry."[38] As we'll see in Chapter 4, those who argue most fervently against government "interference" on behalf of energy efficiency and solar energy are often the most passionate advocates of government "support" of the nuclear power and oil industries.

It is time for all parties to acknowledge that the United States has long had an industrial policy. The argument today should not be over *whether* America adopts an industrial policy—it already has one—but rather over *what* industrial policy to adopt. The previous chapter touched on DARPA's success in creating America's world leadership in computer science. Here's another case history to show the critical link between industrial policy and America's economic vitality.

The Aircraft Industry

America's largest exporter in 1990—by far—was Boeing, with $16 billion in export sales of commercial and military aircraft. One of the few manufacturing industries that America still dominates, aerospace technologies provide America with a $28 billion trade surplus.

Our preeminence in aircraft comes from decades of government support. Twelve years after the Wright brothers' 1903 flight at Kitty Hawk,

71

the government created the National Advisory Committee for Aeronautics (NACA), whose explicit mission was to "supervise and direct the scientific study of the problems of flight, with a view to their practical solution, and to determine the problems which should be experimentally attacked." Within a decade, NACA was a key contributor to research and development in the emerging commercial industry. As the Congressional Office of Technology Assessment (OTA) has written: "NACA pioneered in building and using large wind tunnels, collaborated with both the civilian aircraft industry and the military on designing research projects, and made its test facilities and a stream of test results available to both throughout the 1920s and 1930s." NACA research led to greater engine efficiencies and higher speeds for planes, which in turn helped make overnight transcontinental runs possible, which permitted air travel to boom even in the midst of the Depression. From 1930 to 1934, the United States government helped maintain demand for civilian aircraft with subsidies from contracts to carry the mail. Sometimes the support was indirect, as in the case of Civili Aeronautics Board (CAB) regulations. The OTA notes: "By ruling out price competition, the CAB encouraged the airlines to compete on performance instead, and thus indirectly supported the aircraft manufacturers' commitment to technological excellence."[39]

Total research and development spending in the aircraft industry between 1945 and 1984 came to $109 billion (in 1972 dollars)—$81 billion from the military, $18 billion from industry, and more than $9 billion from nonmilitary federal agencies. Significant spin-offs from military to civilian technology took place as late as the 1960s, when the airframe of the Boeing 707 was made as a "clone" of the KC-135 refueling tanker that Boeing built for the Air Force.[40]

In the 1970s and 1980s, the needs of the military became less and less commercially useful. The civilian aircraft industry has no need for stealthy planes that cannot be seen by the radar of foreign countries. Spillover from military to civilian technology has become rarer and rarer. The airframe companies, Boeing in particular, are now funding most of their research and virtually all their development costs through their own commercial side.

Other countries have caught on to the success of aerospace industrial policy. By 1990, Airbus Industrie, the European aircraft consortium, had captured one third of the passenger jet market, and had replaced

72

McDonnell Douglas as the number two manufacturer (after Boeing). Airbus's order backlog of nearly a thousand planes is valued at almost $70 billion.[41]

Entry into a market once dominated by American companies was made possible by the deep pockets of the governments of France, Germany, Great Britain, and Spain, which helped subsidize Airbus's aggressive low pricing of its planes. The United States government and aircraft industry accuse the Europeans of improperly pumping $26 billion into their company to make it competitive, with European taxpayers covering up to 75 percent of the development costs of new Airbuses. Such accusations miss the point. The cost of developing new airplanes is so high—$4 billion or more for the next "super jumbo"—that government support is crucial, at least initially, and the United States aerospace industry would not have achieved market dominance without it.

If America is to compete in the next decade, and in the next century, three myths must be shattered: (1) Industrial policy does not work ("government cannot pick winners and losers"); (2) America has no industrial policy; and (3) American industry can maintain its position with current government policies. Our major export industries—aerospace, military, computers and software, agriculture, medical technology—have all benefited from a host of direct and indirect government subsidies. They are the largest beneficiaries of government support and are among the only industries that have prospered—not a coincidence. And not surprisingly, aircraft and aircraft equipment, computers, and semiconductors are the only high-technology manufactured products among America's top ten exports to Japan.[42]

European governments have begun spending billions on industrial ventures, not only on the Airbus, but in microelectronic and computer technologies, biotechnology, telecommunications, advanced materials, robotics and automation, transportation systems, and environmental technologies. Furthermore as discussed in the next chapter, the Japanese, having mastered the art of industrial policy on a national level, now seek to turn all of Asia into a Japanese-led industrial machine. Rather than denying the benefits of industrial policy or engaging in futile efforts to stop other countries from exploiting government intervention, the United States government should consider how best to promote its own industries.

How We Succeeded: America's "Free" Economic Security

America owes its industrial success to a variety of fortuitous factors. For much of the nineteenth century and early twentieth century, we spent very little on defense: We had free military security. We also had an astonishing abundance of resources. In 1913, for instance, America was the world's leading producer of copper, phosphate, coal, molybdenum, zinc, iron ore, lead, silver, salt, tungsten, petroleum, and natural gas; we were number two in bauxite and gold. One study, "The Origins of American Industrial Success, 1879 and 1940," concluded: "The most distinctive characteristic of U.S. manufacturing exports was intensity in nonreproducible natural resources; furthermore, this relative intensity was increasing between 1880 and 1920." By the late 1920s, iron and steel products, machinery, automobiles and parts, and petroleum products accounted for more than half of all American manufacturing exports. Automobiles contained roughly half their value in iron and steel, non-ferrous metals, and other fabricated metal products.[43]

As we slowly began to lose our competitive advantage in resources after World War II, other nations might have provided serious competition. But Japan, Germany, France, and the rest of Europe were devastated by the war. American industry further benefited from the tremendous influx of European scientific and technical expertise fleeing Europe during the 1930s and 1940s. All these factors boosted our relative economic might and made our economic policies more successful than they would have otherwise been.

As the world's preeminent industrial power and major producer of raw materials, we could only benefit from free trade. With weak foreign industrial competition, and with basic technologies like software and airframes having both civilian and military application, almost any industrial policy, including one focused on the military, would have been successful.

If we do not understand why we were successful in the past, we cannot hope to understand how to be successful in the future. I am not arguing that America's economic success was wholly accidental or that our economic security was achieved by chance or without effort. Our market-oriented economic system, our native inventiveness and optimism, our entrepreneurship were vital. Rather, I am arguing that one-time factors

74

and nonreproducible conditions played a larger role than is acknowledged. Our economic security, especially in the thirty years after World War II, was unusually easy to achieve compared with that of other nations. Revitalizing America today will therefore require much more effort and strategic planning.

The economist Gavin Wright, concluding his 1990 analysis of the importance of nonreproducible natural resources in American industrial success, wrote: "It is perhaps understandable that Americans have not been inclined to attribute their country's industrial success to what appear to be accidental or fortuitous geographic circumstances."[44] Yet, we need such a reinterpretation of America's past now that America no longer achieves economic security so effortlessly. As historian C. Vann Woodward wrote about the loss of free military security in his 1960 essay "The Age of Reinterpretation":

> If historians waited until the disappearance of free land to recognize fully the influence of the frontier-and-free-land experience on American history, perhaps the even more sudden and dramatic disappearance of free security will encourage them to recognize the effect of another distinguishing influence upon our national history. . . .
>
> So long as free land was fertile and arable, and so long as security was not only free but strong and effective, it is no wonder that the world seemed to be America's particular oyster.[45]

And so long as we had an abundance of resources, a near monopoly on intellectual talent, a lack of competitors, and a military industrial policy with commercial benefits, we could take our economic, energy, and environmental security for granted.[46]

Today, however, every one of those conditions has changed for the worse. Our dependence on imported energy and resources is high. We use far more energy per dollar of GNP than other industrialized countries, and we are the world's largest source of most major pollutants. Our competition is reunited and reinvigorated. Our scientific and technical talent, though still preeminent, is rapidly losing ground by almost any measure, including, for instance, the number of influential patents filed in important new technologies.[47] Equally important, our military-oriented industrial policy, begun in the 1940s and 1950s, and so effective for so long, is now working against us.

75

Unlike thirty years ago, military needs are increasingly divergent from civilian needs. In most cases, civilian technology is far more advanced than defense technology. Private industry leads Defense Department laboratories in such key areas as microelectronics, computers, and telecommunications. It has become rare for private industry to adapt defense technology breakthroughs commercially.

When America was the world's technology leader, the Defense Department forced a strict separation of defense and commercial applications to prevent America's enemies from acquiring crucial technologies, and they backed this separation with tough export controls. That policy had the unintended effect of denying many commercial manufacturers access to important foreign markets, and it also disconnected the United States defense industry from international competition and from the pressure such competition creates for constant improvement and manufacturing excellence.[48]

Perhaps most important, the success of flexible manufacturing has completely undercut a major assumption underlying the military industrial policy: the belief that we can rely on a slow process of defense R&D "spinning off" into civilian technology. This might be called the "trickle-down" theory of R&D funding. Originating technology is without value when a nation cannot develop, manufacture, and market it quickly enough, as we have learned with VCRs, televisions, and a host of other American inventions. As discussed in the Introduction, the Japanese innovate more rapidly than we do, and they market their innovations even more quickly. Defense research, often shrouded in secrecy, diffuses too slowly to produce many high value-added civilian manufacturing jobs.

Time was not a crucial factor for spin-offs in the past because we were the world's leader in most areas of technology; it took years for any foreign commercial competitor to catch up. Time is still not a crucial factor in the development of military technology, because we remain the world's leader in weaponry. Because of the success of flexible manufacturing, however, the key to industrial success has become rapid, incremental improvement—making small changes quickly and inexpensively. This manufacturing paradigm is the antithesis of the United States defense industry, which focuses on slow, quantum changes in technology with no concern for cost. Trying to boost civilian technology indirectly through defense spending is too inefficient a process to succeed in a world of fast-cycle competition.

76

The final reason for the increasing failure of our industrial policy is that in the 1980s, the Reagan and then Bush administrations gave that policy an ever increasing military focus. During the Reagan administration, for instance, federal spending on defense R&D doubled while spending on civilian R&D declined. Equally important, the defense R&D increasingly emphasized the D: development of specific weapons rather than general research. Development is the stage of R&D *least* likely to have commercial spillover. Defense spending on basic materials research, for example, is far more likely to have spin-offs than spending on development of a specific bomber. By 1988, more than 80 percent of defense R&D was for weapons development.

Another instance of overmilitarization of our industrial policy: in 1980, about 75 percent of the Energy Department's R&D was in energy and 25 percent in nuclear weapons and military nuclear power plants. But by 1987, the Department of Energy was for the first time spending more money on nuclear weapons research than on energy. It had become, in effect, the "Department of Nuclear Weapons."

The Bush administration has yet to offer a coherent industrial policy. Some in the administration, including White House Science Adviser Allan Bromley and Commerce Department Undersecretary of Technology Robert White, are in favor of federal support of civilian technology. The administration has increased the annual budget of the National Science Foundation and the value of corporate research and development tax credits.[49] In April 1991, the White House (through Bromley's science office) released a list of twenty-two areas of technological development that should be supported as "critical to the national prosperity and to national security." In a letter accompanying the list, William Phillips, chairman of the National Critical Technologies Panel, states: "We most recently have been reminded, by the spectacular performance of U.S. coalition forces in the Persian Gulf, of the crucial role that technology plays in military competitiveness. It is equally clear that technology plays a similar role in the economic competitiveness among nations."[50]

These powerful words might signal the necessary paradigm shift, but there have been too many outright opponents of industrial policy in the Bush administration working against such changes. Their actions speak louder than Phillips's words. In 1990, the administration fired DARPA director Craig Fields for too strongly favoring the development of dual-use technologies (those with both military and civilian applications), as

77

opposed to technology with purely military applications.[51] According to *The Wall Street Journal*, Deputy Commerce Secretary Thomas Murrin was "squeezed out for pushing industrial-policy programs too forcefully." In fiscal year 1991, the Defense Department spent $311 million in its manufacturing technology program to help support technologies from automatic machinery to machine tools. The 1992 Bush budget proposed slashing that to under $97 million.[52]

In 1991, the administration opposed a plan to create a tiny $10 million fund within the National Institute of Standards and Technology to loan money to small- and medium-sized businesses to develop and demonstrate the commercial feasibility of advanced technologies. Commerce Secretary Robert Mosbacher argued: "We cannot support putting the government in the position of competing directly with private banks and venture-capital firms, nor can we support giving specific advantages to some companies over others for particular commercial products."[53] Here is the quintessential folly: Just as competition from foreign countries with aggressive government-sponsored industrial policies has intensified, the U.S. federal government has abdicated its responsibilities.

After a decade of neglect in funding critical technologies, strong words with half measures are not winning tactics. We can barely afford to lose a few more battles in the trade war; we certainly cannot afford to lose any more time. America's international competitors, especially the Japanese, take a systematic approach to their economic security; a piecemeal American response is doomed to fail. A systematic strategy can be successfully challenged only by another systematic or comprehensive strategy. We must integrate economic, energy, and environmental policy if we are to revitalize America.

Government policy cannot restore our leadership in resource production or reestablish the wartime devastation of our competitors, two of the sources of our success for much of this century. But as I will suggest in Chapters 4 and 5, a wise energy and environmental policy can restore America's resource abundance by promoting energy efficiency and the industrial ecosystem. Another source of our success, our military industrial policy, is no longer adequate to the international economic challenge and must be replaced by a civilian industrial policy, which would pave the way for a new era of economic security.

A United States Industrial Policy

What should the United States do? Just about everything. Applying the lessons of the Persian Gulf War victory, we must invest in people, invest in technology, and adopt a systems approach.

We must harness market forces to promote flexible manufacturing. A wise overall industrial policy should include support for United States technology and manufacturing at every level—from federal R&D, to tax breaks, to regulatory policy, to loans and matching grants. Will mistakes be made? Will funds occasionally be spent on wrong technologies, wrong approaches, wrong industries? Certainly! The surest sign that our industrial policy is not being daring and innovative enough would be if it did not back a few losers. Even a private venture-capital firm is lucky to pick one winner out of five. Thomas Alva Edison would not have invented the light bulb if he had quit after the failure of the first filament. The Japanese have picked a lot of losers; wisely, they manage to advance from their failures as well as from their successes.

If America does not originate most of the technology it uses, and if our manufacturing capability is not superior to that of other countries, either we will have to compete for production through low wages and a weak currency or we will have to import high value-added products. One or the other. Both options lead to decreasing economic security. Between 65 percent and 80 percent of all United States productivity growth since the Great Depression can be attributed to innovation. Today technology-based sectors generate roughly 50 percent of GNP—twice the level of just a generation ago.[54]

What technologies should the federal government support? There are four important national criteria for each technology to meet: (1) Does it contribute to American competitiveness in world markets? (2) Does it enhance national defense? (3) Does it help our energy security? (4) Does it improve our quality of life? These are the key criteria used in developing the White House's own 1991 list of critical technologies. Many other lists exist, but this one is an excellent starting point:

79

NATIONAL CRITICAL TECHNOLOGIES

Manufacturing
- Flexible computer integrated manufacturing
- Intelligent processing equipment
- Micro- and nanofabrication
- Systems management technologies

Materials
- Materials synthesis and processing
- Electronic and photonic materials
- Ceramics
- Composites
- High-performance metals and alloys

Information and Communications
- Software
- Microelectronics and optoelectronics
- High-performance computing and networking
- High-definition imaging and displays
- Sensors and signal processing
- Data storage and peripherals
- Computer simulation and modeling

Biotechnology and Life Sciences
- Applied molecular biology
- Medical technology

Aeronautics and Surface Transportation
- Aeronautics
- Surface transportation technologies

Energy and Environment
- Energy technologies
- Pollution minimization, remediation, and waste management[55]

As quickly as possible, the federal government must pour billions of dollars into these technologies. No new money is needed—just a transfer of funds from the Defense Department, under an updated definition of national security that sees economic security as coequal with, and necessary for, military security. Federal R&D spending, which had been half military, half civilian in the 1970s, shifted to two-thirds military, one-third civilian in the 1980s. The pendulum must swing back and then overshoot, so that civilian R&D ultimately becomes the direct focus of least two thirds of federal R&D funding. DARPA, which has more than thirty years of experience providing venture capital, must devote the lion's share of its resources to dual-use technologies. To restore American energy abundance, the Energy Department must return to spending 75 percent of its budget on civilian energy programs, such as renewable power and energy efficiency.

Although civilian R&D is composed of many elements, such as health, agriculture, and civilian space research, a key component for economic security is support for industrial development. While the German and Japanese governments spend equal amounts of federal R&D funds on defense and on industrial development, *the United States government has lately been spending more than one hundred times as much R&D money on defense as on industrial development.* With the cold war over, there should be broad support for bringing this dangerous imbalance to an end.

A civilian DARPA, with a multibillion-dollar budget, is needed. In 1988, Congress gave the National Bureau of Standards a new name, the National Institute of Standards and Technology (NIST), and a new mission, coordinating government policy on industrial technology and stimulating new ideas in the private sector. NIST should provide extensive R&D support, low-cost loans, venture capital, and matching grants for private companies and universities working on the critical technologies.

Blueprint for a Manufacturing Policy

In 1791, Alexander Hamilton concluded his *Report on Manufactures:* "Not only the wealth but the independence and security of a country appear to be materially connected with the prosperity of manufactures."[56] His words ring true even two hundred years later.

Time and time again, United States companies have failed to market American-originated technologies competitively. Therefore, the focus on manufacturing in the National Critical Technologies list is vital. A massive infusion of R&D money into civilian technologies might not benefit America unless there is a great improvement in our ability to manufacture those technologies. Indeed, without a manufacturing industrial policy, American civilian R&D may well serve to create more potential products—and jobs—for Japanese manufacturers than for American ones.

More important, increasing the number of manufacturing jobs is needed to generate high-paying jobs of all kinds, and hence is crucial to achieving economic security. For although much of the highest-paying work is in manufacturing, many other jobs will benefit from a manufacturing industrial policy. This is a central point of the book, *Manufacturing Matters*, by Stephen Cohen and John Zysman.

Cohen and Zysman argue that manufacturing has both indirect and direct employment benefits. There are two indirect connections:

> (1) through multiplier effects on the demand side: large manufacturing incomes create demands for pizza; shrinking manufacturing incomes reduce the size of the pie; and (2) through wage-setting forces behind the supply side in the labor market for services: eliminate manufacturing jobs in a major way, plus those service jobs directly tied to manufacturing, and the level of wages in the rest of the service sector will drop precipitously as demand for them shrinks and supply mushrooms, in a vortex of impoverishment. This is not a trivial relationship.

There are also a host of jobs closely linked to manufacturing:

> design and engineering services for product and process; payroll, inventory, and accounting services; financing and insuring; repair and maintenance of plant and machinery; training and recruiting; testing services and labs; industrial waste disposal; and the accountants, publicists, designers, payroll, transportation, and communication firms who work for the engineering firms that design and service production equipment; or the trucking firms that move the semifinished goods from plant to plant, up the links of the manufacturing chain.[57]

The industrial program I propose will also create countless high-paying jobs for engineers, physicists, biologists, metallurgists, and computer scientists performing research and development; for teachers and administrators training skilled workers; and for construction workers, architects, and the like rebuilding the nation's infrastructure.

The linchpin is manufacturing, and the intense and systematic effort that will be required to revitalize American manufacturing should not be underestimated. Our major companies have an almost unbelievable bias *against* manufacturing. The headline on a June 1991 *Wall Street Journal* front-page article tells the whole story:

DYING BREED
NO GLAMOUR, NO GLORY,
BEING A MANUFACTURER
TODAY CAN TAKE GUTS

As the article relates, American manufacturing managers make an average of $92,000 a year, while a top marketing executive in a comparable firm earns $230,000 and a controller $160,000. In Japan, the salaries are nearly the same among such managers. As might be expected, only 59 percent of American engineering graduates enter manufacturing, compared with more than 70 percent in Japan.[58]

Moreover, when Fortune 500 executives were asked what area offered the greatest opportunities for advancement in a company, one third said marketing, one fourth said finance, and one fourth said general management; fewer than 5 percent considered production or manufacturing a logical choice. At Reynolds Metals, for instance, only five of the twenty-five executive officers came from the manufacturing plants and all four CEOs the company has had in its history came from a sales background. As one management consultant has said, if the financial and career incentives do not change, "We run the risk of being manufacturing dinosaurs in the 21st century."[59]

Avoiding this fate will require both public and private effort. Individual companies will have to shift to state-of-the-art manufacturing, which means flexible and lean. Mass production provides no career progression for production workers. In contrast, lean production provides workers with a clear career path based on demonstrated problem-solving ability. Higher pay comes from both seniority and from performance bonuses. Thus flexible manufacturers "try to make employees understand that their capacity to solve increasingly difficult problems is the most meaningful type of advancement they can achieve, even if their titles don't change."[60]

83

Companies must learn—or relearn—the benefits of investing in worker training. Guaranteeing that workers will be continually retrained is the best way to ensure that workers will welcome—indeed, insist on—rather than fight the introduction of new technology, such as computer-controlled machinery and industrial robots. The goal is a manufacturing system where the workers themselves are so integrated into the innovation and manufacturing process that they help lead the way to new techniques and new technologies, and share in the resulting profits—in higher wages, bonuses, and benefits.

The nation will benefit greatly when flexible manufacturing is widely used by United States companies. The much-discussed postindustrial, or postmanufacturing, society does not exist, at least not for a country that wants to stay rich. In 1987, for instance, the total value of manufactured goods purchased in the United States was about $1 trillion, nearly twenty times the volume of services exported. Manufacturing at home, with its potential for creating large numbers of high value-added jobs, has far more chance of revitalizing American economic security than exporting services, with its small number of relatively low value-added jobs.

Lean manufacturing achieves higher efficiency, quality, and flexibility the closer each element of the system is to the others, from design to assembly to marketing and sales. As a senior executive at Honda has said: "We wish we could design, engineer, fabricate, and assemble the entire car in one large room, so that everyone involved could be in face-to-face contact with everyone else."[61] As competition between foreign and domestic lean producers intensifies, the advantage in the United States will go to the company that does most of its manufacturing in this country. The more that American companies adopt flexible manufacturing, the more high-paying jobs will be created, both by the American companies and by competitors increasingly forced to manufacture components as well as final products in the United States. As noted in the Introduction, this process is slowly beginning to happen in a few industries, such as clothing.

With a systematic industrial policy, the federal government can accelerate the transition to flexible manufacturing in several ways: by supporting the development of new manufacturing technologies, by accelerating the diffusion of existing manufacturing technologies, and by training technically skilled workers.[62] Direct federal R&D grants, as well as matching grants and low-cost loans, can support the development of the next generation of computer-assisted design and computer-assisted manufacturing. Sematech, a consortium of 14 major United States semiconductor manufacturers, is a good example of a federally funded program aimed at the process of manufacturing. With $100 million from DARPA and $125 million from member companies, Sematech is able to boost the development and testing of new equipment by the 130 or so American companies at the lowest end of the semiconductor food chain (which provide the tools for key processes such as photolithography and chemical etching).[63] The Advanced Technology Program was created at NIST to provide a mechanism for federal guidance and partial support of joint R&D ventures with private companies, such as a group of companies attempting to manufacture a revolutionary data storage system. Federal institutions are already in place to develop state-of-the-art manufacturing; what is needed now is the funding. With its current minuscule budget of $37 million, for instance, the Advanced Technology Program can fund only a handful of projects.

Promoting the spread of existing manufacturing technology may be an even more important job for the federal government than developing new technology. It is worth repeating that the real weakness in United States production is not so much the failure to develop new technologies as it is the inability to exploit them by turning them into high-quality, affordable manufactured goods. One study found that by the late 1980s, probably 40 percent of the Japanese stock of machine tools was computer-controlled (or programmable), compared to 11 percent for the United States.[64]

As of 1987, more than half of the one thousand American manufacturing plants surveyed in the metalworking sector did not have even one computerized machine! Those suppliers with outmoded equipment account for about one million manufacturing jobs. If they do not upgrade quickly, major American manufacturers (such as auto companies) will no doubt increasingly rely on German, Japanese, and Italian firms with state-of-the-art production equipment and superior technical and managerial skills. Such an "out-sourcing" strategy for United States industry will be devastating. Out-sourcing will not only cost America high-paying jobs in supplier industries in the short run, but it will also undermine the competitiveness of our major manufacturers in the long run because overseas sourcing is wholly at odds with the fast-cycle approach to manufacturing. *Our entire industrial base will crumble if American companies use foreign suppliers and foreign companies also use foreign suppliers.*

We must tackle this problem of made-in-the-U.S.A. parts. What is good for General Motors' suppliers is good for the country. Both federal and state programs can make the difference. The Omnibus Trade and Competitiveness Act of 1988 gave NIST the job of creating and supporting Manufacturing Technology Centers (MTCs), nonprofit regional centers for the transfer of manufacturing technology to small- and medium-sized companies. Those centers are intended to "transfer technologies developed at NIST to manufacturing companies; make new manufacturing technologies usable to smaller firms; actively provide technical and management information to these firms; demonstrate advanced production technologies; and make short-term loans of advanced manufacturing equipment to firms with fewer than 100 employees."[65]

In 1991, about $12 million went to fund 5 MTCs, and the present NIST plan envisions increasing the number to 12 by 1995. That number will not suffice. In 1985, the Japanese had 185 comparable testing and research centers providing technology extension services to smaller manufacturers.[66]

America has a proven model for the diffusion of new technologies. The U.S. Agricultural Extension Service has a budget of more than $1.2 billion (31 percent federal), offices in almost every county in every state, 9,650 county agents and a staff of 4,650 scientists and technical experts. The effort has paid off. Studies have found a high rate of return on investment in agricultural research, extension, and farmers' schooling. Agriculture contributes just 2 percent to the GNP, while manufacturing makes up 19 percent. The OTA estimates that 120 Manufacturing Technology Centers with a total staff of 3,120 would be needed just to serve 7 percent of the nation's small- and medium-sized manufacturing firms.[67] That is far too low even as a minimum goal for the program.

The federal strategy should be to help support state-run centers, which would ensure that local needs were met. The Michigan Modernization Service, for instance, is a $4 million state-sponsored industrial extension program; it naturally has a special interest in the auto industry. One of the programs affiliated with it is the Program of Research in Modernization Economics, which "identifies local firms that have complementary production capacities and encourages them to buy from and sell parts and materials to one another and to develop collaborative arrangements."[68] The goal is to strengthen local supplier capacity to

86

meet demands from Ford, Chrysler, and General Motors for higher quality and just-in-time parts delivery, helping to accelerate production cycles for American automakers. The OTA calculates that the federal government could provide 30 percent support for 120 large state-run centers for only $36 million to $144 million a year.[69]

There are a host of other government policies that can directly boost manufacturing: government-supported equipment leasing, accelerated depreciation schedules and capital-cost-recovery programs for manufacturing equipment and facilities, and extending the R&D tax credit to include manufacturing engineering and process R&D. The point is to try a variety of approaches because not every tactic will work. Most approaches will achieve their greatest effect only in combination with other approaches; such is the nature of any systematic approach to a complex problem. Indeed, flexible or fast-cycle manufacturing itself is based on the idea of continually making countless small changes to the product and to the manufacturing system, rather than one or two breakthrough changes every few years.

Roads, Bridges, Mass Transit

The government must restore the nation's decaying infrastructure. Sustained spending on roads, bridges, mass transit, airports, school buildings, communication facilities, and the like is vital to creating a high-performance economy that nurtures industries with sustainably high wages.[70]

A 1990 study by the Economic Policy Institute concluded, "More than half of the decline in our productivity growth over the past two decades can be explained by lower public infrastructure spending."[71] Such spending can also directly provide entry-level jobs as well as basic training in carpentry, plumbing, electrical work, and other skilled construction jobs for tens of thousands of workers. If new buildings constructed with federal support are held to the highest standards of energy efficiency, such spending can also boost energy and environmental security.

Unfortunately, our record on infrastructure has been dismal; spending on new infrastructure has fallen from 2.3 percent of GNP in 1963 to only 1 percent in 1989. At the same time, the U.S. share of major construction contracts worldwide dropped from 50 percent in 1980 to 25 percent in 1988. This decline will continue as the United States loses technological

87

superiority in construction to Japan. *Each year, Japanese contractors spend forty times as much on research into new construction technologies as American contractors* ($2 billion versus $50 million), even though revenues of Japanese contractors are only slightly higher than ours.[72]

The Japanese government has vowed to spend more than $3 *trillion* on public works in the 1990s. No doubt the lion's share of that will go to Japanese contractors. To ensure continued dominance in flexible manufacturing, the Japanese will be investing heavily in an industrial infrastructure program based on innovation in "the rapid diffusion of information-processing technologies in the service and retail sectors, the implementation of automatic warehousing technologies, the development of rail transport to encourage bulk shipments and the creation of state-of-the-art distribution facilities by Japan's retailers."[73] To avoid falling further behind, the U.S. government must make comparable efforts in the 1990s, and spend hundreds of billions of dollars on infrastructure, plus billions on construction technologies.

Since the purpose of the programs I've described is to increase the number of American workers with high-paying jobs, the government should provide assistance only to those American companies whose products have a high domestic content. In the 1980s, even the ostensibly "free enterprise" government of former British Prime Minister Margaret Thatcher invented a requirement that Japanese auto companies who wanted to manufacture in Great Britain must achieve 60-percent domestic content within two years of startup and reach 80 percent a few years later.[74] American companies that seek to benefit from federal support should meet no less stringent domestic content standards. The goal is to promote the industries that build inside this country, and their suppliers inside this country, and the infrastructure they both rely on. Creating a climate ideal for flexible manufacturing and just-in-time supply will restore the competitive advantage of producing in America. Foreigners will find it harder and harder to use foreign labor to compete with American lean producers and will be forced to do more of their manufacturing in this country. For this strategy to succeed, America must have a large supply of highly educated and trained workers.

Investing in People

The final element of a successful industrial policy is investing in people. All else depends on trained workers. There are too few of them now. In the 1980s, American high school students consistently ranked near the bottom of the major industrialized countries of the world in biology, chemistry, physics, and mathematics. Korean thirteen-year olds succeeded twice as often as Americans at solving a two-step math problem, such as averaging. Three times as many could design a simple scientific experiment. The 1983 report of the Commission on Excellence in Education, *A Nation at Risk,* said: "If an unfriendly power had attempted to impose on America the mediocre educational performance that exists today, we might have viewed it as an act of war."[75]

Although Americans widely believe that we invest more than other nations in educating our children, that is true only if postsecondary education is included. In overall public and private spending on schooling from kindergarten through twelfth grade as a percentage of gross domestic product (GDP), the United States is tied for twelfth among sixteen industrialized nations.[76]

Our schools, like our industries, are flabby, with remarkably large numbers of service and supervisory personnel. In both New York and Philadelphia, fewer than half of the school districts' total employees are teachers. In Los Angeles, 50.6 percent of school district employees are teachers.[77]

Improving our current K–12 (kindergarten through twelfth grade) system is vital, but it is a long-term solution. In the coming decade, the United States labor force is projected to grow only 1 percent a year; 85 percent of our work force for the year 2000 is already working. Programs to experiment with new educational approaches—national testing standards, longer school years—might improve our educational system gradually over a period of ten to fifteen years. Those programs could slowly increase the fraction of our high school graduates who are as competent as those of our trading competitors, so that fifteen to twenty years from now all American high school graduates once again would be superior in science, math, and literacy. Unfortunately, we cannot wait that long. The United States must quickly train hundreds of thousands of workers to become technically skilled if it is to compete with the millions of skilled and semiskilled Western European, Eastern European, and Asian laborers who will be entering the world labor force in the next decade. If we cannot upgrade our work force in the 1990s, then no matter how successfully we improve our school systems, good jobs will not be available for Americans as they graduate high school.

If our work force continues its decline, then how will we avoid more urban tragedies like the April 1992 riots in Los Angeles? How will our nation be truly secure? While those riots had many causes, there is little question that the deindustrialization of south central Los Angeles, and the ensuing loss of good-paying jobs, played a key role.

Economic security means a constantly increasing number of high-paying jobs, and since those jobs are in manufacturing, achieving economic security means training manufacturing workers. As American industry trims middle-management fat and begins competing against lean producers, more and more responsibility will be put directly into the hands of blue-collar workers, which requires them to have broad-based technical knowledge. Where shall they learn it? Our schools have failed to teach them the necessary skills.

We cannot continue ignoring the 75 percent of high school graduates who do not go on to complete college. No one is training American high-tech workers. Neither serious private programs nor public programs are readily available.

American corporations spend $30 billion on what is called employee training, but, as Robert Reich has noted, most of that money goes to train executives; college graduates receive far more corporate retraining than high school graduates, particularly at high-tech firms. In contrast yet again, Japanese autoworkers receive more than three times as much training every year as workers in American-owned auto plants in the United States. Japanese and European employers spend three to five times as much money on job training as American companies. In the United States, public funding for worker training and retraining dropped more than 50 percent during the 1980s, from $13.2 billion to $5.6 billion, and the 1992 Labor Department budget proposed further cuts. Overall public spending on workers—employment services, labor market training, special youth programs, direct job creation, employment subsidies, and programs for the disabled—comes to only 0.25 percent of GDP in the United States. The German government spends more than 1 percent of its GDP on its workers.[78]

We would do well to look at Germany's apprentice training system, which sends teenagers to school one day a week and to a job four days a week. Jointly funded and run by private industry and the government, the program has had many benefits: Germany has the lowest rate of youth unemployment in Europe (roughly two thirds of the country's sixteen- to eighteen-year-olds are enrolled) and it graduates some of the finest craftsmen and craftswomen in the world. Larger companies have specialized classes for apprentices. Smaller companies often assign apprentices to master craftspeople, and government technical centers provide additional training. Schools use a uniform curriculum to guarantee a broad level of technical expertise. Upon passing a written and technical exam, the newly graduated journeymen have nationally recognized credentials.[79]

Studies comparing German manufacturers (with 90 percent of the shopfloor workers highly trained) with British manufacturers (only 10 percent highly trained workers) reveal a huge labor productivity advantage in German plants of 60 to 130 percent. "German workers were adept at using computerized wood-working machinery and a linked system for feeding, unloading, and stacking materials," while the British factories rarely had fully linked machines and breakdowns were far more common. In metalworking and cabinetmaking, the Germans made fewer mistakes and required fewer quality controllers. In the clothing industry, German workers were more adaptable, could be retrained more quickly, were better able to focus on short runs of high-priced quality products. Simply put, the German workers are better able to function in a fast-cycle company. Their reward for superior performance was at least 50 percent higher wages than workers in British industry.[80]

The Japanese training system emphasizes lifetime employment at large companies and worker immobility, a culture that may be ill-suited for America. A version of the German nationwide apprenticeship system could be better suited to our mobile work force. Stephen Hamilton, author of *Apprenticeship for Adulthood,* proposes "making a diverse system of apprenticeship available to all youth," including exploratory apprenticeships, such as community service work starting in the middle school years; school-based apprenticeships that combine academic learning with practical work experience; and traditional work-based apprenticeships that could extend from the last two years through two years of

91

technical college.[81] Apprenticeships could encompass not only manufacturing but also many other segments of the labor market, such as computer programming, auto repair, and middle management.

The key to successful education is to link "irrelevant" high school exercises like solving algebra problems with real-world jobs like operating numerically controlled machine tools. Federal and state governments would connect these programs to the Manufacturing Technology Centers, so that apprentices would be trained on the latest equipment, providing a steadily growing labor force for companies adopting new technologies. Indeed, federal support of manufacturing, such as the MTCs, will produce results only when given in tandem with job-training programs.

Such programs will be successful when the stigma attached to manufacturing ends. It is not only engineers and our most talented college graduates who are discouraged from choosing manufacturing as a profession. Consider Oregon's recently approved education plan, which "would be the first in the nation to establish a statewide apprenticeship program and would make students choose between job training or a college preparatory curriculum after 10th grade." The *New York Times* story continued: "The plan has drawn much criticism, particularly for the dual-track idea for high schools. Many educators express concern that it has the potential to stigmatize students who are guided into the job-training track or to discourage young people from pushing themselves to attempt the academic track."[82]

In Germany, by contrast, the master craftsman or craftswoman is not only well paid but highly respected, and in certain fields the German technical universities are considered more prestigious than regular universities.[83] Since today's manufacturing jobs require advanced math, knowledge of materials, systems problem-solving, and a high degree of technical competence, the old notions of low-skilled, dead-end factory work should fade away. When the federal government makes first-class manufacturing technology a central goal for the nation—a matter of national security—the second-class status will vanish.

Federal involvement also brings the government's power to bear on the overall production cycle, with benefits to the country greater even than improving competitiveness in the marketplace. Another goal of an enlightened industrial policy is reducing energy use and energy-related pollution (Chapter 4). The broadest goal is reducing all resource use and all pollution—achieving an industrial ecosystem, where clean production supersedes lean production (Chapter 5).

The production cycle must not merely minimize time and effort. Goods must be designed so that the manufacture and the use of a product employ energy and resources most efficiently, lowering both costs and pollution. Achieving such advanced manufacturing will require the government to make resource- and process-efficiency a focus of its R&D spending as well as its Manufacturing Technology Centers.

In addition, systems thinking must be taught in all programs. The Labor Department understands this. In a 1991 report of its Commission on Achieving Necessary Skills, one of the five job-related "competencies" is "systems." According to the commission, someone who has mastered "systems":

A. *Understands Systems*—knows how social, organizational, and technological systems work and operates effectively with them.
B. *Monitors and Corrects Performance*—distinguishes trends, predicts impacts on system operations, diagnoses deviations in systems' performance and corrects malfunctions.
C. *Improves or Designs Systems*—suggests modifications to existing systems and develops new or alternative systems to improve performance.[84]

Solving America's problems involves the same three steps: understanding systems such as manufacturing and energy, distinguishing trends and system failures, and devising improved or new systems, such as modifications to our existing industrial policy. America's problems are systemic in nature, our competition acts systematically, and so our approach must also be systematic.

In 1985, Budget Director Richard Darman said in response to charges that the Japanese were selling semiconductors below cost in the United States in order to destroy the domestic industry, "Why do we want a semiconductor industry? What's wrong with dumping? It is a gift to chip users because they get cheap chips. If our guys can't hack it, let them go." More recently, Michael Boskin, chair of the Council of Economic Advisers said, "Potato chips, semiconductor chips, what is the difference? They are all chips. A hundred dollars worth of one or a hundred dollars worth of the other is still a hundred dollars."[85] The industrial policy revealed by such shortsighted thinking has helped undermine United

States economic security by undermining the source of high-paying jobs in manufacturing and in a host of areas connected to manufacturing. If permitted to continue, such policies will in all likelihood create a political environment that would make a trade war inevitable.

Avoiding a Trade War

C. Fred Bergsten has written: "A central question for the world of the 1990s and beyond is whether the new international framework will produce conflict over economic issues or a healthy combination of competition and cooperation. History suggests that there is considerable risk of conflict, which may even spill over from the economic sphere to create or intensify political rivalries."[86] Japanese politician Shintaro Ishihara has predicted that "the 21st century will be a century of economic warfare."[87] We must work now to prevent the formation of three warring blocs—a United States-led inter-American bloc, a Japan-led Asian bloc, and a Germany-led European bloc.

Some policymakers, such as Darman and Boskin, believe that the best way to avoid a trade war is to keep America's import market as open as possible. Yet, *free trade in the absence of a robust United States industrial policy is unilateral disarmament.* We are competing against many nations with focused, systematic industrial policies. Without an American domestic strategy for creating high value-added jobs, millions of low-paid foreign laborers will continue taking away American jobs or forcing down our wages. Americans will clamor ever louder for harsh trade sanctions against nations like Japan, which is the most likely route to a trade war. Yet trade sanctions by themselves will be no more effective at revitalizing the United States economy than free trade by itself.

There is no question that the Japanese do not practice free trade at home; they have a restricted domestic market, and their cartels engage in practices that exclude many American products, costing us billions of dollars in exports every year. A decade of ranting and railing by American trade negotiators has had little effect. Japan has been too successful with a policy of favoritism for its domestic suppliers, coupled with a sophisticated industrial strategy to replace lost lower-wage jobs with higher-wage jobs. The Japanese see their economic policies as the basis of their national security and therefore vital to their well-being—exactly as we have seen our military policies. Moreover, their economic policies

94

have the same primary purpose as our military policies: to avoid foreign coercion. The Japanese will not cave in to demands to weaken their economic security at the very moment in history the United States might be able to mount a serious industrial challenge to that security.[88]

Rather than trying to punish the Japanese, the United States should focus on upgrading uncompetitive American industries. In some instances, however, temporary trade protection may be a worthwhile tool. First, some industries have been hurt or wiped out by unfair foreign trade practices. Second, certain American industries, like steel and motorcycles, have benefited from temporary trade protection, but only when they have used the breathing space to become more efficient. Third, the transition from mass production to lean production can be difficult.

We can expect some of the traumas of a newly industrialized nation. It is commonly accepted that newly industrializing countries should protect their budding industries from foreign competition until they are strong enough to compete worldwide. In Europe, the competition from the Japanese auto industry is considered so fierce that the European Community has extended quotas against Japanese imports for seven years after the elimination of intra-Europe trade barriers in 1992, to give their automakers time to retool. Certainly the United States, which has suffered greatly from being far more open to Japanese trade than the Europeans, could benefit from the judicious use of temporary trade protection. Finally, it bears repeating that one of the reasons the Allies were so successful in the Persian Gulf was that we had more than five months to prepare our battle plan, train our soldiers in the desert, and test our high-tech weapons under unusual conditions. Had we been forced to confront the Iraqis immediately, the outcome might have been catastrophically different. In an analogous fashion, limited trade protection could, in some cases, give industries time to prepare for foreign competition.

Pork-barrel politics can be counted on to have a great impact on policymaking. To minimize its influence on the decisions over which industries to protect, the White House and Congress should establish a quasi-independent Economic Security Board, such as the Federal Reserve Board. To be selected, industries would have to demonstrate how they are being hurt by unfair foreign competition. They would have to produce goods with a high proportion of domestic content. The few industries chosen by the board would get a breathing space of limited duration, perhaps three years, in the form of quotas or tariffs on imported goods. The board would work with federal agencies to give target industries low-cost loans, matching grants for R&D and worker retraining, and access to advanced equipment and technical expertise needed to become fast-cycle (through organizations such as the Manufacturing Technology Centers). At the end of the allotted time, trade barriers would be phased out and the industry would sink or swim on its own.

Such a United States policy, used wisely, need not lead to a trade war. At worst, aggrieved foreign nations could justify responding with their own temporary protection. Anathema to many, such protection should be invoked infrequently. To use the language of military strategy, its primary purpose would be to deter predatory foreign business practices. Foreign countries would learn that their rapacity would not destroy American industries but would rather lead to even fiercer competition.

To summarize: *Protectionism should be the last resort. It is useless without a comprehensive domestic industrial policy. It would probably be unnecessary if we adopted all the other programs proposed here, but it should be in the arsenal for use when needed.*

The best way to "protect" American high-paying jobs is through a new industrial policy aimed at promoting domestic fast-cycle manufacturing and energy-efficient infrastructure, which will in turn boost the profitability of American retailers and service and financial companies. Most elements of this policy require either very little money or a real-location of resources—for example, from defense R&D to civilian R&D. The funds for more education and training—civilian intelligence—could come entirely from cuts in the military intelligence budget.

A small beginning has been made. The National Security Education Act of 1991, introduced by Senate Intelligence Committee chairman David Boren and Senate Armed Services Committee chairman Sam Nunn, will take $150 million from the intelligence budget to support foreign language and regional studies programs.[89] America, however, must spend fifty times that amount—$7.6 billion—merely to restore spending on worker training and retraining to what it was in 1980. And yet $7.6 billion is only about 25 percent of the current military intelligence budget. We need—and we clearly can afford—a multibillion-dollar National Security Education and Training Act of 1993 aimed at training scientists, engineers, manufacturing laborers, and skilled craftspeople working on

96

research, development, manufacturing, critical technologies (including energy and the environment), infrastructure, and on and on.

Our economic security can once again be relatively free, because the United States can restore its long-term economic vitality with no net increase in federal spending. We need only reorient priorities from our post-World War II military-oriented industrial policy to the civilian industrial policy outlined here. The changeover will not increase the burden on the vast majority of American families. Quite the reverse, it will reduce their economic burden while it increases their incomes.

Nevertheless, an aggressive program to restore economic security has two elements with a high *short-term* cost: rebuilding our infrastructure and reducing the budget deficit. These will require hundreds of billions of dollars in the 1990s. Since the 1980s saw both these problems grow as money was shifted to the military and to the wealthy, it is clear where the money should come from.

Tax increases are not required to achieve the industrial policy I recommend here, as long as America is willing to continue living with budget deficits for a while. In theory, deficits are not a danger if they are incurred to pay for investment in future growth, such as research and development, education and training, and infrastructure. Such borrowing eventually pays for itself in higher productivity, higher growth rates, and higher revenues from increased wages. Still, the deficit and the interest on the debt have begun to get unwieldy, and reducing this government borrowing would probably boost economic growth.

If taxes need to be raised, it is only to reduce the deficit while sustaining the necessary federal spending on economic security. The money should not come from the 80 percent of Americans who have failed to grow richer in the 1980s. The top 10 percent of American families should reassume their fair portion of the load, particularly since by 1989, those families possessed *70 percent* of all privately held wealth in America. Any new tax increase should rightfully fall upon them. According to Robert Reich, a "federal income tax as progressive as it was in 1978 would require the top 10 percent of income earners to pay about $950 billion more than they'll otherwise pay in the 1990's."[90] That would make a respectable dent in the deficit, without raising anyone else's taxes.

97

As I will discuss in Chapters Six and Seven, a comprehensive ten-year program of defense cuts can free up the hundreds of billions of dollars needed for our infrastructure without sacrificing military security, since that narrow aspect of national security is assured for the foreseeable future. Indeed, the new foreign aid program I will outline holds the promise of increasing our military security (and our economic, energy, and environmental security) by dealing with the root causes of conflict and weapons proliferation.

The proposed economic security policies will create far more jobs than are lost because of defense reductions. In addition, worker-retraining programs could target regions particularly hard hit by Pentagon cutbacks.

Cuts in military spending, properly redistributed, will increase our overall national security. While this may be a new concept to Americans, such thinking has been an essential component of Japan's strategy for years. The Japanese understand the balance required, and they have debated whether to institute what they call a "comprehensive security cost" of roughly 3 percent of GNP, which would include "expenditures for 'economic security' items [e.g., food and resource stockpiling, energy research, etc.], Official Development Assistance (ODA), and military defense."[91]

We in the United States can now also redefine security and we must reorient our industrial policy accordingly if we are to restore our economic vitality. Because our problems are systemic in nature, they can be solved only with a comprehensive, well-funded program. If we take a scattershot approach, adopting only a few of the policies outlined above and then underfunding them, little will change. Indeed, as I hope to make clear in the next chapter, even if we adopt all of these policies, we will still have a very long way to go to match the Japanese.

98

3

Japan's Economic Security System

I believe that [Japan] will come out of this recession even stronger than it's been in the past. . . . If you take the figures the IMF [International Monetary Fund] released two weeks ago about long-term sustainable growth rates . . . by early in the next decade, the economy of the United States and the economy of Japan would be about the same size. . . . On the basis of investments that have already been made, by the mid-1990's, Japan will have a manufacturing base that's larger than that of the United States.

—Kenneth Courtis, Deutsche Bank in Tokyo
May 8, 1992, congressional testimony[1]

Japan, a few slivers of barren land in the Pacific Ocean, has but 3 percent of the world's population and 0.3 percent of its habitable land. In 1987, Japan relied on imports for more than 99 percent of its natural gas, oil and petrol, iron ore, copper, nickel, bauxite, manganese, molybdenum, and titanium. In 1988, it imported 93 percent of all the world's exported nickel ore, 57 percent of all the available copper ore, and 30 percent of all the exported coal and iron.[2]

With virtually no natural resources, little land, and 123 million people, Japan has nevertheless achieved a gross national product (GNP) 60 percent that of the United States. It has been growing much faster than any other industrialized country for decades, and, in industry after in- dustry—computers, office equipment, telecommunications, medical equipment, motor vehicles, banking—has become a world leader, often at the expense of the United States.

How does a country with so little achieve so much? Answer: The

Japanese invest heavily in people and in technology, and they use a systems-oriented strategy. The pattern should sound familiar. It is how we won the Gulf war, and it is how individual Japanese companies have outcompeted American companies.

But fast-cycle manufacturers represent only the spokes in a relentlessly turning wheel; they are the micro level of the overall Japanese economic plan. No country with so little could be so successful without a systematic national and international strategy—a national security doctrine always aimed at one goal: economic security.

The Japanese investment in people—the remarkable achievement of their educational system, and their continual retraining of workers—is well known. For instance, in 1989, the Japanese provided their new automobile assembly workers 380 hours of training, while Americans provided their new auto assembly workers 46 hours of training.[3] Also well known is Japan's investment in technology: In 1990, Japan, with half the population, outinvested the United States in new plants and equipment by $660 billion to $510 billion. Between 1985 and 1991, Japan's investment in new plant and equipment totaled $4,800 per worker, compared with $2,300 per worker in the United States. And a 1992 study by one federal panel concluded that Japan has surpassed the United States in total business spending on research.[4]

This chapter will focus on Japan's astonishing, and relatively unknown, economic strategy. The United States has other major competitors, and the economist Lester Thurow, for one, argues in his 1992 book, *Head to Head*, that the German-led European bloc will win the global economic competition in the twenty-first century. I, however, believe the Japanese-led Asian bloc will be our tougest competitor.

Financial crises and business slowdowns come and go for every country, and America, Germany, and Japan have all had troubles in the early 1990s. But in the long-term—and the long term is the subject of this book—what matters is how much a nation saves and invests in the future (R&D, infrastructure, and the like), how it educates its children and trains its workers, and whether its national strategy is sensible and strategic. Japan deserves special focus, I believe, because it pursues economic vitality with a systematic approach, which gives it a unique adaptability in the face of changing circumstances and helps maximize its advantages in saving, investing, educating, and training.

Japan and Comprehensive Security

The Japanese think of security in a different way than Americans. They regard themselves as safe and strong only with a vibrant economy.

As Nobutoshi Akao, former chief economic officer at the Japanese embassy in Washington, said some years ago: " 'Economic Security' is an expression used more often in Japan than in any other advanced industrialized country." *The Economist* wrote in 1989: "That the country's security depends on its economic strength is the main premise of Japanese foreign policy." A variety of other analysts have recently made a similar point.[5]

Japan's comprehensive security doctrine, which emerged in the late 1970s, consists of both military and economic security policies. Its non-military goals include attaining energy security and food security. As the authors of *Japan's Quest for Comprehensive Security* wrote in 1982:

> Comprehensive national security for Japanese decision makers, therefore, appears to include not only overt threats from an increasingly menacing Soviet military machine or from major geophysical catastrophes, but also to include major threats to the economic livelihood and standard of living of the Japanese people from the denial of access to markets for Japanese goods. . . . It implies, too, that it will be necessary to take positive steps to shape a significant part of the national environment in such a way as to protect national interests from international competition, not only in one's own market or within one's own territory, but also in other markets and in other territories.[6]

The doctrine of comprehensive security represents a paradigm or common orientation that drives Japan's economic security system. What are the elements of the system? The Japanese policies I will examine here are those aimed specifically at maximizing the number of high value-added jobs—those high-paying jobs, such as fast-cycle manufacturing, that involve adding a high value to goods and services.

A critical element is the role of the Ministry of International Trade and Industry (MITI), which coordinates Japan's industrial policy. For example, between 1961 and 1981, it has been estimated that MITI gave out roughly $6 billion to computer makers. In the 1980s, Japanese government subsidies, tax benefits, and loans to its computer industry ex-

101

ceeded $7 billion. In addition, over the past thirty years, the Japanese computer industry has been the beneficiary of more than $25 billion in Japanese government contracts.[7]

Another element is their flanking maneuvers. One of the thorniest issues in United States-Japan trade relations is our trade deficit. The U.S. strategy on the trade deficit has been to focus on one number: the overall direct deficit. To lower that number while increasing their own economic vitality, the Japanese use a variety of ingenious tactics. They have moved some *assembly* plants to the United States, lowering the deficit by the value added by American workers to what remain largely Japanese *manufactured* goods. They have similarly moved assembly plants to other countries, like Thailand, while still keeping the highest value-added jobs in Japan, and then export to America out of those countries, debiting them, instead of Japan. Direct overseas investment by Japanese manufacturers has risen from the $2-to-$3-billion range of 1982–1985 to more than $15 billion in 1989. Finally, while the Japanese have increased their trade surplus with the United States in computers, office machinery, and electrical and power-generating machinery, they have offset the dollars gained by increased purchases in American commodities—cork, wood, breakfast cereals, meats, fish, scrap metal, tobacco, fruits, vegetables, coal, and paper—not exactly a list of high value-added products.[8]

In 1990, Japan's trade surplus with the United States in just three areas—computers and telecommunications equipment, cars and trucks, and industrial equipment—totaled more than $50 billion. Nevertheless, Japan's rapid and novel flanking maneuvers, as a military strategist might call them, helped to lower its overall trade surplus with the United States by more than $10 billion between 1987 and 1990, satisfying American trade negotiators who are foolishly content to believe that exporting raw materials and importing high-technology goods, precisely like a Third World country, can maintain United States economic security. Mirroring America's indirect attack on Saddam Hussein's strategy in the Gulf war, the Japanese have also followed Sun Tzu's military lessons and successfully attacked our trade strategy by using multiple indirect attacks.

Cartels—Keiretsu

A key reason Japan can control its trade so easily to maximize its wealth is that 70 percent of its global trade has a Japanese company at each end of the transaction: An overseas subsidiary will export parts or finished goods back to its domestic partner. In Europe, the corresponding proportion is less than 50 percent; in the United States, a pitiful 20 percent. Japan's intracompany trade is fostered by the cartel system of its major firms, called *keiretsu*. This cartel is both horizontal, such as Mitsubishi, which has almost 190 member companies making different products, and vertical, such as Toyota, with 175 primary suppliers and 4,000 secondary ones. Member companies own large blocks of shares in each other and overlap corporate board membership. The six largest cartels account for roughly 25 percent of Japan's GNP. The keiretsu run the gamut of companies—in banking and finance, raw materials, shipping and transportation, materials processing, industrial equipment, manufacturing, trading, and retailing.[9]

Such a cozy arrangement brings many benefits. Cartel members easily coordinate industrial policy with MITI and the Japanese government. The cartel's own banks provide low-cost capital and are very patient and understanding lenders who do not bail out or foreclose at the first signs of trouble. The interconnectedness minimizes friction, accelerating fast-cycle manufacturing and the just-in-time supply system.

Intrakeiretsu trade is a key feature of the system. As one Japanese auto executive explained the supply system: "First choice is a keiretsu company, second is a Japanese supplier, third is a local company." Once a supplier company is a member of a keiretsu, the cartel sends quality control and other experts to help it fit into the high-speed distribution system. Ultimately, the cartel sets the new member's profit margin and influences every facet of its business. When one Japanese auto parts supplier testifying before the U.S. House Judiciary Committee was asked why he didn't leave the keiretsu, he explained, "No one else would buy from me. All my family wealth is in my company. It would be economic suicide."[10]

What are the impacts of keiretsu? A 1991 GAO report said that twenty-two of fifty-nine United States companies interviewed provided specific cases of Japanese companies delaying delivery of equipment six months to two years or rejecting orders outright. The same parts were, it was

103

reported, made available to the Japanese competitors of these United States companies. According to the GAO, one small American computer company lost $65 million in sales in 1989 and had to abandon the growing laptop computer market because a Japanese supplier refused to sell the company high-quality displays.[11]

The auto industry provides a sobering case study. Vehicles and parts now account for three quarters of Japan's trade surplus with the United States. The Japanese have built eight auto plants in the United States. The startling result: In the first five months of 1991, Japanese car companies shipped more autos *back* to Japan from their American manufacturing plants than American automakers sold in Japan. The Japanese transplants have been joined by about 250 Japanese suppliers, in spite of the fact that America is the world's biggest producer of auto parts. American companies that once supplied Japanese manufacturers are replaced by suppliers from within the cartel. A 1991 Commerce Department study concluded that the transplants "record a large and growing overall trade deficit, particularly with their foreign parent firms, mainly due to the extensive use of imported inputs to their manufacturing operations."[12]

A detailed audit by the U.S. Customs Service of Hondas made in Canada concluded that Hondas determined by Customs to cost $8,146 to manufacture are being sold to United States consumers with a sticker price of $6,635. Honda controls its cartel member suppliers so that they "sell to Honda at a price below their cost of manufacture and continually operate at a loss." The Customs report states: "Rather than basing prices on market-force factors such as actual North American costs, profit or customer-supplier negotiations, Honda prices within North America are developed and fixed in accordance with the dictates of Honda Japan." The report also found that, contrary to Honda's claim that most of the material for the Honda Civics came from North America, at least 62 percent originated outside North America. Moreover, even parts that were not imported, such as the engine, are still primarily intracartel. According to the Customs report: "Of approximately $775 of materials or parts for the engine assembled in Ohio, only three parts ($9.06) and $42.69 of raw materials are sourced from U.S.-based companies that do not have an equity relationship with Honda." Honda's own accounting reveals that the single largest item of local content added at Honda's engine plant in Ohio was depreciation of the factory's equipment; yet the

Customs Service charges that most of that machinery was imported from Japan. A University of Michigan study found that only about 16 percent of the Honda Civic's content consisted of parts purchased from United States-owned suppliers. In March 1992, the Bush administration ruled that Honda owed millions of dollars in tariffs because Civics imported from Canada did not contain enough North American parts to qualify for duty-free treatment.[13]

Japan's Asian Industrial Policy

The systematic economic approach Japan is taking in Asia makes its efforts in the United States look almost haphazard. Because the United States is an advanced industrial society, the Japanese are limited in how much they can integrate us into their industrial policy. The economies of Asia are far less advanced, and therefore easier to influence. In the following discussion, the Newly Industrializing Economies or NIEs are Hong Kong, Singapore, South Korea, and Taiwan (also known as the Four Dragons). Indonesia. Malaysia, the Philippines, and Thailand, four of the members of the Association of South East Asian Nations, will be referred to here as the ASEAN nations.[14]

Japan's regional industrial policy in Asia has been called a "new division of labor" and "flying geese in V-formation."[15] The goal is simplicity itself: to integrate the Asian economies into an economic flock with Japan at the head, followed by the NIEs, and then ASEAN, together with coastal China (and eventually Vietnam and Bangladesh). Japan provides leadership and direction and produces the highest value-added products because of its tremendous capital surplus, its technological superiority, and its economy's size (it produces two thirds of the region's annual output). The made-in-Japan products might be luxury cars or state-of-the-art consumer products (camcorders, laptop computers, even "thinking" vacuum cleaners that adjust themselves to a carpet's dirt-level) that are cram-packed with microelectronics and microprocessors.

The Four Dragons are experiencing rising wages and so have begun to lose cost-competitiveness in products requiring much labor; they are expanding in the high value-added items like advanced electronics, automobiles, and semiconductors. The ASEAN countries, at the rear of the formation, continue to be primary suppliers of basic materials like oil,

105

rubber, and timber, but they have also begun to manufacture low value-added products. For example, a single Malaysian Matsushita factory will become the world's largest manufacturer of room air conditioners for the global market; Sony now builds color TVs and compact disk players in seven Malaysian and Thai plants; and Sumitomo Electric is moving labor-intensive assembly of auto-wiring systems to Indonesia.[16] Japan itself retains most of the high value-added R & D laboratories; it provides the plant equipment and machine tools needed to build the overseas factories, and, of course, Japan keeps the profits from the companies it owns.

The challenge to America is very real. *Already the Four Dragons account for 10 percent of the world's exports in manufacturing—the United States' share is 12 percent.*[17] In 1991, the Asian nations led by Japan will for the first time generate more real economic growth than either the European Community or the combined economies of North America. In one month—August 1991—the four Dragons had a combined trade surplus with the United States of $1.5 billion. Together, they generate twice the merchandise exports of all the countries in Central and Latin America combined, even though the latter have six times the population. One American economist estimates that manufactured imports from East Asia could cost America 700,000 jobs by the year 2000.[18]

The potential gain for East Asia is great. As one Japanese economic journalist has written:

> The region's growth rates are among the highest in the world, and according to the proponents, will remain so in the future. It is projected, for example, that by the year 2000, the per capita real GDP of developing ASEAN countries will reach those of South Korea and Taiwan in 1980, the figures for South Korea and Taiwan in 2000 will reach those of the higher-income Hong Kong and Singapore in 1980, which in turn will surpass the per capita real GDP of Japan in 1980. Even China will close the gap with its per capita GDP in 2000 approaching the 1970 South Korean level. Together the Pacific economies will become one gigantic engine of growth.[19]

Intra-Asian trade has risen so rapidly that in 1989 Japan's trade with Asia exceeded its trade with America. More than half of Japan's imports from Asia are manufactures (although many, if not most, of these come from overseas factories owned and operated by Japan). A 1987 report

106

by the Japanese Ministry of International Trade and Industry, MITI, noted the "growing tendency for Japanese industry, especially the electrical machinery industry, to view the Pacific region as a single market from which to pursue a global corporate strategy."[20]

Yen Diplomacy

Asian countries are not entirely sanguine about possible Japanese hegemony and exploitation. They were victims of Japanese aggression before and during World War II, and are fearful of a return to the "Greater East Asia Coprosperity Sphere," as the Japanese called their rapacious strategy in the 1930s and 1940s. Nevertheless, with America's economic influence waning and America flipping from being the world's largest creditor to the largest debtor, the United States itself has urged Japan to increase its contribution to the Western alliance, in part by increasing financial flow to the developing world, both through greater overseas development aid and a recycling of Japan's tremendous surpluses.

The Japanese have been happy to oblige. Indeed, they have integrated increased aid and investment to the developing world into their overall economic strategy.

The ever-adaptable Japanese surpassed the United States in total overseas development assistance in 1989. Japan's overall foreign aid to Asia that year was more than $4 billion—three times the United States level. In the past, Japan's development aid was aimed only at creating new markets in developing countries and securing new supplies of resources; the aid also benefited Japan because it was tied to purchases of Japanese equipment. In contrast, United States aid is showered upon projects that American companies do not necessarily build.[21] Japan's new strategy for Asia is a far more sophisticated plan, coordinating overseas development assistance, trade, and foreign direct investment "to construct a regional economy managed from Tokyo," or, put another way, "to keep Japan's flock in formation."[22]

The strategy, called the New Asian Industries Development Plan or New AID plan, was developed by the Ministry of International Trade and Industry in 1986 and announced by MITI Minister Tamura in January 1987. A Japanese trade official explained the difference between the New AID plan and earlier forms of economic cooperation with the developing world:

107

In the area of Japan's economic cooperation up to now, aid for infrastructure and humanitarian objectives such as telecommunications equipment, dam construction, and hospital construction was the core, but the New AID Plan is cooperation directly in the area of industry, and this is what is "new" about this plan. Moreover, this cooperation is not just up to the government, but hopes for direct investment by Japanese firms. This, too, is a new type of private-public cooperation activity.[23]

To set up the New AID Plan in a given country, Japanese officials first determine what are the most promising export industries. They develop a master plan to nurture those industries, and the foreign ministry sets up a joint steering committee with the target country to decide how to put the plan in place. Japanese experts are sent to help. Everything is carried out in a classically systematic fashion—Japanese money and know-how achieve success through myriad organizations, most of which are connected with MITI. The Japanese provide surveys and trained people to design new infrastructure, such as industrial export zones. The legal, tax, and investment incentives needed are set up to bring in Japanese private investment. The Association for Overseas Technical Scholarships, a quasi-public corporation under MITI guidance, assists direct investment in developing countries "by training developing country personnel at the investing firm in Japan." Japan's Overseas Economic Cooperation Foundation provides aid to build the physical infrastructure, such as ports, telecommunications, and industrial parks. A variety of organizations, including the Japan External Trade Organization and the Japan Overseas Development Corporation, provide technical cooperation and personnel to improve local standards of management, production technology, product development, marketing, promotion and distribution—the entire production cycle. Japanese governmental organizations also coordinate investment by Japanese firms. Financing requests under the New AID Plan now have priority. In 1987, then Prime Minister Nakasone announced that $2 billion would be devoted to the ASEAN-Japan Development Fund. Most of the money would go for bilateral joint ventures, and the rest for regional joint ventures among ASEAN countries, and for the Japan-ASEAN Investment Corporation to purchase equities and bonds in joint ventures.[24]

All this points to Japan's old dream of dominating Asia, once the cornerstone of its war policy. Japan denies it. According to one MITI division director describing projects in the Malaysian and Thai governments: "Agencies are doing their work [according to a development plan], but Japanese experts enter and give advice on the basis of the recipient side's request. Since their side is making industrial policy, one cannot say that Japan is pushing ideas on them. Japan is offering experience, and the other side makes choices."[25]

No one is reassured by such explanations. Japan's ultimate designs were revealed in a 1988 report commissioned by MITI titled *Promoting Comprehensive Economic Cooperation in an International Economic Environment Undergoing Upheaval: Toward the Construction of an Asian Network*. The report calls for an oversight organization that it dubs the Asian Brain, which would coordinate Japanese development aid, direct foreign investment, and trade throughout Japan, the NIEs, and ASEAN to determine who produced what in the region. From Japan, the Asian Brain would direct Asia's industrial policy to maintain a three-tier division of labor with Japan on top. Ever understanding about appearances, the report recommends that some of Japan's development aid be rerouted through South Korea and Taiwan to avoid the problem of "overpresence" of Japanese bilateral assistance. The Asian Brain would be an Asian MITI and its potential influence vast, since by one forecast, Japanese direct investment in Asia will be $18 billion each year in the 1990s. Although the report was only a policy statement, it represents the ideal for which Japan is striving.[26]

Can Japan create the Asian Brain? Will countries sign on to a regional division of labor? Why not? Who in Asia can resist the irresistible pull of Japan—not just the offers of foreign aid and investment, but the lure of export-led growth and the promise of a rising standard of living?

The Flying Geese

Consider Malaysia, a modest-sized country of eighteen million, with an overt "Look East" policy designed by Malaysian Prime Minister Mahathir to help lead the nation along the road paved by Japan and the Four Dragons. The Malaysian economy had been limping along until the government liberalized investment laws to allow foreigners to own some export-related manufacturing companies completely. Since then, Japanese investment has ballooned—$1.5 billion in 1990 alone. Some 250 Japanese manufacturing operations and 300 nonmanufacturing businesses have been built, creating tens of thousands of new jobs.[27]

In return for this substantial upgrading of their industrial base, Malaysians have become increasingly dependent on Japan's technology and capital, and subject to Japan's larger plans. Says a Malaysian politician, "One of the consequences of Mahathir's Look East policy is that we have been absorbed more and more into an industrial programme which is dominated by Japan." This industrial policy takes a variety of forms. The Japanese use their foreign aid to promote their own businesses and to foster Malaysian dependence. In 1982, Japan made a multimillion-dollar loan to the Perwaja national steel project to buy experimental smelting technology from Nippon Steel. Overall trade between the two countries is lopsided in Japan's favor. In 1989, Japan's trade surplus exceeded $1 billion, and reached $2 billion in the first ten months of 1990. Part of that surplus reflects the flow of Japanese manufactured parts for final assembly in Japanese-owned Malaysian plants.[28]

With dependence on Japan come risks. According to one Malaysian economist, a few years after a local manufacturer becomes locked into joint production of a specific product, the Japanese cite "market developments" as the reason to raise the original contract requirements and lower the price. In other instances, Japanese companies informally collude on wages, as happened in 1990 after Sony raised salaries offered to skilled technicians by 30 percent, and other companies complained. With assistance from Japanese officials, more than one hundred Japanese companies informally agreed to limit competition for engineers. Typically, Malaysians have the same complaint about Japanese management that are heard worldwide: Local people cannot advance beyond mid-level administration and real decision-making remains in the hands of Japanese executives.[29]

Studies by the Japan External Trade Organization and the Japan International Cooperation Agency for the Malaysian government spell out exactly what products Kuala Lumpur should specialize in to capture more Japanese investment. Japan recommends that Malaysia promote joint-venture production of facsimile machines and word processors and expand its production of minicomputers, precision casting, and computer peripherals. Malaysia is free to ignore Japan's blueprint for success, and Japan is free to favor other ASEAN countries with its investments. Malaysian Prime Minister Mahathir seems happy with the arrangement, so happy that in December 1990 he proposed an East Asian trade bloc led by Japan but excluding the United States, Australia, and New Zealand.[30]

Indonesia sells half of its exports to Japan, which amounted to about $11 billion in 1989. Those exports are more than 60 percent oil and gas, but manufactured products have risen from a 6.7-percent share in 1986 to 20 percent in 1989. So the "flying geese" process does mean economic growth, even at the back of the formation. Imports from Japan, primarily machinery and equipment, come to only $3.3 billion, so Indonesia runs a hefty surplus. Nevertheless, the complaints about Japanese business practices connected with their estimated sixteen hundred joint ventures in Indonesia are widespread. Most electronics and motor vehicles manufacturers import up to 90 percent of their parts and materials from Japan. Japanese managers fill most, if not all, of the senior management positions. In the oil, gas, and financial services industries—businesses dominated by American and European investors—Indonesians are able to obtain both management skills and technology from their foreign partners, but such transfers are far less common in the Japanese-dominated textiles and electronics industries.[31]

Although not the preferred investor, Japan gets the business in Indonesia because it is the primary source of capital. Part of the reason is its tied-aid credits—foreign aid with strings attached. A report from the U.S. Export-Import Bank calculated that from 1984 to 1987, Japan and France together offered some $14.5 billion in tied credits to support global sales from their countries. The United States offered under $1 billion (which, the report estimates, has cost American firms up to $800 million a year in lost overseas sales). Further: "The Japanese know the most about Indonesia," according to one Indonesian businessman engaged in joint ventures with both the United States and Japan. "Better yet, they are prepared to stay with you for the long term. We don't have to worry about [leveraged buy outs] or bankruptcies."[32]

Thailand, with a population of fifty-five million, has the fastest-growing economy of the ASEAN countries. In 1991, Japanese economic aid totaled about $500 million, compared with only $20 million from the United States. In direct investment, the United States lags behind Japan, Taiwan, and South Korea. The share of foreign investment provided by

111

the United States has declined from more than 30 percent in the 1970s and early 1980s to under 10 percent in 1989, while Japan's share has soared to almost 70 percent. The Thai government approved $3.6 billion in Japanese investment in 1989 compared to $565 million for the United States, according to one estimate.[33]

The Japanese have been opening factories in Thailand at the incredible rate of one every three days, straining both the infrastructure and the skilled-labor pools.[34] Since 1985, forty-six Japanese electronics companies have been established in Thailand, boosting exports of microwaves, VCRs, and color TVs from Japanese companies in Thailand to the United States, but giving the appearance of a reduced American trade deficit with Japan. By 1991, Thailand's exports of electronic equipment to the United States had exceeded $300 million, a *4,000-percent* jump from 1988. In Japan's Asian division of labor, it is natural that Japanese electronics companies have now moved key production facilities from Singapore, where the average yearly wage in 1986 was $300, to Thailand, where the comparable rate for the same year averaged $75.[35]

The Japanese have made a strong effort to stay ahead of the Four Dragons. For instance, they supplied more than half of Taiwan's and Korea's imports of technology products in the late 1980s (over twice the American share). Japan is responsible for roughly one third of the total investment in Taiwan since 1952. Some twelve hundred Japanese companies have branches in Taiwan; in contrast, Taiwan has forty to fifty, mainly small, procurement companies in Japan (even though Taiwan is Japan's fourth largest trading partner). Most of Taiwan's exports to Japan are handled by Japanese trading companies within Japan. Those exports, which came to a respectable $8 billion in 1990, consist of a significant share of the Japanese domestic market for golf clubs, electric fans, telephones, and wood furniture. Taiwan's imports from Japan, on the other hand, came to $16 billion—double the exports. Most of those imports are industrial components (auto chassis, photosensors, semiconductors, and bicycle gears of special metal alloys), essential for producing high value-added exports, while the remaining imports are mainly machine tools and heavy industrial equipment. As *The Wall Street Journal* observes: "It is Taiwan's industry, rather than consumers, that is hooked on Japanese products."[36]

Thus Japan is certain to stay ahead of Taiwan. Taiwan will not be far

112

behind, however, since it has learned Japan's lesson of emphasizing economic basics—education, infrastructure, and foreign investment. Of all doctoral candidates in electrical engineering at United States universities, a startling one in four is from Taiwan. The Taiwanese government has announced plans to spend $300 billion by 1997 on ports, airports, highways, and high-speed trains. In particular, Taiwan helps maintain its close-to-the-leader place in the flying geese formation by its increasing role as an investor in the third-tier nations. In the first half of 1988, the Thai Board of Investment approved 186 projects with Taiwan, compared with 171 from Japan. Taiwan became the second largest investor in Malaysia in 1987, and the largest investor in the Philippines in the first quarter of 1988.[37]

Even Korea, whose thirty-five-year subjugation by the Japanese did not end until Japan's defeat in World War II, cannot resist a close economic association with Japan. A poll of Korean businessmen revealed they preferred Japanese to American suppliers two-to-one: "Koreans complained about mediocre product quality, slow delivery times, and poor service, and added that U.S. companies were reluctant to accept small orders." Fast-cycle manufacturing provides the Japanese their edge.[38]

Japan is South Korea's chief source of imports even though Korea bans the import of at least 258 Japanese products. Ironically, while Japanese cars are banned in Korea, Japan is a major source of car parts for South Korean auto manufacturers. Half of Korea's exports to Japan are textiles, food, timber, and minerals. More than 60 percent of Japan's exports to Korea are high-tech machinery, transport equipment, and electronic products. The Japanese strategy is to export machinery and components to Korea, but rarely share technology. The South Korean strategy is still largely based on the high-volume shipments of finished goods to open export markets (such as America or Europe), rather than an emphasis on quality and technology.[39] This is not the road to surpassing Japan. As one business magazine put it: "South Koreans are often confident to the point of arrogance in believing they will eventually overtake the US and Europe economically, but frequently appear convinced they will not catch up with the Japanese."[40]

Japanese economic security policy is systematic in both its means and its end. It focuses every aspect of Japanese policy-making toward achieving its end—the integrated, regionwide system that keeps Japan leading the geese. This is how Japan attains its ideal of national security. If Japan succeeds in doing for Asia in the 1990s what MITI did for Japan in the 1960s, American workers will be competing with tens of millions of additional high-skilled foreign workers.

It might seem that a natural response for the United States would be to develop a Western Hemispheric bloc (starting with Canada and Mexico) to match Japan's Asian industrial policy or the growing strength of the European Community (EC). Yet many problems will complicate any attempt to create such a United States-led bloc.[41] And in the absence of a national industrial policy to systematically generate high value-added jobs for our workers, a free-trade zone in the Western Hemisphere would do little more than accelerate the loss of high-paying American jobs. Neither Germany nor Japan is foolish enough to try to integrate themselves into a regional bloc brimming with lower-paid workers without a strong domestic industrial policy.

Nevertheless, all by itself, the United States has twice Japan's population, with GNP still 40 percent higher than Japan's. Adopting the domestic industrial policy outlined in the previous chapter would go a long way toward keeping us competitive—but it would not be enough.

Another key challenge from Japan is in the area of energy. Energy security is a central component of Japanese comprehensive security. The Japanese government's greater investment in new energy technologies—five times the level of United States investment as a percentage of total federal R&D—promises to keep Japanese businesses more competitive and to make them the world leaders in this increasingly important component of world trade. The United States cannot hope to match Japan, to revitalize our own economic security, and to do so in an environmentally sustainable way, without a major reformulation of our energy policy.

4

Achieving Energy Security While Saving Money

People do not want electricity or oil . . . but rather
comfortable rooms, light, vehicular motion,
food . . . and other real things.

—Amory Lovins
Soft Energy Paths[1]

America's current energy policy damages our economic and environmental security and makes us dangerously dependent on imported oil. America needs a new program, one that eliminates the barriers to the wider use of energy sources that cost the least and do the least environmental harm. By updating our definition of security and reallocating resources and dollars accordingly, we can easily fund such a policy. And since a market-oriented policy would be much more efficient than our extremely wasteful strategy, federal spending will be reduced by tens of billions of dollars a year. Therefore, the total cost to the nation of such a policy is negative. Moreover, the new program will create many new high-paying jobs and free up considerable domestic capital for more productive uses. It will put tens of billions of dollars back into the hands of American businesses and American consumers boosting both competitiveness and living standards. Schools and low-income households will particularly benefit from energy efficiency.

As I will show, with new energy-efficient technologies, the United States can reduce its electricity use by up to 70 percent, at a cost far below that of building new power plants. And although many people think affordable renewable power is decades away, wind power, for example, is already cheaper than fossil fuels in many areas of the country. In this chapter, I will examine the myriad flaws in our energy policy and suggest what is needed to spur the use of efficient and renewable power.

The simplest energy policy (though not the most cost-effective) is to supply more traditional energy sources—more coal, oil, and nuclear. No new thinking or action is required. Only one part of the energy system—the supply—need ever be considered. Since regulations have traditionally permitted electric utilities to make more profits primarily by selling more energy, more energy use is what utilities have encouraged. Ever-increasing demand has been built into our laws.

Energy supply, however, is only one element of the overall energy system, which includes delivery, use (i.e., demand), and pollution. Pollution is the waste by-product created by inefficient processes at every stage of the system. Pollution in the energy system is analogous to wasted "time" in Colonel Boyd's fast-cycle theory; both are due to friction. A new, systematic approach to energy security will achieve more efficiency and less pollution, but will require a basic shift in the way we think about energy.

One strong impediment to change is the widespread myth that not much can be done about our energy (and environmental) problems without great sacrifice to our life-style and our economic growth. That myth has some of its origins in the gas lines and lowered thermostats people associate with the energy crises of the 1970s. President Carter added to the myth in his speeches to the nation, when he said that a different energy policy would require sacrifice. Carter's legacy persists to this day. According to a front-page *Wall Street Journal* article: "The Bush administration is resisting any notion of mounting a major conservation effort, as officials fear reminding voters of the Carter years, during which President Carter actually donned a sweater when he turned down the heat at the White House. In any event, previous efforts at conservation have proved short-lived."[2]

On the contrary, efficiency measures such as home insulation and fuel-efficiency standards for new cars have been remarkably successful and long-lasting. Today, those measures alone save the equivalent of thirteen million barrels of oil a day over 1973 levels, making energy efficiency the largest new source of oil for the United States by far. Since 1979, the United States obtained more than seven times as much energy from improved efficiency as from all net expansions of the energy supply. In spite of these improvements, America has a long, long, way to go. *If*

116

we were as efficient as the Japanese and Western Europeans, we would save close to $200 billion a year in energy costs.

Energy *efficiency* means providing the same or better energy services using less energy. *Conservation*, in contrast, generally achieves lower energy use by giving up some quality of service. Conservation is turning down the thermostat. Efficiency is insulating your house or using new high-performance windows. It is efficiency, not conservation, that I will be focusing on in this chapter.

An energy policy based on efficiency will not require sacrifice. On the contrary, it is America's current energy policy that has required sacrifice, forcing Americans to live with lower incomes, less capital spending, slower growth, a bigger federal deficit, a larger trade deficit, greater reliance on Middle East oil, and far more air pollution than is necessary.

Nevertheless, President Bush's pro-fossil fuel, pro-nuclear energy strategy explicitly rejects a broader, more systematic solution and instead embraces a narrow supply-side approach based on subsidizing traditional sources. The Bush plan is likely to form the basis of the nation's actual energy policy for the 1990s if he is reelected in 1992. In any case, it is worth examining in detail because its optimistic projections probably represent the best-case scenario for the supply-side approaches, and thus serve to highlight their inadequacies.

The National Energy Tragedy

Of the energy consumed by the United States each year (85 quads or quadrillion BTUs), nearly half is produced by burning oil (40 quads). The Bush administration's 1991 National Energy Strategy has many tactics for increasing oil extraction, including opening for exploration part of Alaska's Arctic National Wildlife Refuge, and tax credits for enhanced oil recovery. The strategy estimates that these initiatives would reverse the steady decline in United States oil production of the last several years, increasing domestic oil production 1.8 million barrels per day above levels otherwise projected for the year 2000. By 2010, however, domestic oil production would again resume its steady decline, but consumption hardly changes, and so by 2030 America would be importing 70 percent of its oil.

117

Under this strategy, energy from coal, the dirtiest fossil fuel, would rise from 19 quads today to 28 quads in 2010 to 32 quads in 2030. The use of natural gas, the cleanest-burning fossil fuel, would rise only slightly over the next ten to twenty years, and by the year 2030 consumption would be back at the 1990 level.

Renewable energy use would rise from 7 quads today to 22 quads in 2030. That growth would come mainly from significantly increased burning of municipal solid waste (which rises more than 1000 percent), increased use of liquid fuels made from biomass such as ethanol, and a 25-percent increase in hydroelectric power. Solar and wind power do not play a major role in this scenario.[3]

Nuclear power is a key element of the National Energy Strategy, which includes proposals to accelerate the review process for new nuclear power plants by limiting public comment. The strategy would also make it more difficult for states to block nuclear waste respositories within their borders. Under the Bush strategy, by 2030, nuclear energy production would double from current levels; this is a 3400-percent increase over the decline that the strategy says will otherwise occur over the next forty years without new pronuclear policies.

In large part, all this additional capacity is needed because the National Energy Strategy projects that total energy consumption will rise by two thirds over the next forty years, even though it rose hardly at all between 1973 and 1988.

This is the best-case scenario for the supply-side or business-as-usual approach. It is the "best case" because many of its assumptions are optimistic—too optimistic. For example, nuclear power is unlikely to double in capacity over the next forty years, given continued widespread public opposition and the fact that no one has ordered a large nuclear reactor in the United States since 1978 (and scores of orders that were made before that time have been canceled or delayed). The strategy also cites the present average cost of electricity from nuclear power at 9.9 cents per kilowatt-hour, and sanguinely assumes that new reactor designs, not yet developed, will bring the costs down to 6.6 cents per kilowatt-hour.

Similarly, domestic oil production is also unlikely to increase sharply, given that United States oil production has been declining steadily since

118

1985. Few experts expect even a leveling off. The title of an article in the 1991 edition of the *Annual Review of Energy and the Environment* tells a more likely story: "Policies to Increase U.S. Oil Production: Likely to Fail, Damage the Economy, and Damage the Environment."[4] Moreover, one must read the small print of the National Energy Strategy to learn that a key reason domestic oil production rebounds is that the price of petroleum is assumed to rise steadily in the 1990s to nearly $30 per barrel, and so strategy initiatives to increase production are of secondary importance to price incentives. Nowhere does the strategy report that such a price would cause our trade deficit in petroleum alone to reach $80 billion a year in the year 2000.

Under this best-case scenario for a supply-side energy policy, energy use rises 60 percent over the next forty years, the trade deficit soars, our reliance on Middle East oil grows, and carbon dioxide emissions rise 25 percent in twenty-five years.

The strategy would *decrease* our energy and military security, with the United States 60 percent dependent on imported oil by the late 1990s; *decrease* our environmental security, as the increased combustion of petroleum products exacerbate a host of serious environmental problems, from urban smog to acid rain to global climate change; and *decrease* our economic security, as the bill for imported oil sucks scarce capital out of the country, and as other countries employ their citizens in the manufacture of the new energy-related technologies we have neglected. Should the assumptions about cheaper nuclear power or increased oil production prove incorrect, our national security would weaken even more.

Prior to developing this strategy, the Department of Energy (DOE) held eighteen meetings around the country, which produced twenty-two thousand pages of testimony from industry, citizens, and experts. It is remarkable that such an inadequate energy strategy could be the product of so much effort, until we learn that the effort was scorned. An April 1990 DOE summary of its public hearings stated:

> The loudest single message was to increase energy efficiency in every sector of energy use. Energy efficiency was seen as a way to reduce pollution, reduce dependence on imports, and reduce the cost of energy.[5]

119

The original strategy developed by the DOE and leaked to the press in February 1991 contained a variety of measures to promote energy and fuel efficiency as well as renewable sources such as solar power. But news reports indicated that the White House red-penciled most of those proposals.

For instance, there is scarcely a word in the National Energy Strategy about how to reduce the demand for gasoline. Although the transportation sector is the largest user of petroleum, no proposals encourage motorists to reduce their use of it or require automakers to provide high-mileage cars. Worse, the administration proposed *reducing* federal funding for mass transit. Proposals widely urged by energy experts for reducing dependence on Middle East oil—oil import fees, gasoline taxes, higher fuel-efficiency standards for cars, a strong push for energy efficiency— were dismissed because "the cost would be very high—in higher prices to American consumers, lost jobs, and less competitive U.S. industries." How both Germany and Japan, *whose citizens pay three times as much as we do for gasoline,* still have higher growth rates than the United States is not explained. Turning a deaf ear to demand-reduction policies means ever more energy insecurity, since roughly two thirds of the world's proven oil reserves lie in the Middle East, a point I will return to in Chapter 6.[6]

Achieving Energy Security

In the past, discussions of energy security have focused on the need to be free from foreign dictation, the need to preserve our independence. Therefore, the primary threat has been seen as vulnerability to oil supply disruptions that could be overcome only with high economic and social costs.[7] This has made "stable supplies" the focus of energy security analyses, which in turn emphasizes the importance of military power for preventing trade disruptions. Even by this narrow definition, however, the strategy falls short, since it is forced to conclude: "The National Energy Strategy review . . . revealed that our Nation and the world are likely to depend *more* on Middle East oil suppliers under any realistic scenario for the foreseeable future."[8]

Such a 1970s definition of energy security is wholly inadequate in the 1990s, when energy policy is so intertwined with economic and environmental problems. A broader definition is now required. As Amory Lovins noted more than a decade ago, energy *services,* not energy *supplies,* are the nation's primary goal: "People do not want electricity or oil . . . but rather comfortable rooms, light, vehicular motion, food . . . and other real things."[9]

The pursuit of energy supplies can lead us astray. Here's a definition for the 1990s: *The goal of energy security is to assure adequate, reliable energy services in ways that maximize economic competitiveness and minimize environmental degradation.*[10]

This kind of energy security cannot be achieved with a supply-side approach focused narrowly on traditional energy sources. Once again, we must seek a systematic approach, a new energy paradigm. Supply-side policies remain important, but not to the exclusion of those aimed at every other element of the energy cycle, particularly demand and pollution.

A better way to decide among energy options is "least-cost energy planning." Least-cost planning offers a way to decide among competing power plant types or efficiency options: We invest in new energy production only when we have fully exploited less costly options, which can include saving energy. The least-cost technique is found by calculating all the costs over their expected lifetimes, "from design through construction and operation to retirement."[11] This comprehensive "life-cycle" calculation is analogous to the flexible manufacturing strategy of examining the entire production cycle for inefficiencies.

Pollution complicates life-cycle calculations because it is difficult to determine its costs to society. One way to handle the effects of pollution, such as carbon dioxide, in a least-cost framework, is to put a "carbon tax" on power plants based on the amount of carbon dioxide they produce. This automatically raises the price of polluting power plants relative to efficiency techniques or renewables. A similar tax could be used for other emissions, such as sulfur dioxide. Another approach sets overall targets for carbon dioxide emissions and then mandates that utilities meet those targets in a least-cost fashion. When we harness market forces through least-cost planning, energy efficiency can produce a sizable fraction of the new energy "generation" far more cheaply and cleanly than new plants.

Reducing Electricity Use

What is the range of energy savings possible using more efficient energy technology? A best-case scenario from Rocky Mountain Institute, an energy research organization, projects that the United States could save about 70 percent of the electricity it uses, at an average cost of about 1.0 cent for every kilowatt-hour saved. The Electric Power Research Institute, an industry-supported research center, believes that about 38 percent of the United States' electricity could be saved at an average cost of about 2.5 to 3.0 cents per kilowatt-hour saved. Analyses by the Solar Energy Research Institute (a government laboratory) and others fall in between the two.[12] Detailed studies for other countries reveal similar potential. For instance, Swedish energy experts have calculated that Sweden could save 50 percent of its electricity at an average cost of 1.2 cents per kilowatt-hour.[13] By way of comparison, the cost of electricity for a new United States coal-fired plant is about 7.0 to 8.0 cents per kilowatt-hour.

While Rocky Mountain Institute and the Electric Power Research Institute may not agree on the exact savings possible in the United States, in a notable jointly authored article, they both agree that such savings require no sacrifice:

> Electricity, like other forms of energy, can be saved by demanding fewer or inferior services—warmer beer, colder showers, dimmer lights. No such options are considered here. . . . In fact, many new devices actually function better than the equipment they replace: they provide more pleasing light, more reliable production and higher standards of comfort and control.[14]

If improving energy efficiency is more economical than building new power plants, why isn't everyone installing such equipment? Many are. As *The Economist* reported in its special thirty-page August 1991 survey: "Energy and the Environment," the Louisiana division of Dow Chemical began an "energy contest" in 1981 to find capital projects that cost under $200,000 with a payback time of under one year. In 1982 they found twenty-seven projects requiring a Dow investment of $1.7 million with an average return of 173 percent (a seven-month payback). In 1988,

Dow found ninety-five projects with a total cost of $21.9 million and an average return of 190 percent. The September 1991 *Business Week* cover story, "Conservation Power: The Payoff in Energy Efficiency," detailed a variety of efforts. For instance, the Bank of America retrofitted its San Francisco office and is now saving $400,000 a year on its energy bill, a two-year payback.[15]

Nevertheless, utilities have been slow to change because regulations couple utilities' profits to their sales of electricity, a policy that discourages investments in conservation and efficiency. Very recently, some states have allowed utilities to earn a profit when they help their customers save energy, by allowing the utilities to keep a fraction of the money they save. Consumers end up paying lower electric bills, and utility stockholders benefit as well. Such win-win regulatory reform must be put in place in every state, as soon as possible.

Consumers are also reluctant to use new efficient technologies. The up-front cost is often high, the payback time is often longer than the typical two-year horizon of most consumers, and the benefits of such technologies are not widely known.[16] The utilities, on the other hand, with their financial strength and long-range planning, can cover their costs over a twenty-to-thirty-year period.

More than sixty utilities, serving almost half of all Americans, now offer rebate programs to help people buy energy-efficient devices, such as compact fluorescent lighting. But instead of promoting these important programs, the White House perversely eliminated most of the original DOE proposal to do so. The National Energy Strategy instead calls for an IRS Technical Advice Memorandum stating that "direct payments by utilities to customers that are industrial or commercial firms for making efficiency investments are taxable income" and the same for residential customers.[17]

Fortunately, the advantages of some new energy-efficient equipment are overwhelming. Compact fluorescent lamps consume 60 percent to 75 percent less energy than incandescent bulbs while delivering the same amount of light. And even though they cost more, they last ten times longer, which over time saves not only replacement cost but the labor required to replace them (in commerical buildings). As Rocky Mountain Institute and the Electric Power Research Institute write: "One can recover the cost of the fluorescent lamps and still save many dollars over

123

the life of each lamp. One can thus make money without even counting the savings in electricity. *This is not a free lunch; it is a lunch you are paid to eat" (emphasis added).*[18]

The concept is so attractive, Southern California Edison decided that giving away eight hundred thousand compact fluorescent lamps was more economical than building new power plants. The Office of Technology Assessment reported in May 1991 that a lighting retrofit by the U.S. Postal Service achieved an astounding 368-percent annual return on investment—a payback period of a mere three months. The Postal Service ended up with a brand-new lighting system that had more pleasing light with less glare and that cost less to maintain.[19]

In the original version of its energy strategy, the DOE included a proposal to set efficient lighting standards, but the final version contains a plan merely to label light bulbs. Ironically, two months earlier, another government agency, the Environmental Protection Agency (EPA), had announced that by replacing the lights in one EPA office, electricity use, costs, and power plant emissions were reduced by a whopping 57 percent.[20] The EPA said that if all buildings upgraded their lighting, about 11 percent of all the electricity used in this country would be saved and costs would drop by $18.6 billion year; at the same time, the national output of sulfur dioxide, the principal cause of acid rain, would be cut by 7 percent, and output of carbon dioxide would fall 5 percent. By April 1992, the EPA was reporting that lighting electricity could be cut cost-effectively by up to *80 percent,* creating even greater savings and even deeper carbon dioxide reductions. This win-win situation would involve no sacrifice; quite the reverse, it would not only benefit the environment, but it also might well spell the difference between success and bankruptcy for borderline businesses.

Such was the case for the Southwire Company, which over a period of eight years was able to save 60 percent of its gas and 40 percent of its electricity through a variety of efficiency measures. During a rough financial period, these savings were almost equal to all of the company's profits and may have saved four thousand jobs at ten plants. For Southwire, energy and fuel efficiency was a lifesaver, not a hardship.[21]

Many businesses have profited from greater efficiency. The Milwaukee steelmaker Charter Manufacturing Company split the cost of a $1.5 million high-efficiency melting system, cutting the company's costs by $10 a ton, saving 60 million kilowatt-hours over ten years, and permitting the utility to save $2 million. A $3 million investment in new motors, lighting, and other improvements by Kraft General Foods Group in Framingham, Massachusetts will reduce the electricity cost in a gallon of ice cream from 7.5 cents to 2 cents.[22]

It is a woeful misconception that regulations requiring higher energy- and fuel-efficiency are antigrowth. As I will discuss in the next chapter, tough environmental regulations spur the development of sophisticated pollution-control products, which can give American firms the edge in the rapidly growing international market for environmentally friendly technologies. Sweden, for instance, has the largest percentage of energy-efficient buildings in the world and exports the greatest fraction of building technology worldwide. The Swedes have strict building standards, and their National Council for Building Research spends five times more on such research than the United States government and American utilities combined, as a percentage of gross national product. Not surprisingly, while the United States building sector adds $6 billion to our annual trade *deficit*, Sweden's building sector, when scaled to the American economy, achieves the equivalent of a $60 billion trade *surplus* every year.[23]

Since energy is an essential element of every production cycle, its continued overuse by American companies relative to those in other countries can only contribute to America's competitiveness problems and make United States businesses more vulnerable to fluctuations in the price of energy. The savings from efficiency are so large that improvements such as compact fluorescent lighting will inevitably become more widespread, even though the government has chosen to largely ignore efficiency and instead implement tax breaks and regulatory encouragement for the oil and nuclear industry. One result of current United States energy policy will be to assure that as energy-saving devices become more widely introduced, American companies will be manufacturing far fewer of those products than they might under a wiser policy.

The whole world needs improved energy technology. Our industrialized trading partners are committed to stabilizing greenhouse gases, which guarantees a huge market for efficient products, just as ozone depletion created a market for chlorofluorocarbon replacements. In addition, the environmental basket-cases of Eastern Europe—East Germany, Poland, and Czechoslovakia—depend on coal for 70, 78, and 60 percent of their energy, respectively. They cannot hope to develop in an

125

environmentally sustainable fashion without cleaner, more efficient power.

The developing world, the former Soviet Union, and China—the majority of people on this planet—have the same problem as Eastern Europe. India and China in particular have massive coal reserves, and if they are forced to depend on fossil fuels for economic growth, their contribution to the greenhouse effect will dwarf America's in the next century. Today, the level of suspended particulates owing to coal combustion in the cities of northern China is ten times that found in most of the United States, and pollution in China is estimated to cause economic losses equal to 2 percent of GDP. If China were to triple its coal use over the next thirty years—a move necessary to achieve a modest 5-percent annual growth rate using traditional energy planning—it would be an ecological nightmare for both China and the world.[24] The nations that build the technologies that are both environmentally benign and more cost-effective than new coal plants will not only keep their energy bills low and help clean up their own environment, but they will also employ their citizens in the manufacture of such technologies for other countries.

I have begun by discussing reduced electricity use. But reducing oil use should be the centerpiece of attaining energy security, particularly for a country that sends $50 billion outside its borders each year to pay for oil and spends another $60 billion each year to keep the Persian Gulf shipping lanes open.

Reducing Oil Use

During the Reagan years, federal funding for energy conservation was cut by 70 percent. New-car efficiency standards were rolled back in the mid-1980s. Not surprisingly, this misguided domestic energy policy, coupled with a decline in the price of oil, caused dependence on Persian Gulf oil to surge—or *gush*—from ninety million barrels in 1985 to more than six hundred million barrels in 1989—an increase of more than 500 percent. By the end of 1990, this growing addiction was a key reason hundreds of thousands of American soldiers found themselves in Saudi Arabia. What should be done now to kick the habit of foreign oil?

126

New energy-efficient products, such as high-performance windows that permit less heat to escape, can mean significant energy savings: The energy lost unnecessarily by United States buildings through their windows equals twice the entire output of the Alaska pipeline.

While such measures are useful, indeed critical, Detroit must be the principal target of our policy: Nearly two thirds of all oil is used in our cars, trucks, and airplanes.[25]

The average car on the road gets only about 20 miles per gallon; new cars get about 27. America could reduce oil consumption by two million barrels per day by the year 2005 by raising the average fuel economy for new cars from 27 miles per gallon to 40 miles per gallon. This savings is *more* than we import from the Persian Gulf, and it is five times the oil production rate possible from the Arctic National Wildlife Refuge, according to Department of Interior estimates. Moreover, the efficiency savings are permanent, they help the environment, and they are a straightforward extension of existing automobile technology. In contrast, the Interior Department estimated in 1991 that the Arctic National Wildlife Refuge had less than a 50-percent chance of containing any economically recoverable oil.[26]

The efficiency standard for new cars is called CAFE, for Corporate Average Fuel Economy. There are two basic arguments advanced against raising CAFE standards: safety and effectiveness. Let's start with the safety debate. Both Detroit and the administration have argued that meeting increased CAFE standards would require much smaller and lighter cars, which, it is argued, would decrease auto safety. Secretary of Energy James Watkins labeled one bill to raise CAFE standards the National Highway Death Act. Such arguments are doubly flawed.

First, higher efficiency does not necessarily mean smaller cars. In the 1970s, automakers began by reducing vehicle weight, but in the 1980s they used improved technology to raise mileage. A study by the Center for Auto Safety concluded that between 1974 and 1991, technological improvements accounted for 86 percent of the improvements in mileage, and only 14 percent were due to weight loss or a shift to smaller cars.[27]

Second, and more important, higher efficiency does not mean less safety. Between 1974 and 1991, average new-car fuel efficiency doubled from 14 miles per gallon to 27; emissions of nitrogen oxides, carbon monoxide, and hydrocarbons decreased more than 75 percent; and traffic

127

fatalities per 100 million miles traveled have fallen from 3.5 to 2.1.[28] The safety improvments have occurred steadily throughout the 1970s and 1980s. From 1975 to 1980, fatalities per 100 million traveled vehicle miles decreased only from 3.4 to 3.3, but since 1980 they dropped significantly, to 2.5 in 1985 and 2.1 in 1990. Researchers at Lawrence Berkeley Laboratory have found no correlation between fuel efficiency and automobile safety.[29] An October 1991 study by the United States General Accounting Office stated that its statistical analyses "support the view that the automobile weight reductions since the mid-1970s have had virtually no effect on total highway fatalities."[30]

Most major automakers were able to develop new cars, or modify old ones, to increase driver safety and fuel efficiency simultaneously. Honda's 81/82 Civic had a 10-percent weight *increase,* but a 10-percent improvement in gas mileage compared to the 79/80 Civic, and yet had a 40-percent lower death rate (measured over the same time period). Volkswagen replaced the Beetle with the Rabbit, a vehicle with a similar weight and wheel base, and yet had a 25-percent improvement in gas mileage and a 44-percent lower death rate. General Motors' 86/87 Nova weighed 2 percent more than the 84/85 Chevette, had a 4-percent improvement in gas mileage and a 50-percent-lower death rate. All of these replacement cars also had far superior crashworthiness as measured by the National Highway Transportation Safety Administration.[31]

Studies by the General Accounting Office (cited above) and the Office of Technology Assessment conclude that improved mileage need not compromise safety. The OTA concluded in an October 1991 study: "In our view, significant improvements in fuel economy should be possible over the longer term—by 2001, for example—without compromising safety." To the extent that new fuel-efficiency standards reduce the number of large vehicles on the road, everyone will be safer. According to the GAO, the reduction in weight of the overall fleet was part of the reason highway safety improved since the mid-1970s.[32]

Indeed, improved technology holds the promise of making fuel-efficient cars safer than the larger cars they replace. Had Detroit (or Washington) been concerned about auto safety, it would not have resisted putting air bags in cars for twenty years (or resisted enacting laws making them mandatory). Small cars with air bags are far safer than larger cars without air bags.

The solution to the safety problems lies in the free market. If an automobile rating system were developed and every new car were labeled with both the mileage and the safety rating, automakers would soon be competing to provide high-safety, high-fuel-efficiency cars. Very soon, air bags costing $100 may be available. It is disingenuous for the White House to say that it opposes higher fuel-efficiency standards because of the threat to auto safety, *when federal funding for highway safety research has been cut 40 percent since 1981—to a mere $35 million a year.* That meager funding level is shocking given the terrible cost and tragedy of traffic accidents—$70 billion, 45,000 deaths, and 4 million injuries every year.[33]

Given the can-do attitude the White House and Congress adopted in their decision to go to war and the display of American technological ingenuity in the Gulf war, it becomes absurd—I might say un-American— to shun wise national policy on the basis of a can't-do attitude about automobile technology. Many other nations are eager to meet the challenge. At the end of 1991, Honda came out with its 1992 Civic VX, which is expected to get 48 miles per gallon in the city, 55 on the highway. With fuel efficiency comparable to that of more slowly accelerating two-seater minicars, the VX has a powerful 92-horsepower engine, and is far more roomy; it seats five and is almost large enough to be classified as a compact car. Moreover, the VX's engine does not incorporate any brand-new technology.[34] Volvo of Sweden has developed the LCP 2000, a fuel-efficient research vehicle that surpasses the United States crash standard while attaining 63 miles per gallon in the city and a mind-boggling 81 mpg on the highway!

Eventually, "intelligent vehicles" interacting with "intelligent highways" hold the promise of significant advances in safety. The European effort called PROMETHEUS (Program for European Traffic with Highest Efficiency and Unprecedented Safety) is a collaboration of twenty automobile manufacturers and seventy research institutes from six countries. The goal is to reduce the risk of collisions by 50 percent by the year 2000, while enhancing the efficiency of highway transportation through advanced collision-avoidance systems, advanced traffic-control technology, microelectronics, and automotive engineering. The $800 million project stems from Europe's broad industrial policy initiative Eureka. Such programs might be able to double or triple the number of cars a

129

road could handle, and "save up to 20 percent of fuel consumed." Japan, not unexpectedly, also has an active program for developing intelligent transportation technology.[35]

In this country, however, U.S. automakers are among the leading opponents of higher efficiency standards. Without regulatory pressure on American automakers to build new highly fuel-efficient cars, the inevitable result will be that high-mileage foreign imports will capture an even larger share of the U.S. auto market, especially if, as the National Energy Strategy predicts, the price of oil rises steadily over the next forty years. The way to improve the competitiveness of American automakers is *not* for the federal government to ignore the industry. Indeed, if the DOE honestly believes its own projection for rising oil prices, it should do everything it can to prevent Detroit from shooting itself in the foot yet again.

Increased efficiency standards are only part of the solution. The government must help automakers meet those standards in a timely fashion. It must help them speed up their production cycles through policies such as those discussed in Chapter 2 to promote flexible manufacturing— including increased spending on new manufacturing technologies, worker training, manufacturing technology centers, and the like. Such policies also will help United States car companies compete with the Japanese.

The second argument given against raising fuel-efficiency standards concerns effectiveness: Making available highly efficient new cars is no guarantee customers would purchase them. Fuel costs are perhaps only 20 percent of the total operating costs over a motor vehicle's lifetime, which reduces the incentive to purchase more fuel-efficient vehicles.

There are two solutions. The first is a system of revenue-neutral rebates and "feebates" for cars. When registering a new car, the buyer would pay a fee or receive a rebate depending on the efficiency of the car, which would increase consumer interest in fuel-efficient cars by putting the costs of inefficiency up front on the window sticker. An additional rebate could be given for trading in old, fuel-inefficient cars, which would speed up the process of getting those often highly-polluting cars off the road.[36]

The second option is to raise the gasoline tax. The National Energy Strategy rejects a gasoline tax because "significant gross national product [GNP] losses were estimated to result from a large motor fuel tax increase." The argument sounds reasonable until we look at our strongest competitors. The Germans and Japanese achieve high rates of growth with gasoline taxes that are five times ours. The argument that a gas tax would hurt the GNP assumes (1) that it is better to give money to foreign suppliers of oil than spend the money in America and (2) that the taxes are not spent in ways that would increase the GNP. Gas taxes could, however, boost GNP by reducing the federal deficit or by increasing funds for energy R&D, which has had phenomenal payoffs in the past and can be expected to do so again in the future.

Rejecting a gas tax because it might hurt the GNP is too short-sighted a complaint, even if it were not false. We must not ignore the broad benefits of reduced oil use that are difficult to include in GNP calculations, such as decreasing both pollution and reliance on foreign sources. Many analysts have recommended a higher price for gasoline for the simplest reason: A higher price reflects the "full social cost" of gasoline, which includes the money the Defense Department spends to safeguard the oil supplies in the Persian Gulf, federal subsidies to the domestic oil industry, the health costs and environmental damage caused by burning oil, and the jobs lost due to the outflow of capital from the United States to pay for imported oil.[37] This full or true cost has been estimated in 1990 at $50 to $100 per barrel *above* the actual cost. By underpricing oil, we inevitably overuse it, with severe environmental and economic consequences.

The military spending alone devoted to keeping the shipping lanes open is a subsidy not merely of United States domestic use, but of the oil used by our major trading competitors. The Pentagon spends tens of billions of dollars every year to protect oil going to Japan and Germany. Theodore Moran suggests that an American gasoline tax should be called a "national security premium."[38]

America has so far made the much more costly choice of trying to improve energy security by devoting major financial resources every year to prepare for military intervention in the Persian Gulf, instead of using minor resources to reduce American energy dependence. The superior way to increase our security is to redirect a small fraction of the $60 billion the Pentagon spends each year on the Persian Gulf toward measures such as fuel efficiency, thereby reducing the need for that spending. The military approach *undercuts* energy security, since it leads to overuse

131

of oil and hence additional pollution. The demand-reduction approach, on the other hand, not only achieves energy security, but also helps reduce our entanglement in Middle East politics.

Many researchers believe that fuel efficiency will cost *less* than the gasoline it replaces. Researchers at the University of Michigan and the American Council for an Energy-Efficient Economy have concluded that each gallon of gasoline saved by raising the average fuel efficiency of new cars from 27.5 mpg to 44 mpg in 2000 would cost fifty-three cents— far below the current price. In other words, while improved fuel efficiency would raise the price of a car, the increased cost would be more than offset by the reduction in gasoline use. Similarly, a 1991 National Academy of Sciences study on responses to global warming concluded that policies such as improving vehicle efficiency would have a cost "less than or equal to zero."[39]

In the short run, energy-efficient technologies hold the promise of maintaining steady economic growth while keeping in check energy demand and the emission of greenhouse gases and other pollutants. This literally provides the world breathing space as we make the inevitable transition to renewable forms.

Renewable Energy

From a systems perspective, the best energy sources are those that are constantly replenished, such as the wind, falling water, plant matter, and heat and light from the sun. Their energy cycles create the lowest net pollution. People seem to believe that wind and solar power are years, if not decades, away from being practical, but that is yet another energy myth.

In the 1980s, the cost of wind-generated electricity dropped by roughly 80 percent, to under 7 cents per kilowatt-hour. At some sites, average capital and operating costs for new windmills can be as low as 6 cents per kilowatt-hour. That is cheaper than the cost of electricity for a new coal-fired plant. Early design problems have been largely solved, and wind turbines can now be mass-produced cheaply. For the nation's largest utility, California's Pacific Gas and Electric, wind will supply the energy for the next power plant. And the Midwest has even more wind resources than California. A 1991 study by Pacific Northwest Laboratory

132

for the DOE calculated that there is enough wind potential nationwide to produce all of the electricity the country uses. The cost of wind power is expected to fall below 5 cents per kilowatt-hour (kWh) by 1995. James Birk, director of the Electric Power Research Institute's Storage and Renewables Department, said in 1992, "We have good reason to expect that within 10 or 12 years, wind will have delivered energy costs of 3.5 cents/kWh, making it one of the lowest cost electrical generation technologies available."[40]

Solar energy is another unsung success story. Solar thermal energy, focusing the sun's heat and light onto oil-filled pipes and creating steam to drive a turbine, is down to 8 cents a kilowatt-hour, which is competitive with some conventional power sources today. It is likely to decline below the costs of coal-fired plants in the first decade of the next century. The costs of manufacturing photovoltaic cells, which convert sunlight directly to electricity, have declined from $60 per kilowatt-hour in 1970 to $1 in 1980 to 30 cents or less today and will continue declining.

If the price of fossil fuel plants (coal, oil, natural gas) reflected the full social costs due to environmental degradation (such as global warming) and adverse health effects (such as increased asthma and lung disease), solar and wind power would do even better by comparison. A 1989 study by the California Energy Commission concluded: "Fossil fuel electricity generation technologies have significantly higher total societal costs than renewable-energy technology."[41] Research done for the New York State Energy Research and Development Authority and the U.S. Department of Energy concluded that the *environmental* costs of electricity came to about 5.7 cents per kilowatt-hour for coal-fired generation, 2.7 cents for oil-fired, and 1.0 cent for gas-fired, but under 0.4 of a cent for solar and under 0.1 of a cent for wind. A German report prepared for the Commission of the European Communities concluded that wind energy would have been cost-effective in the mid-1980s if social costs had been included in the market prices of conventionally generated electricity.[42]

From a utility's perspective, the most valuable energy is that required to satisfy peak power demand. It is such peak demands that drive construction of new power plants. In California, demand peaks daily in the late afternoon and yearly in the hot summer, and this is exactly when solar and wind power have their greatest potential. With a modest energy storage capability, wind and solar could meet as much as half of Cali-

fornia's peak demand and one third of its total electric energy requirements. More work on energy storage technology is required to increase
the utility of solar and wind power. Interestingly, solar-thermal systems
can be adapted to energy storage and are potentially more economical
than batteries, particularly if the liquid that transports heat from the
solar collector is used to store the heat.[43]

These advances have all come in the 1980s despite a crippling cut
of 85 percent in federal funding for solar and other renewable forms of
energy (from more than $750 million in 1980 to less than $100 million
in 1988). By contrast, Japan's funding for such R&D doubled during the
1980s; the Japanese now spend more money on solar energy than we
do, as do the Germans, despite their smaller economies.

The long-term nature of such R&D makes it difficult for American
companies to support, given their focus on the next quarter's profits. In
the 1980s, United States market share in photovoltaics declined from
80 percent to 40 percent. Recently, ARCO decided it could no longer
afford to support its ARCO Solar subsidiary, the world's largest photovoltaic manufacturer (with 15 percent of the world market) and technology that was considered state-of-the-art. A German company, Siemens
A.G., bought it. Although in 1980 we led the world in every renewable
energy technology, today we lead in none. If the federal government
cannot take a long-term view in energy, economic, and environmental
planning, who can?

An accelerated R&D program could allow renewable energy to provide
41 quads of energy cost-effectively—one half of current energy use—by
the year 2030, according to a 1990 interlaboratory white paper by five
of the nation's national laboratories. *The additional cost of this program
would be a mere $160 million a year for 20 years.* If, on the other hand,
we continue the current level of funding, the report predicts renewable
energy will provide only 22 quads of energy by the year 2030, which is
also the estimate of the White House's National Energy Strategy.[44]

With accelerated R&D, the equivalent of 4.5 million barrels of oil per
day (9.6 quads per year) of renewable energy will be available by the
year 2010, all of it directly replacing oil and natural gas. The equivalent
of 9 million barrels of oil per day will be available by 2030. This direct
replacement comes primarily from biofuels, such as ethanol and synthetic
gasoline made from energy crops. Biofuels do not add net carbon dioxide
throughout their life cycle, for although they give off carbon dioxide when

134

they are burned, they absorbed an equal amount of carbon dioxide while growing. With an aggressive R&D program, a cost-competitive process for deriving ethanol from biomass appears possible by the year 2000.[45]

An Energy Industrial Policy

The supply-side approach to our energy problem leads to only a partial solution: providing more energy supplies. A systems approach is superior because energy is a means and not an end. People don't want electricity or oil per se; they want good lighting and good transportation. Only an approach that sees energy as one part of a system can produce wise policy that gives people what they want, good jobs, for instance.

In traditional energy supplies, the trend is toward lower employment. For instance, between 1980 and 1988, coal mining jobs in the United States fell from 246,000 to 151,000—a 40 percent drop—despite a 14 percent increase in total coal production. The same contraction is seen in the American oil and gas industries. Those industries provide relatively few jobs because fewer people are needed to use increasingly automated and expensive equipment. They are exceedingly *capital*-intensive industries compared to more *labor*-intensive industries, such as manufacturing. In Alberta, Canada, for instance, the oil and gas industries generate only 1.4 jobs for every $1 million worth of capital investment, while manufacturing yields 9 jobs. Thus, devoting resources to manufacturing energy-efficient appliances will provide more jobs than devoting the same resources to providing more energy.

Efficiency will produce even more jobs when people who reduce their use of energy take the savings from their utility bills and spend it on products from industries that are more labor-intensive than conventional energy generation. A study in Oregon revealed that spending $1 million in the utility industry generates roughly 12 jobs, while $1 million spent throughout the state produces 35 jobs.[46]

A study by the New York State Energy Office found that for the same amount of energy generated (or saved), compact fluorescent lights provided over twice as many jobs as new coal plants, and over three times as many jobs as existing oil plants. A study for Idaho concluded that stricter energy-efficiency standards for buildings would reduce residential electricity use by 46 percent; that the energy savings were greater

135

than the extra construction costs; and that for every 1.5 million kilowatt-hours conserved, one new job would be created. A University of Alaska study concluded that state spending on weatherization (installing weatherstripping, insulation, storm windows) "creates more jobs per dollar of outlays than any other type of capital project—almost three times as many direct jobs as highway construction."[47]

Similarly, building windmills and other solar-based energy sources will provide more jobs than mining and burning coal. The following chart from the Worldwatch Institute's *The State of the World 1991* gives the numbers:

United States Direct Employment Generated by Electricity-Producing Technologies[48]

Technology	Jobs (per billion kilowatt-hours a year)
Nuclear	100
Geothermal	112
Coal (including mining)	116
Solar Thermal	248
Wind	542

Compared with our current energy industrial policy, a new policy aimed at encouraging better technologies would have myriad benefits: cheaper energy, abundant domestic supplies, reduced reliance on foreign sources, reduced trade deficits, decreased pollution (both local and global), development of new United States industries, and many more manufacturing jobs. Everything about this policy recommends it.

The level of debate in this country has sunk so low that supply-siders ignore the German and Japanese models—as well as common sense—and equate "industrial policy" with "anti-free market," "socialistic," "central planning."

Tainting solutions one disagrees with by labeling them "industrial policy" is not only absurd, it is also dangerous to our economic security. Denying that America has an industrial policy is the first step down the wrong road. The United States has had an industrial policy since its inception. By industrial policy, I mean any government policy that systematically favors one industry or one set of technologies. Industrial policy is systematic (and not always obvious) in the sense that a variety of tools (some fairly obscure) are used, including direct funding, tax breaks, and regulations. As I discussed in Chapter 2, our largest export industry is aerospace, thanks to a targeted industrial policy dating back to 1915. We won the Gulf war in large part because of a military industrial policy.

Our primary trading competitor, Japan, has no aversion to industrial policy, as we have already seen. In particular, energy security is an essential component of its doctrine of Comprehensive National Security, which is why Japan devotes 22 percent of government R&D to energy, whereas we devote a pitiful 4 percent.[49] The question is not whether we should adopt an energy industrial policy, but whether we should adopt the one laid out in the National Energy Strategy that favors the nuclear power and oil industries.

The domestic oil industrial policy proposed in the National Energy Strategy is a complex array: R&D funding for advanced oil recovery technology, the opening up of federal lands to oil exploration (including the Arctic National Wildlife Refuge and the Outer Continental Shelf), regulatory relief for oil pipeline and horizontal well-drilling, a variety of tax incentives for oil producers, revised trade and export policy aimed at boosting non-Middle East oil imports and investment in non-Middle East production, and increases in the Strategic Petroleum Reserve. This elaborate policy is, alas, costly and ineffective. In the National Energy Strategy's own best-case scenario, reliance on Middle East oil rises, the price of oil rises, the trade deficit rises, overall oil use rises, and emissions of carbon dioxide rise. All of those will be accompanied by great sacrifice to our own life-style and economic growth. Nothing about this policy recommends it.

America's Pro-Nuclear Industrial Policy

The nuclear power industry, the other major beneficiary of the strategy, hardly competes in a free market. In the 1980s it received some $100 billion in direct federal subsidies; one estimate for direct federal subsidies for the year 1984 alone came to $15.6 billion, nearly as much as the total retail revenue from nuclear energy output that year.[50] Indirect

137

federal support and subsidies abound. The Price-Anderson Act limits the liability the nuclear power industry assumes for any accident; one estimate for the cumulative value of this indirect subsidy to the industry by 1988 is $111 billion (in 1985 dollars).[51] The government has indirectly subsidized the industry by more than $9 billion (according to the General Accounting Office) for uranium-enrichment services.[52] What happens to the nuclear waste after the plant is finished with it, and what happens to the entire nuclear plant when it reaches the end of its life, are not included in the stated cost of the electricity generated by nuclear plants. Nevertheless, even though its stated price reflects neither the subsidy nor the full life-cycle cost, nuclear power remains uneconomical.

Nuclear energy advocates have argued that one reason it remains uneconomical is the vast amount of government red tape nuclear plants must go through to be certified. Such red tape is reasonable, given that without government support and the government's assumption of disaster liability, the nuclear industry would probably not exist. If all red tape were removed *and* if all federal subsidies were removed, *and* if the nuclear plant owners had to assume all liability for accidents and waste disposal, it seems doubtful that the plants would ever be economical. A study for the Commission of European Communities estimated the *external* cost of nuclear power in West Germany (including government subsidies and environmental factors) at between 6 and 13 cents per kilowatt-hour.[53] Add that to the National Energy Strategy's best-case future cost for nuclear power, 6.6 cents per kilowatt-hour, and nuclear power becomes far more costly than other sources of energy.

The National Academy of Sciences, among many others, recommends a new look at nuclear power. Since "nuclear reactor designs capable of meeting fail-safe criteria and satisfying public concerns have not been demonstrated," a "new generation of reactor design is needed." But nuclear power should be pursued only if it is economical compared with other forms of energy, including efficiency, a subject most analyses do not treat. For instance, a 1990 *Scientific American* article recommending expanded use of nuclear power concludes: "No mention of costs was made in this article expressly."[54]

As noted earlier, the National Energy Strategy's industrial policy for nuclear power includes new regulations to accelerate the review process for new nuclear power plants by limiting public comment and making it more difficult for states to block nuclear waste repositories within their own borders. The strategy aims money at "reducing the economic risk of building a nuclear powerplant," through research and development for a new plant design and through the creation of a "temporary Government [uranium] enrichment corporation," to lower fuel costs.[55]

This particular industrial policy is pointless, according to the strategy's own best-case scenario: The tax-supported, subsidized cost of nuclear power falls from 9.9 cents per kilowatt-hour to 6.6 cents, yet nuclear power provides roughly the same 6 quads of power in 2015 as today, and rises to only 12 quads in 2030. But more energy—cheaper, safer, cleaner—can be provided by efficiency. Similarly, according to the study by five national laboratories discussed earlier, expanded R&D for renewable energy could provide an additional 20 quads of clean power by 2030—as opposed to a mere 6 quads from problematic nuclear.

Sound bites and media hype notwithstanding, the debate over industrial policy is not about *if* but about *which*. Industrial policy promoting the nuclear and oil industries works against least-cost planning; it encourages energy sources that are not the most cost-effective, not the cleanest, and not the most job-producing. Such policies, which include the National Energy Strategy, attempt to dictate which energy sources the country should use, and thus are far more "centrally planned" and "anti-free market" than those policies that harness market forces to ensure that the least-cost energy sources are used. The sensible energy industrial policy opens the door to efficiency in the near term and renewable energy in the long term.

Research and Development

Investment in energy-efficiency R&D is very cost-effective. During the heyday of energy-efficiency support in the Carter years, the DOE funded a variety of projects that have paid off handsomely. The big successes were improvements to compact fluorescent light bulbs; high-performance windows; and low-energy heat pumps, water heaters, and air conditioners. These projects required tiny federal government investment, $2 million or $3 million apiece. A 1991 analysis by the Lawrence Berkeley Laboratory revealed that three projects receiving a total of $6 million in federal funds have already realized savings of $5 billion and will eventually generate savings of $82 billion—a return on taxpayer investment of 14,000 to 1! Furthermore, the technology is all made-in-the-U.S.A. Not all R&D projects can produce such dramatic payoffs, but even if these three projects alone had to justify the entire federal investment in energy conservation R&D over the past decade, they would represent a 50-to-1 return. One of the projects, the $3 million DOE investment in high-performance windows, will eventually save as much energy as the Interior Department believes could be found from drilling in the Arctic National Wildlife Refuge.[56]

Merely promoting the research and development of new technologies will not ensure that they are manufactured and marketed. Indeed, it is precisely in these latter two areas of the production cycle that American businesses fail. To ensure success, the federal government must promote policies that guarantee a demand for the best new products. This can be accomplished through a variety of regulations. Again, a systems approach is called for.

Energy Conservation at Federal Facilities

One way to guarantee demand for United States energy-efficiency products is through programs for reducing energy use in federal buildings. Federal buildings and facilities used $3.5 billion in energy in 1989. A 1988 law requires a 10-percent reduction in energy use in federal buildings by 1995, but federal energy use has actually increased 7.9 percent since 1988. A key reason for this dismal performance is that federal spending on energy-efficiency improvements declined from $297 million in 1981 to $45 million in 1989. An independent study of federal energy use concluded that the government could save $864 million a year if it took advantage of available, off-the-shelf energy-saving products.[57] Many studies indicate that the energy efficiency of all United States buildings could be doubled by the year 2010, saving the nation $100 billion per year, which suggests the government could save $1.75 billion annually in its own buildings.[58]

The government should change its course, and accept an energy-reduction mandate: Every five years for the next twenty, energy use must decline 15 percent. Meeting this mandate means overcoming a key road block to federal investment in new equipment—Washington's budgetary process, which makes it difficult to get money for investments that take even two to three years to pay for themselves. To solve that bureaucratic problem, the Alliance to Save Energy recommends that the DOE set up

140

an energy-efficiency investment fund to lend money to federal agencies for efficiency improvements, at the same time allowing those agencies to retain two thirds of any energy costs savings. As both the EPA and the Office of Technology Assessment have documented, such efficiency improvements are very profitable, with rapid paybacks, so the fund would quickly become a huge revenue generator.

To support the development of a strong domestic industry in energy-efficient technologies, I believe the proposed DOE fund should invest only in new equipment with a high domestic content, at least 60 percent in the beginning, and eventually 80 percent or more. Such policies are needed to combat the informal but pervasive Japanese practices (discussed in the previous chapter) that in effect mandate high levels of Japanese content.

Low-Income Housing

Energy bills are a genuine hardship for low-income families. After rent, energy is the largest monthly expense of such households. Yet energy is of lower priority than food and must compete with many other necessities, including medical care. Poor families often find they have no money to pay for energy at the end of the month and simply do without.[59]

The Department of Housing and Urban Development (HUD) spends between $2 billion and $3 billion every year subsidizing the energy bills for 3.6 million federally assisted housing units. The Department of Health and Human Services (HHS) Low-Income Home Energy Assistance Program spends another $1.4 billion to help cover heating and cooling costs in roughly 6 million low-income households; typically HHS covers 50 percent of the bill. In both the HUD and HHS programs, some of the energy bill is borne by the occupant, unless there is another subsidy. Yet in most states, low-income families still are faced with annual home-energy bills exceeding $750, even after receiving energy aid. An OTA study concluded: *"There seems little question that increased use of existing, proven technologies would reduce a large fraction of the $4 billion in residential energy paid for by the government in federally owned and assisted households"* (emphasis in original).[60]

A 1988 HUD study estimated a potential for saving 30 percent of the energy used in public housing with an average payback of 4.5 years for capital invested in such simple measures as weatherstripping and insulation.[61] As noted earlier, many studies show that at least 50 percent of the energy used by buildings can be eliminated cost effectively. Rather than subsidizing low-income households to overuse energy, HUD and HHS should subsidize retrofits, which would ultimately save the taxpayers $2 billion a year and at the same time drastically reduce the hardship that energy bills bring to millions of low-income households. Such a program would have more societal benefits than almost any other equivalent transfer payment the government has today. Since this would be a federal program, HUD and HHS should also specify that the retrofits be done with equipment that has high domestic content.

All new low-income housing that HUD builds should meet the highest energy-efficient standards. The initial cost of the building may be slightly higher, but that extra cost is quickly paid back in energy savings, which means both reduced federal energy subsidies *and* a lower total monthly bill (rent plus utilities) for the occupants.

Regulatory Policy

Overall federal regulatory policy should be aimed at moving the entire country in the same direction as federal buildings—installing energy-efficient technology, made in America. Federal power supply agencies, such as the Tennessee Valley Authority, should be mandated to conduct least-cost planning.[62]

Certain products, such as compact fluorescent light bulbs, are so beneficial that standards mandating their use should be established. Building codes for residential and commercial buildings need to be revised everywhere to encourage greater efficiency. Incentives should be provided to government agencies and businesses that significantly surpass minimum standards. Federally subsidized mortgages should go only to homes that meet energy-efficient standards. State utility regulations must be altered to allow utilities to make money when they save energy through efficiency. Least-cost planning must be made the norm nationwide. In time, targets for reducing carbon dioxide emissions should be set for all energy producers.

As for autos, new-car fuel efficiency standards should be raised from 27 mpg to at least 40 mpg by the year 2000, and even higher after that. Safety regulations should be strengthened. The rebate/feebate system should be put in place.

Funding for urban mass transit should be increased, not cut. It is often argued that mass transit exists only because of taxpayer subsidization far in excess of collected fares, while road use is largely covered by users fees (primarily gasoline taxes). The California Energy Commission, however, notes that while gas taxes cover 70 percent of total road construction costs, they do not cover "maintenance costs, vehicle facility costs (such as parking lots), loss of property tax revenues from land set aside for roads and other facilities, social service costs (i.e., police, ambulance, court, legal) and health and environmental costs." The commission cites one study concluding that the full public subsidy for users of public roads is twice as large as the subsidy for mass transit.[63]

Infrastructure

The infrastructure program described in Chapter 2 should be carried out in an energy-efficient manner. Buildings in need of repair must receive energy retrofits. Not only government buildings and low-income housing can benefit, but also schools. The annual energy bill for the Chicago public school system, $58.5 million, exceeds the budget for supplies and books *combined*.[64] Since school energy bills are huge, the potential savings are also huge. Yet only a few school systems have started to take advantage of energy efficiency.

Iowa has a local energy bank to fund such retrofits of their schools and provide necessary technical assistance. Iowa's North Kossuth Community School District invested $44,000 on energy improvements and saved $23,000 the first year—"enough money to hire another teacher," according to the Iowa Department of Natural Resources. The Dubuque Community School District upgraded the efficiency of its pool system, ventilation system, and boiler controls in one high school at a cost of $101,000 and cut energy costs $44,000 the first year—a two-year payback "with enough money saved to create several new faculty positions." Philadelphia public schools have an energy conservation program that created savings of $6 million a year. In Wisconsin, the town of New Berlin was able to save an average of nearly $10,000 a school through energy improvements.[65]

Honeywell's School Services Program guarantees that a heating, air-conditioning, and lighting upgrade will pay for itself in an agreed-upon number of years, usually six or seven—or Honeywell pays the difference.

143

Schools get the latest equipment, or repair of their old equipment, without providing capital up front: Costs are paid from the savings provided by the reduced use of energy and the lower operating costs of the improved equipment. Usually the savings are higher than projected to attain a six-year payback, and the schools keep the difference. In the case of the Scotch Plains-Fanwood School District in northern New Jersey, savings exceeded projections by almost $150,000 a year.[66]

The DOE could set up School Energy Banks with every state to fund energy retrofits. Since these programs pay for themselves, there is no net cost to the taxpayer. The government's primary role is providing the up-front capital and the technical expertise, where needed.

A neglected element of "infrastructure" is trees. Most American cities are now "urban heat islands," where summer temperatures downtown are 5 to 9 degrees Fahrenheit higher than in surrounding areas and are rising at a rate of more than 1 degree per decade in many cities. Before mechanical air conditioning, people cooled their houses in the summer by painting the exteriors white and surrounding them with trees. As such practices disappeared, the urban heat problem has increased, creating additional peak demand for air conditioning at a cost of $1 billion a year to ratepayers. In addition, episodes of urban smog have worsened.[67]

Unfortunately, in tough economic times, cities and states cut back on forestry budgets. For example, New York City reduced its forestry budget from $5.2 million in 1990 to $660,000 in 1991. The city is losing an estimated fifteen thousand trees every year. The director of Cornell University's Urban Horticulture Institute, Nina Bassuk, told *The New York Times*, "Eight trees are dying or being taken down for every one that's planted." Other cities have similar problems.[68]

Yet, researchers at the Lawrence Berkeley Laboratories estimate that if municipalities planted trees and painted the outsides of buildings white, energy would be saved at a cost of under 1 cent per kilowatt-hour—making this program far cheaper than any new energy supply. They estimate that "an aggressive research program and beginning of 'whitening and greening' can advance heat island mitigation by ten years, saving $10 billion in energy cost, and $20 billion in avoided generation and air-conditioning investments."[69] The improvements in the urban environment—and the many aesthetic benefits provided by trees—are free.

144

The DOE should begin working with states, cities, and utilities to revitalize this essential element of urban infrastructure.

The broad program for promoting energy efficiency outlined here would dramatically reduce the need for new power plant construction, which in turn would help free considerable domestic capital and help make the infrastructure program I propose achievable. Consider, for instance, the crude-petroleum and natural gas sector. From 1975 to 1987, the capital used by that sector exceeded the GNP that originated in that sector by $100 billion. That gap equals 13 percent of the total gross fixed capital formation of the entire manufacturing sector during the same period. That $100 billion gap represents capital that could have been allocated more productively, for instance, to new manufacturing plant and equipment. As researchers at the Center for Energy and Environmental Studies at Boston University explain and warn:

> The inefficient allocation of capital that is suggested by the gap adds to the US deficit in trade and capital accounts. For example, a portion of the decline in US exports is due to outdated production facilities, especially in manufacturing, some of which could have been replaced by capital diverted to the oil and gas sector. Similarly, the "lost" capital represented by the gap is not available to finance the federal government deficit. This increases the government's dependence on foreign sources of capital and contributes to the shift in the US position from the world's largest creditor nation to the world's largest debtor nation in the past decade.[70]

For a country that already underinvests in new plant and equipment compared with our foreign competition, every billion dollars of misallocated capital severely hurts our economic competitiveness. Every federal policy that encourages scarce capital to go to economic sectors that are inefficient and environmentally harmful endangers our security. Every billion dollars of federal subsidy that pulls with it billions more dollars of private capital to industries like oil extraction is doubly wasted: Taxpayer money that could have gone to useful investments (like infrastructure and worker training) is wasted, and private capital is misspent. Yet another reason for not drilling in the Arctic National Wildlife Refuge is that the billions of dollars needed to find, retrieve, and transport

145

whatever oil might be there could be better allocated to more productive investments.

A similar danger is posed by planned government policies to artificially boost the nuclear power industry. Not only do huge construction projects, such as nuclear power plants, drain the national economy of scarce capital, but they also create regional labor shortages, slowing construction and raising costs of other infrastructure projects that are far more vital to this nation, such as schools, low-income housing, and public buildings.[71]

Training

In order to put in place the necessary energy policy, America will need thousands of electricians, carpenters, architects, design engineers, interior decorators, utility executives, federal employees, urban planners, building managers, corporate executives and the like with state-of-the-art training in the efficient use of energy. We will need thousands of scientists and engineers to research, design, and test a host of renewable and energy-efficient technologies. Yet there is virtually no federal funding for training the needed energy experts.

Professor Arthur Rosenfeld, director of the Center for Building Science at the Lawrence Berkeley Laboratory (LBL) told Congress in April 1991: "An absurd situation that demonstrates the need for Conservation and Renewables fellowships exists at the LBL Center for Building Science. At any given time we have about six fellows who have been sent by their governments to collaborate in our productive programs and learn about building science and technology. *None of them is American!*" (emphasis in original).[72]

The federal government should establish a special program of fellowships and low-interest college loans for training these experts. An apprenticeship program aimed specifically at training skilled craftspeople should be established (as part of the larger program described in Chapter 2). The government should increase the number of federal employees who attend the numerous existing shorter-term energy training courses. Such courses cost only a few hundred dollars and stand to produce greater savings to federal agencies than the cost of sending their employees.

146

Tax Credits

There is no need to establish a nationwide Energy Department fund to lend money to businesses for new efficient technology, since some utilities are already providing such loans. Indeed, some utilities are paying for such installation outright. A New England utility paid half of the $1.3 million cost of installing high-efficiency lighting, heating, and cooling systems at the *Boston Globe* newspaper building; the newspaper will get its investment back through savings in just two years. Contrary to current rules, the federal government should exempt from taxation all rebates that utilities give customers for conservation and efficiency. Tax credits should be phased out for nuclear power and fossil fuels. Tax credits for renewable energy should be made available for a limited period, perhaps through the year 2000, to make up for past favoritism to traditional energy sources and to help give the renewable industry time to mature. Such credits are not anti-free market since they would reflect the lower social cost of renewable power. Another way to level the playing field for renewables would be to incorporate environmental costs into energy taxes.

Revenues

Most of these recommendations are cost-free or pay for themselves quickly. In that sense, the energy industrial policy proposed here can return America to the golden era of "free" energy security. Reorienting the priorities of the Department of Energy, shifting money from testing and building nuclear bombs and from promoting nuclear power, could easily pay for new R&D, energy fellowships, temporary renewable tax credits, and the like. For instance, the accelerated R&D program for renewable energy put forward by five government laboratories can be achieved with an increase in funding of only about $160 million a year for twenty years.

Moreover, by phasing out direct and indirect subsidies for nuclear power and fossil fuels, the federal government can save billions of dollars each year. The last comprehensive survey of government energy subsidies was made in 1985, and estimated that subsidies for nuclear, petroleum, natural gas and coal came to more than $30 billion a year.[73] Since then,

147

the subsidies have been reduced somewhat, but they still favor nuclear and fossil fuel over renewables and energy efficiency.

Although the energy policy outlined here would either pay for itself or make money, higher prices for fossil fuels and nuclear power are needed, to reveal their full negative costs to society and thereby create incentives to reduce excessive consumption. A 1991 *Scientific American* article estimated yearly societal burdens of energy production and consumption as follows:

Hidden Societal Burden of Energy Production and Consumption[74]

Corrosion	$2	billion
Health Impacts	$12 to 82	billion
Crop Losses	$3 to 8	billion
Radioactive Waste	$4 to 31	billion
Military	$15 to 54	billion
Employment	$30	billion
Subsidies	$43 to 55	billion
Total Yearly Burden	$109 to 262	billion

Contrary to the popular argument, energy taxes do not work against the free market. The free market does not determine the true cost of any form of energy, including oil, coal, gas, or nuclear. Until the price of energy reflects its full social cost, energy will continue to be overused, causing economic and environmental harm. Correct pricing will speed the introduction of the cleanest and most beneficial forms of energy— energy efficiency and renewables. The interlaboratory white paper discussed above achieves its best-case scenario of 41 quads of renewable power in 2030 with only an accelerated R&D program, and notes that carbon taxes will promote even faster and greater market penetration of renewables.

If any element of this energy policy should be considered a sacrifice, it is paying higher prices for energy. Yet other more productive and more growth-oriented nations pay far higher prices than are proposed here. Moreover, since the United States willingly took on such large budget deficits in the 1980s, higher taxes in the 1990s were inevitable; how can paying off IOUs be called a sacrifice? I recommend a carbon tax of twenty dollars per ton of carbon, which translates into about six cents per gallon of gasoline, plus an additional gasoline tax of twenty to twenty-five cents per gallon. Those taxes should be phased in slowly, over a five-year period, to allow energy producers and users a long adjustment period. At no point will we come close to Europe's or Japan's gasoline tax of *two dollars per gallon* or more.

These energy taxes could be used to raise some $50 billion annually in new revenues, but they should not. I believe that the 80 percent of Americans whose wealth stagnated or declined in the 1980s should not see a higher tax burden in the 1990s. Their income taxes should be lowered proportionally to cover the rise in their energy bills. In other words, the federal government will not take away more of most people's money; it will just take the money in a different way in order to reveal the true cost of energy (while at the same time allowing people to keep a higher fraction of the money they make from their jobs).

The government should keep the energy taxes paid by the richest 20 percent of Americans. This roughly $10 billion in increased revenues should go to (1) transportation infrastructure that has energy and environmental benefits, such as mass transit, and (2) programs to help low-income families with energy costs.

The government could have an explicit income-support program to compensate low-income families for higher energy taxes, but a variety of other programs would be more useful. The poor will not be disproportionately hurt by energy taxes, and indeed should end up with lower energy bills overall, if the Energy Department joins with HUD and HHS on a comprehensive program to ensure that low-income households receive subsidized weatherization and energy-efficient retrofits. The Department of Transportation could put in place a special program to help low-income families buy fuel-efficient cars, and provide a bounty for trading in old, polluting, gas guzzlers. Another useful program would be vouchers for mass transit, since many of the poor live in cities.

Energy taxes promote economic security, energy security, environmental security, and military security. They should be labeled national security or environmental security taxes. Such taxes are widely considered politically unfeasible, although they represent only about 1 percent of GNP. Certainly, they would be difficult to put in place without strong presidential support. I believe that the public would accept taxes targeted

149

to specific national problems if the long-term benefits were explained clearly, if the short-term burden on the majority of Americans was minimized, and if they were phased in slowly over several years.

In October 1990, the California Energy Commission concluded that a combination of tighter state energy standards, more aggressive utility programs to reduce energy demand, and expanded R&D into efficiency technologies and policies had the potential to *reduce* California's electricity use 2.5 percent a year through 2009. According to the commission, such a program would eliminate the need for 37,000 megawatts of generating capacity, and "pave the way for a renewable future."[75] The United States as a whole should be able to achieve a similar improvement, but only if the federal government strongly encourages, rather than discourages, wise energy policies.

On its own merits, it is easy to defend a shift to a systems-oriented energy policy based on energy efficiency in the near term and renewable energy in the longer term. Such a policy is pro-growth and pro-environment. America's decision on energy will significantly affect the quality of life of future generations, and, because of the threat of global warming, it will affect not only United States national security, but global security as well.

5

Environmental Security and the Industrial Ecosystem

*If you place a frog in a pot of boiling water, it will
immediately try to scramble out. But if you place the
frog in room temperature water, and don't scare him,
he'll stay put. Now, if the pot sits on a heat source,
and if you gradually turn up the temperature . . . the
frog will become groggier and groggier, until he is
unable to climb out of the pot. Though there is
nothing restraining him, the frog will sit there and
boil. Why? Because the frog's internal apparatus for
sensing threats to survival is geared to sudden
changes in his environment, not to slow, gradual
changes.*

—An Old Parable[1]

People are like frogs. We are not adept at adapting to threats that creep
up on us gradually; slow-growing threats do not force us to confront the
failure of our current thinking and to reorient ourselves. A Pearl Harbor,
a *Sputnik*, even an unexpected hole in the ozone layer—those can inspire
drastic change. But a slow erosion of our standard of living or a slow
increase in our planet's temperature—these bring shrugs and yawns.
Ignoring the early warning signs of environmental problems is particularly perilous because most are difficult or impossible to reverse once
they start wreaking havoc.

The word "environment" comes from *viron,* meaning "circle"; the
emphasis is on interconnections. Environmental security will be achieved

151

only when humankind recognizes how it is bound to the intricate earth ecosystem: the atmosphere, the oceans, and the land. As Jim MacNeill, director of the Environment and Sustainable Development Program at the Institute for Research on Public Policy in Ottawa, Canada, has observed: "Global warming is a form of feedback from the earth's ecological system to the world's economic system. So are the ozone hole, acid rain in Europe and eastern North America, soil degradation in the prairies, deforestation and species loss in the Amazon, and many other environmental phenomena."[2]

The case for redefining security to include environmental issues has been made with increasing urgency over the last few years, in part because the waning military tensions of the cold war have coincided with the growing visibility of global ecological dangers that threaten the "security" of many nations and require international solutions. This chapter focuses on the environmental problems I view as the greatest threats to security, such as global warming and disputes over scarce water supplies in the Middle East. I will discuss some of the international and national policies required to move us toward environmental security.

Ultimately, the United States, and the world, must develop an industrial ecosystem—where industrial processes minimize both the input of all resources (such as energy and water) and the output of all contaminants (such as air and water pollution). Many companies are already moving in this direction and the federal government has a critical role to play in accelerating the trend.

Global Environmental Problems

The ozone layer shields life on earth from the sun's harmful ultraviolet rays. The discovery in 1985 of a hole over Antarctica in the ozone shield was, as the National Academy of Sciences wrote, "the first unmistakable sign of human-induced change in the global environment. . . . Many scientists greeted the news with disbelief. Existing theory simply had not predicted it."[3] Scientists have known since 1974 that the principal cause of ozone depletion is chlorofluorocarbons (CFCs), which are used as refrigerants and solvents. Some nations, including the United States, had taken steps in the 1970s to limit their use. But no theory predicted the development of a gaping hole in one place, rather than a gradual thinning of the entire ozone layer.

It was not until the stunning revelation of the ozone hole that the nations of the world took the unprecedented step of negotiating the Montreal Protocol on Substances that Deplete the Ozone Layer. The 1987 agreement called for a 50-percent reduction in CFC production by 1999. Then, in June 1990, some ninety-three countries agreed to halt *all* CFC production by the year 2000. The world was recognizing that the long atmospheric lifetime of the CFCs (75 to 140 years) means that they will continue to destroy the ozone layer for several decades after we all stop releasing them into the atmosphere.[4]

Ozone depletion continues to exceed worst-case fears. In April 1991, the EPA announced that the ozone layer over United States latitudes was disappearing at the rate of 4 percent to 5 percent a decade, twice as fast as had been predicted just a short time before. An additional two hundred thousand skin cancer deaths may result over the next fifty years in this country alone. Then, in early 1992, NASA scientists announced that they had detected record levels of ozone-destroying chemicals above the Northern Hemisphere, raising the possibility that an ozone hole could develop over populated parts of the United States sometime in the next few years.[5]

Just as trace levels of ozone are crucial for life on earth, so, too, are trace levels of carbon dioxide and other gases. These gases trap heat at the earth's surface and lower atmosphere, keeping the earth about 33 Centigrade degrees (60 Fahrenheit degrees) warmer than it would otherwise be. Life on earth as we know it is made possible by this natural greenhouse effect. With far fewer greenhouse gases, we would have the unbearably cold climate of Mars; with far more, the unbearably hot climate of Venus. For decades, scientists have been worrying that humanity was altering the natural greenhouse, but their concerns grew in the last decade, partly because the eight hottest years of the century all occurred since 1980.

The public and media began worrying in earnest in 1988 (which until 1990 was the warmest year on public record), a year that had heat waves, fires, floods, drought, and a superhurricane. James Hansen, director of NASA's Goddard Institute for Space Studies, told Congress he was "99% confident" that the warming trend since 1900 was real and that we should accept the idea that the greenhouse effect was responsible.[6] Since then, the national and international scientific community has come to a broad consensus that global climate change poses a serious danger.

In June 1990, the science working group of the United Nation's Intergovernmental Panel on Climate Change (IPCC) asserted:

> We are certain of the following: . . . emissions resulting from human activities are substantially increasing the atmospheric concentrations of the greenhouse gases: carbon dioxide, methane, chlorofluorocarbons (CFCs) and nitrous oxide. These increases will enhance the greenhouse effect, resulting on average in additional warming of the Earth's surface.[7]

Atmospheric carbon dioxide concentrations have risen roughly 25 percent from preindustrial levels. The earth's surface temperature is already estimated to have risen between 0.3 and 0.6 degrees Centigrade in the last one hundred years. The expected doubling of heat-trapping greenhouse gases over preindustrial levels by the middle of the next century is projected to raise the average temperature of the earth between 1 and 5 degrees Centigrade over the next one hundred years. This view is shared by both the IPCC and by the National Academy of Sciences in the United States.[8]

The science involved is full of uncertainties and unknowns. The global carbon cycle remains a complex and poorly understood interaction among the oceans, the land, the atmosphere, and humans. The oceans may act as a reservoir for half of all newly created carbon dioxide and ocean circulation depends critically on the global temperature balance. The land has forests and plant life that convert carbon dioxide to oxygen. The atmosphere's climate can be catastrophically altered by small changes in its composition. Last, there are humans, who exacerbate the carbon dioxide problem in many ways, such as by burning fossil fuels and destroying forests.[9] Complex computer models try to predict the climate's future behavior (so-called general-circulation models), but they have many limitations. With so many uncertainties and unknowns, not every scientist is convinced that global warming is occurring. Nevertheless, the

IPCC study had more than 95 percent of the global team of two hundred scientists agreeing.[10] The two-year congressionally mandated study by the National Academy of Sciences, National Academy of Engineering, and Institute of Medicine involved nearly fifty scientific and policy experts.

The likely effect of even modest warming cannot be known for certain. In part this is because a 2.0-to-2.5-degree Centigrade warming, near the middle of the expected range, would make the earth hotter than it has been in the 10,000 years of human civilization, hotter than it has been in 125,000 years, when humans existed in primitive hunter-gatherer communities; so there is no historical basis for determining the outcome.[11] For the United States, the National Academy study foresees possible degradation of agriculture, forests, grasslands, marine and coastal environments, as well as reduction of freshwater supplies and great damage to coastal structures.

The sea level has risen by some 15 centimeters (6 inches) or more this century. Warming is likely to raise the sea level farther. A 1-foot rise (which is in the middle of the expected range) would pose a serious problem for Bangladesh, the Nile Delta, China, Japan, and the Netherlands. One third of the world's people live within forty miles of the sea, where the land is richest and lowest. As the sea level rises, we can expect millions of environmental refugees. The United States itself has more than one half of its population living on or near a coast. A 3-foot rise in sea level, for example, would increase the part of Charleston, South Carolina, that floods every ten years from 20 percent to 45 percent. Louisiana already loses fifty square miles to open water every year. The EPA reported to Congress that a 3-foot sea level rise by 2100 could drown up to 80 percent of America's coastal wetlands. Global warming may also create more severe storms, which, coupled with rising sea levels, threaten severe flooding and intrusion of salt water into groundwater aquifers (a particularly serious problem in a world already running low on fresh water).[12]

The National Academy study notes that while humankind can probably adapt to global warming given enough time, effort, and money, "in the unmanaged systems of plants and animals that occupy much of our landscape and oceans, however, the rate of change of some key processes may be slower than the pace of greenhouse warming, *making their future questionable*" (emphasis added).[13]

*   *   *

Under the National Energy Strategy, emissions of carbon dioxide are projected to rise 25 percent over the next twenty-five years. Remarkably, the document claims, "This country has taken a lead in adopting prudent strategies to reduce greenhouse gases," and, "The United States has been a leader in both actions and research on possible climate change and its implications."[14] Unfortunately, the reverse is true. A set of guidelines distributed by the Bush administration prior to a United States-sponsored conference on global warming in April 1990 urged American delegates to avoid using "specific numbers" as well as discussions of "whether there is or is not warming." A key recommendation was "Don't get into an advocacy position on the merits of various policy proposals." At the 135-nation World Climate Conference in November 1990, United States negotiators, essentially alone in the world, blocked efforts to have the industrial nations set specific targets for reducing emissions of carbon dioxide.[15]

In May 1992, the Bush administration succeeded in watering down a U.N.–sponsored international treaty on global warming so that the treaty would not set binding targets and timetables on carbon dioxide reductions. Sadly, the greenhouse debate in the United States remains uninformed at the highest levels of government and policy-making. In April 1992, President Bush had expressed concern that carbon dioxide limits would "commit the United States to a course of action that could dramatically impede long-term economic growth in this country."[16] The view that programs to minimize global warming must hurt the economy is common, yet reflects a lack of understanding of what is now possible with new energy technologies.[17] The energy policy needed for the United States to cut its emission of carbon dioxide is not antigrowth; as discussed in the previous chapter, it will increase competitiveness, revitalize the economy, and put billions of dollars into the hands of consumers, businesses, and the government.

Our major industrial trading partners do not believe that antiwarming policies are antigrowth. They have committed to substantial action. Japan has pledged to stabilize carbon dioxide at 1990 levels by the year 2000; Australia, New Zealand, and most European nations believe they can reduce their emissions by 20 percent without hurting economic growth. Germany has promised a 25-percent reduction by the year 2005.[18] What makes these doubly impressive is that all of these countries already

156

produce far less carbon dioxide per capita—and per dollar of GNP—than the United States.

Global Warming as a National Security Threat

As the world's largest producer of greenhouse gases, the United States has not only a national but a global responsibility to reduce emissions. In the long term, global warming has the potential to threaten the American way of life far more than Saddam Hussein ever did. Rising average temperatures may well make hot summer droughts, such as occurred in 1988, more common, endangering the breadbasket of central United States and inducing further water shortages. Sea level rise could require the United States to spend hundreds of millions of dollars to protect its coasts. The United States should consider global warming a serious national security threat and respond accordingly.

Many analysts have singled out global warming as a security threat.[19] One argument is that global environmental degradation has the potential to affect international relations and in some cases worsen existing conflicts or create new ones. Rising sea levels, decreased availability of fresh water, and changing agricultural patterns could increase regional rivalries and regional conflicts. In particular, global warming could create tens or even hundreds of thousands of environmental refugees, a traditional source of political instability and tension between nations.

For military security threats, we routinely plan for a worst-case scenario, such as our old worries over the "bolt out of the blue" strike by the Soviets that could theoretically destroy half our nuclear arsenal. This unlikely scenario is a prime justification for our still spending in excess of $50 billion a year on strategic nuclear forces. Similarly, during the Gulf crisis a key justification for choosing war over economic sanctions was that worst-case analyses showed that Hussein *might* have one nuclear bomb, if not more, within a year. It was argued that a war now would avoid higher casualties later. The "worst-case analogy" of Hitler, Munich, and appeasement was used.

When dealing with major environmental problems, a worst-case scenario cannot be ruled out because, as the National Academy of Sciences explains, "The behavior of complex and poorly understood systems can easily surprise even the most careful observer." The hole in the ozone

157

layer is one example of an unexpected outcome that has exceeded worst-case fears. A worst-case analysis of the greenhouse effect would be a temperature increase of 5 degrees Centigrade over the next one hundred years, a drastic shock to the ecosystem, given that the last time the earth's average temperature changed 5 degrees, it took some ten thousand years, following the last Ice Age.[20] A 5-degree-Centigrade rise in one hundred years might create a Desert Age. The National Academy study could not preclude "radical changes" to the ecosystem, such as significant melting of the Antarctic Ice Sheet "resulting in a sea level several meters higher than it is today"; "radically changed major ocean currents leading to altered weather patterns"; or a runaway greenhouse effect if initial warming melts the high-latitude tundra or permafrost, causing a sudden release of large quantities of methane. That would be an ecological catastrophe of unimaginable proportions: widespread drought, desertification, starvation, flooding, and tens of millions of environmental refugees.

Doing nothing in the face of the real threat of severe environmental damage is economic "appeasement" to short-sighted political and business interests. Climate change may be irreversible, making any delay doubly dangerous. If preliminary actions to forestall the greenhouse effect were particularly onerous, caution might be more justifiable, but as seen in the previous chapter, the United States can achieve large-scale reductions in fossil fuel production while sustaining economic growth, reducing dependence on imported oil, and achieving myriad other benefits. Two California utilities have already pledged to reduce their carbon dioxide output by 20 percent over the next twenty years; the United States should commit to a similar reduction nationally, since we can do so while saving money. The adoption of energy-efficient standards and technologies is often called a no-regrets policy: We respond to global warming incrementally in ways that would be wise for other reasons, while waiting to see if further research shows we need to take drastic measures.

On the other hand, if we wait even ten years to act, we may have to reduce carbon dioxide emissions much more, and at a more rapid pace, forcing dramatic life-style changes and drastic reductions in fossil fuel use, all at great cost. Put another way, global warming threatens to constrict the choices available to both the government and the people. Our ability to act independently will be diminished. In this sense, global warming is like many traditional security threats—for instance, an oil embargo by a foreign power.

The economic security implications of a do-nothing energy policy for the United States are also dramatic. The National Academy says starkly: "If climate change occurs, and no mitigation or adaptation actions are undertaken, a substantial reduction in real income is likely over time." Adaptation will be expensive—hundreds of billions of dollars in the United States alone, according to the academy. The Netherlands already spends 6 percent of its GNP to keep the sea water out—the same fraction of GNP we spend on defense. On the other hand, mitigation efforts, such as energy efficiency, will actually save money (and have myriad benefits to economic and energy security) and hence be far superior to adaptation. Moreover, mitigation reduces the likelihood of the worst-case effects, such as a tremendous rise in the sea level, that would be particularly difficult and expensive to adapt to. And while humans can use technology and other means to adapt, the ability of plant and animal life to adapt to climate change is problematic at best.[21]

Even if global warming never occurs, the pledges by the other industrial nations to stabilize or cut emissions will guarantee an enormous market for energy-efficient and renewable energy technologies—technologies that companies in other countries are already racing to develop. Japan announced in 1990 that it plans to develop a host of technologies to avoid or reduce global warming, including energy efficiency, and "manufacturing technology with low emission of CO_2."[22] The Ministry of International Trade and Industry (MITI) has established the Research Institute of Innovative Technology for the Earth to develop environmental technologies. In June 1991, MITI published its "Long-term Outlook for Energy Supply and Demand," which emphasizes reconciling three goals: "affluence," "preservation of the global environment," and "energy security."[23] By investing in the technology to reconcile these goals, Japan may ultimately achieve all of them. If the United States sees these three goals as incompatible, we may achieve neither economic security, environmental security, nor energy security.

One energy technology whose global spread could raise serious security problems is nuclear power. Peaceful nuclear power provides countries with a cover for doing nonpeaceful work and gives them a rationale for pursuing enrichment facilities, reprocessing plants, and other technologies that can be used to develop bomb-grade material and nuclear

159

components. In addition, were nuclear reactors to become widespread, the threat of a terrorist attack leading to radiation leakage would become a significant security concern. As seen in the last chapter, however, perhaps the biggest problem facing nuclear power is that even with huge government subsidies, it is too expensive compared with other energy sources, including energy efficiency. Finally, subsidizing this industry so it can achieve a wider presence in the Third World seems unwise, given that our fear of nuclear weapons proliferation was one reason we decided to go to war with Iraq.

Resource and Environmental Threats to Traditional Security

Wars over resources date back to ancient times; the Trojan War may have been fought over tin, not Helen.[24] The word "rival" derives from a Latin word meaning, "one who uses a stream in common with another." The United States has been blessed with abundant resources. Those blessings, together with the diverse suppliers from whom we can obtain many strategic resources, plus our inherent ability to substitute among many resources, led a number of studies over the past two decades to conclude that oil is the only commodity whose cutoff (or threatened cutoff) poses a serious threat to the national economy.[25] The recent war in the Persian Gulf was, in part, a resource war. Saddam Hussein justified his invasion of Kuwait in part by arguing that its oil policies amounted to economic war against Iraq, and the conflict would not have seized the attention of the United States and the world so strongly had oil supplies not been at stake.

Other countries less lucky than ourselves have growing demands on their scarce resources. Those demands will lead to conflict or to the ecosystem collapse that results in environmental refugees. Such traumas could, in turn, threaten American national security if the conflict were in a part of the world important to the United States, or if the refugees fled in large numbers to this country.[26]

A key resource problem is the growing scarcity of fresh water everywhere, especially in the Middle East. Water scarcity will complicate all efforts to achieve lasting peace in that region. By the year 2000, Jordan's water needs are projected to exceed supply by 20 percent; Israel's by perhaps 30 percent. The West Bank aquifer supplies 25 percent to 40 percent of Israel's water.[27] Before 1967, only 3 percent of the river's basin was within Israel's borders. One reason Israel went to war in 1967 was that Syria and Jordan were trying to divert the flow of the Jordan River.

Turkey's Ataturk Dam on the Euphrates River will irrigate seven thousand square miles—an area the size of Israel, enabling Turkey to double its farm output and its electrical production. But the downstream effect on Syria and Iraq could be significant. At one point, Turkey's president suggested that Turkey might curtail the flow of water to force Syria to withdraw its support for Kurdish separatists in eastern Turkey.

In 1970, Egypt was feeding itself. By 1986 it was importing half its food. As the population has exploded, the Nile Delta has become increasingly polluted and per capita food production has declined. The Aswan Dam cannot keep up with the energy needs of the growing population; drought periods make matters worse. By 2025, Egypt's population is expected to grow to ninety-four million from fifty-four million.[28] Water shortages in countries along the Nile's drainage system upstream of Egypt—Sudan, Ethiopia, Uganda, Kenya, Tanzania, Zaire, Rwanda, and Burundi—have forced each of them to take more water from the river. Ethiopia controls the Blue Nile tributary that is the source of about 80 percent of Nile water entering Egypt. Ethiopia has said it can do with that water whatever it wants and may divert up to 40 percent of it. In 1980, Egyptian President Anwar Sadat warned, "If Ethiopia takes any action to block our right to the Nile waters, there will be no alternative for us but to use force."[29] In March 1991, a senior adviser to President Hosni Mubarak of Egypt said, "We need not only military security, but economic security. And that also means questions of the environment and the security of water supplies. Because if water becomes scarce, it could become a source of serious conflict throughout the region." As one American analyst has argued: "Water security will soon rank with military security in the war rooms of defense ministries." Certainly, any Middle East peace agreement must include solutions to water scarcity.[30]

Many other areas of the world are running low on water. California is a classic case. The sharing of the Colorado River by the United States and Mexico has been a source of tension between the two countries in the past and could be again if global climate change reduces the river's flow. Climate change can exacerbate water scarcity problems by affecting precipitation, evaporation, flooding, drought, and agricultural demand for water.[31]

The United States and the world need to start thinking about how to use water more efficiently. As with energy, water is overused because it is underpriced. In California, the Federal Bureau of Reclamation subsidizes water to some of the nation's richest farms; in the Central Valley, farmers pay as little as ten dollars for an acre's worth of irrigation water, while a few hundred miles away in Los Angeles, the same amount of water can cost city authorities six hundred dollars.[32]

The United States must spur the development and use of equipment and agricultural techniques that require less water. In the next century, these water-efficient technologies will be almost as important in global trade as energy-efficient technology. Some simple devices, such as low-flow shower heads, save both energy and water. Water-efficient technologies should be part of any aggressive environment, energy, and resource R&D program.

Environmental refugees are a growing concern. Consider the tragedy of Bangladesh—the result of a chain reaction. Deforestation of the Himalayas limits the ability of the uplands to store water and to moderate its flow into the streams that feed the Brahmaputra River, worsening the flooding where the river flows into the Bay of Bengal. The terrible 1988 flooding, their worst ever, left two thirds of the country under water for several days, and created countless refugees for India.[33] In the Western Hemisphere, as discussed in Chapter 1, the Haitian exodus to the United States was at least partly due to environmental degradation.

Mexico, to take a desperate example close to home, has serious environmental problems, which are playing a greater and greater role in that nation's economic problems and therefore contribute to the steady exodus northward. In this sense, hundreds of legal and illegal environmental refugees enter the United States every day. The facts are straightforward and depressing. Because much of Mexico is dry, farmland is scarce. What little exists is at risk. Soil erosion is significant in 70 percent of the good agricultural lands. Nearly 900 square miles of farmland are lost each year to desertification, the relentless process in which good farmland is turned into worthless sand. About 400 square miles of farmland are lost each year because water is no longer available and the soil has eroded. About one tenth of irrigated lands has become very salty.

162

Yet, even as cropland is lost, population grows. The country cannot support its present population of nearly 90 million. In 1986, Mexico reverted to being a net importer of food. By the year 2000, there may be another 20 million Mexicans; by 2025, the population is expected to reach 150 million. In 1990, Mexico City, with 19 million people and 32,000 industrial polluters, exceeded maximum ozone limits four of every five days, more than twice as often as Los Angeles. Boutiques now sell oxygen for $1.60 a minute. Nevertheless, some 2,000 newcomers move to the poisoned city every day because conditions in the countryside are so bleak.[34]

Forests

We are losing one of the world's most essential renewable resources: forests. This loss illustrates how environmental problems are intertwined. Each year an area the size of New York State loses its trees. One of the consequences is the more rapid overheating of the planet. Deforestation accelerates global warming in a variety of ways, including the destruction of plants that otherwise would have removed carbon dioxide from the atmosphere, and the burning and/or decay of those plants, which releases more carbon dioxide into the atmosphere. Deforestation also creates environmental refugees, as in the case of Haiti and Bangladesh.

Furthermore, many ecosystems are fragile, such as the tropical rain forests, and once destroyed may not be recoverable. Rain forests harbor the majority of species on the planet, an awesome biological diversity. On a single tree in Peru, researchers found as many ant species as are found in all of the British Isles. In only 10 one-hectare plots in Indonesia it is possible to find 700 tree species, equal to the number of tree species native to all of North America. These forests contain countless undiscovered medicines and foods. Globally, nearly a quarter of all medical prescriptions are for compounds derived from plants and microorganisms.[35] If a very promising anticancer drug, taxol, can be found in the rapidly vanishing ancient forests of the Pacific Northwest, who knows what cures can be found in the near limitless abundance of the tropical rain forests? In all the world, there are at least 75,000 plant species with edible parts, but in the course of history humankind has used no more than 10 percent of them, and today relies heavily on a mere 20 species, such as wheat, rye, millet, and rice. At the rate the rain forests are being cut down, we are losing some 4,000 to 6,000 species a year—which is more than 1,000 times greater than the normal rate of species loss before *homo sapiens* ruled the earth. By the year 2000, we may have lost as many as 20 percent of all the species now living.[36]

Deforestation often occurs because trees are underpriced or mispriced. Countries that grant short-term logging concessions provide no incentive for loggers to replant, thereby turning a potentially renewable resource into a one-time cash crop. Flat royalties encourage loggers to remove only the most valuable trees. In the Philippines, such short-sighted policies turned 17 million hectares of rich forests into 1.2 million in less than a century. Rain forests can be more valuable if uncut and used to harvest renewable goods such as medicines, fruits, rubber, oils, and cocoa.

Even the United States, the land of the free market economy, is saddled with remarkably unsound forestry practices. It sells timber on public land far below cost, sometimes for only 10 cents on the dollar. Some economists estimate the U.S. Treasury loses more than $100 million a year on timber sales. Accounting practices at the Forest Service are so unusual that it can make money on lumber sales even when the federal government loses money on the sale; when managers of the Bridger-Teton National Forest wanted to reforest bare spots created by an earlier timber cutting, they paid for the project with the sale of timber clear-cut from another area! The Forest Service, operating under a law written more than sixty years ago when timber prices were far lower,. can actually sell timber at market rates of up to $50 per thousand board feet, but return only 50 cents per thousand to the Treasury.[38]

Deforestation, environmental degradation, and global warming are all connected to population growth. World population is expected to grow from 5.3 billion in 1990 to 6.2 billion in the year 2000 to 8.5 billion in the year 2025. This growth rate, nearly 1 billion people per decade, is astonishing considering that it took 130 years for the world's population to grow from 1 billion to 2 billion. Population pressure means that more land is cleared for housing and agriculture and that more energy is used. One billion people need a great deal of land, food, and fuel. Population growth was responsible for almost two thirds of the increase in carbon dioxide entering the atmosphere between 1950 and 1985.[39]

The vast majority of the population growth will take place in the developing world. Ethiopia's population is expected to rise from 47 million today to 112 million in 2025, Nigeria to rise from 113 million today to 301 million, Bangladesh from 116 million to 235 million, and India from 853 to 1,446 million.[40] What will happen to topsoil, forests, the climate, and regional security under such explosive conditions?

Environmental Degradation by the Peacetime Military

The damage to America's environment by our nuclear weapons program is not of the same scale as most of the ecological problems previously discussed. Nevertheless, it deserves discussion because it shows that our cold war paradigm of national security as only military security had a significant impact on our environment, just as it did on our economy.

As the cold war waned, stunning revelations showed that the Department of Energy grossly mismanaged the facilities that produce nuclear weapons material. Since 1944, to take one case, 200 billion gallons of contaminated water entered the Columbia River and the groundwater around the Hanford nuclear reservation in Washington State. Between 1943 and 1956, officials there deliberately exposed the public to large amounts of airborne radiation. The Centers for Disease Control (CDC) concluded that some residents near Hanford received higher doses of radioiodine than people living near Chernobyl. The CDC estimates that more than 30,000 children may have increased their likelihood of contracting thyroid cancer fivefold to fifteenfold. A 1986 General Accounting Office (GAO) report found that eight out of nine DOE weapons sites examined have "groundwater contaminated with radioactive and/or hazardous substances to high levels. . . . Six facilities have soil contamination in unexpected areas, including offsite locations." According to an internal Du Pont study, severe contamination "may extend well beyond the period which land control can be anticipated and indeed may exist for centuries or millennia." A 1985 internal Du Pont memo publicized in congressional hearings revealed more than thirty serious reactor accidents at the Savannah River plant, some involving melting of radioactive fuel and radiation releases beyond the site boundary.[41]

The Departments of Defense and Energy have been largely exempt

165

from environmental laws and oversight by EPA and state regulations. They work in secret, and they are essentially responsible for cleaning up after themselves. The result is that the Defense Department is widely regarded as the largest producer of toxic waste in the world, and the DOE now estimates that it will have to spend nearly $30 billion over the next five years alone to clean up only seventeen nuclear weapons plants in twelve states. Estimates for the total clean-up bill range between $100 billion and $200 billion.[42]

The end of the cold war has greatly reduced the national security importance of the entire nuclear arsenal in general and the need for weapons modernization in particular. President Bush's 1991 announcement of deep cuts in tactical weapons, together with a scaling back of strategic forces under the START treaty, should result in nuclear force levels at least half their current size. And deeper cuts are possible still, as discussed in the next two chapters. Thus, for the foreseeable future, there will be an excess of warheads, nuclear material, and plutonium components, which all can be "recycled" (that is, reused in other bombs) to a far greater extent than now contemplated.[43]

There is no military security gain from creating more nuclear material, designing a host of new nuclear warheads, and testing them (and, as discussed in the next chapter, the potential military security gain from a global ban on all nuclear testing is considerable). The environmental cost of continued operation of weapons plants by the DOE is significant, but immeasurable. The dollar cost of the nuclear warheads program is $7.5 billion per year (which does not include all of the tens of billions of dollars for weapons plant cleanup).[44] America's overall security would benefit if the DOE put in place a moratorium on the production of nuclear materials and new weapons. That would allow the DOE to devote more resources to cleaning up its mess, to dismantling warheads, and, most important, to pursuing a wise nonmilitary energy program.

Achieving Environmental Security

Not all pollution deserves to be labeled an environmental security threat. Indeed, to do so would render the term meaningless. Most pollution does not threaten "a substantial reduction in real income," as global warming does. Most environmental problems are confined to a single nation, often a single site, and are not international. Consider the definition of national security offered in Chapter 2: "A threat to national security is whatever threatens to significantly (1) degrade the quality of life of the people, or (2) narrow the range of policy choices available to their government." This definition, applied to environmental security, would include global warming and the loss of the ozone layer, but exclude many domestic pollution problems. Global warming threatens both to degrade our quality of life significantly and to narrow the range of choices available to our government and ourselves. This definition also encompasses traditional security threats such as invasion, nuclear war, and oil embargoes.

Once seen as a national security threat, global warming will become a factor in domestic United States energy policy, although as the previous chapter argued, energy policies that mitigate global warming are wise policy choices in any case. Internationally, we should give negotiating a treaty to mitigate global warming as high a priority as we gave achieving nuclear arms control during the cold war. We should immediately join our allies in setting targets for carbon dioxide emissions.

We in the United States should become aware that resource and environmental issues can cause or contribute to conflict and instability— the same kind of traditional security concerns that we have always had. The Gulf war should boost such awareness. Every step the United States can take to reduce the importance of oil is valuable, such as fostering energy efficiency and the growth of alternative energy. Since water scarcity is a threat to Middle East peace, and the region's traditional military security is important to us, we should devote resources to its solution, including foreign aid and technical assistance.

More broadly, the United States should rethink its entire foreign aid program. Not only do we give the lowest percentage of our GNP in overseas development aid of all twenty-four Western industrialized members of the Organization for Economic Cooperation and Development, but our overall foreign aid also has a heavy bias toward military assistance. As noted in Chapter 1, a 1982 draft report for the U.S. Agency for International Development concluded that El Salvador's conflict stemmed in large part from "problems of resource distribution in an overcrowded land." Yet, in 1986, the United States gave El Salvador $122

167

million in military aid, compared with $21 million we gave for environmental measures in all of South and Central America and the Caribbean Basin.[45]

Most regional instability has nonmilitary origins. American aid should focus on promoting sustainable development in the Third World, and include technical training and assistance, private sector cooperation on environment-saving technology, the creation of training and research centers devoted to new energy technologies, and debt relief. American ecological aid should exceed military aid. Chapter 7 will discuss such a foreign aid program, which does not require an increase in total spending on foreign aid, but rather a shift in priorities away from military aid.

In particular, since runaway population growth in the developing world threatens political stability everywhere, population planning, funding birth control, and technical training, become tools of statecraft far more important than a new missile or fighter plane. The National Academy of Sciences recommends that same policy for a different reason—raising living standards in an environmentally sustainable fashion: "Control of population growth has the potential to make a major contribution to raising living standards and to easing environmental problems like greenhouse warming. The United States should resume full participation in international programs to slow population growth and should contribute its share to their financial and other support."[46]

The point of changing the definition of national security is to change our way of thinking about and dealing with all national security threats. Redefining security is a paradigm shift. Military force rarely provides a lasting solution to an international problem, especially one with a nonmilitary origin. New approaches are needed for environmental problems, just as they are needed for economic, energy, and military problems. By definition, no security that is achieved in an environmentally unsustainable fashion can long endure.

This suggests another definition of national security: "The objective of national security is to achieve major national values, such as freedom from foreign dictation and improvement of living standards, in an environmentally sustainable fashion." The concepts of "living standards" and "environmentally sustainable" are partly redundant. But the redundancy will occur only when environmental costs are fully calculated in the

168

figures for GNP and living standards. As I have argued, a key reason that we have environmental problems is that the true cost to society of basic resources—energy, water, trees—is not reflected in their nominal cost. This leads to overuse, misallocations, distorted priorities, inefficiency, and waste.

As one 1989 study explained: "A country could exhaust its mineral resources, cut down its forests, erode its soils, pollute its aquifers, and hunt its wildlife and fisheries to extinction, but measured income would not be affected as these assets disappeared."[47] We measure income in misleading ways. Spending on pollution increases the gross national product. The wreck of the Exxon *Valdez* actually *increased* the nation's GNP by the amount of money spent on the attempt to clean up the oil spill.

The narrow focus on GNP as the measure of a nation's standard of living is no more valid in the 1990s than the focus on military strength as a measure of a nation's national security. Environmental economics is the rapidly growing field that attempts to correct these deficiencies to include in GNP calculations the costs of environmental degradation, pollution-related health problems, and resource-replacement. These systemic or "green" calculations are becoming more widely used in Europe, as are demands in this country for greater use of "full social cost pricing." One recent attempt to make the necessary corrections to GNP is called the Daly-Cobb Index of Sustainable Economic Welfare (ISEW), which includes depletion of nonrenewable resources, loss of farmland from soil erosion, air and water pollution, and global environmental damage, as well as adjustments for income distribution inequality. The ISEW shows that per capita welfare rose 42 percent between 1950 and 1976 in the United States, but then declined 12 percent through 1988.[48]

Calculating the cost of pollution is difficult and controversial. For instance, how much is air pollution responsible for the dramatic 80-percent increase in deaths from asthma between 1979 and 1988, and what is the "cost" of that debilitating disease?[49] Nevertheless, wider use of environmental economics is crucial if we are to move toward a systems-oriented solution to our problems. However crude the new environmental paradigm is, it is vastly superior to the existing paradigm, which deals with the issue by ignoring it and pretending that environmental taxes and regulations are an impediment to economic growth rather than a

169

boost to sustainable welfare. Moreover, the new environmental paradigm is based not on a centrally planned political agenda, but rather on a more efficient, market-oriented vision of the future.

Industrial Ecosystem

The ultimate goal for the nation must be a wholly new strategy of sustainable economic growth. Two researchers at the General Motors Research Laboratories in Warren, Michigan, put it this way:

> [T]he traditional model of industrial activity—in which individual manufacturing processes take in raw materials and generate products to be sold plus waste to be disposed of—should be transformed into a more integrated model: *an industrial ecosystem.* In such a system the consumption of energy and materials is optimized, waste generation is minimized and the effluents of one process—whether they are spent catalysts from petroleum refining, fly and bottom ash from electric-power generation or discarded plastic containers from consumer products—serve as the raw material for another process [emphasis added].[50]

The industrial ecosystem—a felicitous phrase—is the next evolutionary stage after fast-cycle manufacturing, which is already aimed at minimizing the time and effort wasted in the production cycle. Much as fast-cycle manufacturing is called lean production, resource-efficient manufacturing is called "clean production."[51] Ultimately, the best companies will integrate the two approaches, creating "lean-and-clean" production.

Many large companies already mount strong efforts in resource efficiency. The payoff is handsome. For example, a series of relatively inexpensive changes at ARCO's Los Angeles refinery have cut yearly waste from 12,000 tons in the early 1980s to 3,400 tons in the late 1980s. The company saves $2 million a year in disposal costs alone; it makes money selling spent alumina catalysts to Allied Chemical and spent silica catalysts to cement makers. These "hazardous wastes" once had to be disposed of in landfills for hundreds of dollars a ton. Such high-efficiency production cycles were spurred on by regulations developed in the Carter administration to reflect long-term environmental costs of hazardous-waste disposal, which had raised the price of landfill disposal from under $20 a ton to $200 a ton or more in the space of a few years. ARCO's story is not unique. The 3M Company calculates that since 1975 its Pollution Prevention Pays program has eliminated more than 500,000 tons of waste and pollutants, saving $482 million; another $650 million has been saved by conserving energy. To 3M, environmental reduction and green products are a way to increase competitiveness and achieve product differentiation.[52]

The techniques required to achieve clean production include substituting less toxic materials; redesigning products to require fewer toxic inputs; reformulating production processes; improving operations, maintenance, and monitoring of production processes; and recycling, cleaning, or reusing production chemicals.[53] Changes must be made in research, development, product design, and manufacturing. In other words, the same kind of systematic approach to the production process that is required in lean production to minimize time is required in clean production to minimize pollution.

The American Telephone and Telegraph Company adopted a systems approach in the late 1980s, and in its thirty-five plants worldwide has been able to save several million dollars reducing its use of air toxins by 60 percent; its use of CFCs, 55 percent; and its use of manufacturing wastes, 8 percent. By recycling a toxic solvent used in making herbicides, Dow Chemical has cut the amount of solvent waste in half, saving $3 million a year. At one Louisiana facility, Dow spent $15 million on waste reduction projects in 1990 and by mid-1991 had already saved $18 million in toxic waste disposal and raw material costs. By altering the process for making plastics and paint products at one Texas plant, Du Pont cut the plant's wastes by two thirds, saving $1 million a year. *The Wall Street Journal* noted in a June 1991 article on pollution prevention: "In a major shift, chemical companies are viewing waste not as an unavoidable result of the manufacturing process, but as a measure of its efficiency."[54]

In industries such as pharmaceutical production, automotive manufacture, microelectronics, and photographic film processing, pollution prevention programs have reduced waste—sludge, solvents, oil, and paint—from 80 percent to 100 percent. Payback times ranged from one month to three years.[55]

What overall reductions are achievable? The Office of Technology Assessment has estimated that United States manufacturing wastes can be cut in half with existing technologies, and that another 25 percent could be eliminated with more research and development. The federal government has a role to play, both in promoting R&D and in creating regulations that encourage efficiency. Other countries are very active in this area. France, for instance, created a Clean Technology Commission, which, in 1984, contributed about $3.4 million to 60 pilot projects such as solvent recycling and production redesign. The Netherlands Organization for Technology Assessment has a regional clean-technology program that has put in place 45 projects to cut production waste. Roughly half of the projects resulted in savings, and half didn't affect cost.[56]

Also, regulations overseas are often much stricter. The Japanese Energy Conservation Law of 1979 "set tough standards for energy usage in air-conditioning equipment, refrigerators, and automobiles, leading to many product improvements that have enhanced international position." Environmental quality standards in Germany, Sweden, and Denmark have surpassed ours in many areas. Germany is debating taxes on packaging and products to reflect the cost of disposal. The German environmental minister has proposed requiring car manufacturers to be responsible for ultimate disposal of the cars they make. This, in turn, has spurred companies such as BMW to design cars whose plastic body parts are both easily removed and specially labeled so they can be grouped by type for recycling.[57]

If America is to be the leader in this important area, one pervasive myth must be squelched—that environmental regulations are antigrowth. One economic impact analyst at the EPA has written: "The notion that additional environmental protection necessarily endangers international trade is to date unsubstantiated."[58] I would say that in stronger fashion: Many of our trading competitors have stricter environmental regulations than we do, yet maintain trade surpluses and higher growth rates.

In fact, strong environmental regulations can benefit U.S. trade. Michael Porter, head of the Harvard Business School's Competition and Strategy group, explains: "The United States relaxed environmental, safety, and other standards under the Reagan administration. Tough and forward-looking standards once encouraged U.S. firms to innovate in ways that gave them advantages in sophisticated product segments. Today, other nations are often out front in such areas, giving their firms an edge in winning foreign markets." Porter has found that Germany, with perhaps the world's strictest regulations in stationary air-pollution control, apparently holds "a wide lead in patenting—and exporting—air-pollution and other environmental technology." In contrast, about 70 percent of the air-pollution-control equipment sold in the United States today is produced by foreign companies.[59]

Just as flexible manufacturing can bring jobs back to America, clean production can boost economic security. Spending on pollution-control creates high-paying jobs, by some estimates 15,000 to 20,000 for every $1 billion spent.[60] The key is ensuring that as much of that money stays in America as possible, putting Americans to work.

Of course, it is more efficient to avoid creating the pollution in the first place, and companies that minimize inputs and outputs will have a competitive advantage over more wasteful companies. That is why the dominant manufacturing process of the twenty-first century will be the industrial ecosystem (or the even more advanced "lean-and-clean" production). Although many American companies are making strides in clean production, overall the United States is less efficient than other countries, particularly because of our overuse of energy. For instance, it takes more than twice as much energy to make a ton of paper in North America as it does in the Pacific region, in part because of the higher use of waste paper in the Pacific. *American companies produce roughly five times the waste per dollar of goods sold as the Japanese do and more than twice that of the Germans.*[61]

Since high-efficiency, low-waste production strengthens not just United States economic security, but also energy and environmental security, the United States government must take steps to see that American companies become the world's leaders.

The first and most important step minimizes government involvement in day-to-day business decisions: We must enact federal regulations that ensure that manufacturing inputs (such as water and energy) and outputs (such as solid waste) reflect their true social cost. Manufacturers can then make the most cost-effective decisions. The government should correct the market's failure to value a variety of products properly, including water depleted from under the ground, fossil fuels, paper from virgin pulp, and power generated while emitting sulfur dioxide or other pollutants. In 1989 the United States put a tax on chlorofluorocarbons as an incentive to curtail their use and spur the development of substi-

173

tutes. Environmental taxes should be phased in slowly to allow time for adjustment. I would propose returning the money to the American taxpayer in the form of lower income taxes, at least for the 80 percent of Americans who did not grow wealthier in the 1980s. The leftover money can be used for the programs described below.

Second, the government must make resource- and process-efficiency a focus of its R&D spending. The trend in the 1980s was in the wrong direction. Between 1980 and 1989, the EPA's budget for R&D was cut more than 25 percent. One promising sign is the White House's list of National Critical Technologies, which includes "pollution minimization, remediation, and waste management." Federal funding for other technologies on that list, especially materials and manufacturing, should also emphasize recyclability and the industrial ecosystem. Not only can new technologies create jobs and opportunities for trade, but they can also lower costs of pollution control. New technologies helped lower the estimated cost for the steel industry of controlling coke-oven air pollution from $4 billion to only $250 to $450 million. In the late 1970s, certain chemical companies avoided a projected per-plant cost of $350,000 for benzene emission control with a new process that substituted other chemicals for benzene and virtually eliminated control costs. In 1971, the oil industry projected that phasing out lead in gas would cost $7 billion a year. In 1990, with roughly 99 percent of the lead phase-out completed, the actual yearly costs are between $150 and $500 million.[62]

The third step the government can take to encourage the industrial ecosystem is to have the Manufacturing Technology Centers, discussed in Chapter 2, provide local businesses with advice on how to design manufacturing processes that reduce resource use and production waste. The Georgia Institute of Technology Industrial Extension Offices, for instance, already include assistance in energy conservation and hazardous waste management. Some MTCs could also function as regional centers where the environmental consequences of new manufacturing processes could be tested without an EPA permit, saving companies time and money.[63]

These federal programs can be especially helpful to small companies that might be hard hit by an environmental regulation, but cannot afford to do the R&D needed to develop a new production process. The government might also consider tax incentives for pollution-reducing technologies, and loans to small companies to pay for new pollution-reducing

174

equipment. Federal and state job training and apprenticeship programs can be targeted to industries that are adversely affected by environmental regulations.

The federal government can improve its environmental regulatory strategy, by moving away from crude "end-of-pipe" regulations that force individual companies to meet strict or arbitrary reductions quickly. In some cases, pollutants are so dangerous they must be banned outright. In general, however, end-of-pipe regulations are flawed because they focus on pollution *after* it has been created, because they can cause tremendous expense and dislocations, and because they do not encourage companies to work harder at pollution control once they have met the arbitrary reduction level.

Such problems can be minimized in a variety of ways. Gradually phased-in environmental taxes can more accurately reflect social costs, while allowing users time to adjust. A scaled rebate/feebate system would give greater rewards the more reductions are achieved (and greater fines the more targets are missed), spurring polluters to continually improve their technology. Incentives can reward firms for replacing the most polluting technologies with innovative equipment.[64] Tradable emission rights can allow whole regions to meet targeted reductions, allowing companies that are highly efficient at reducing pollution (and exceed targeted cuts) to make money from those that are less efficient.

Wherever possible, the government must encourage efficiency in manufacturing. Once the market is given a clear cost signal, it is much more efficient than the government at determining the best way to achieve a desired result. The government's role is determining what prices are incorrect, aiding the R&D process, and diffusing new technology. A key rationale for a government role: The industrial ecosystem is a matter of national security; it benefits economic, energy, and environmental security. Promoting energy efficiency and the industrial ecosystem can restore America's resource abundance, which, as discussed in Chapter 2, was a key source of America's success earlier in the century.

People—like frogs—are poor at adapting to slow changes. Nevertheless, we are not altogether like that frog in the opening parable—we are in no danger of boiling to death. Global warming and other environmental dangers do not threaten humankind with extinction. The question is not whether we will survive, but whether we will thrive—or perhaps whether the majority of Americans will thrive, since the wealthiest 20 percent are likely to do well under almost any scenario.

In the chapters so far, I have presented a comprehensive new national security paradigm with specific policy proposals aimed at ensuring that America thrives economically and environmentally in the next century. I have so far focused on the nonmilitary aspects of security. Military security, of course, must remain a vital element of any new paradigm. The next two chapters explain how and why we can safely make deep cuts in military forces and military budgets without harming military security. I will also propose a military program, and a new foreign aid program that can increase our military security—as well as our economic, energy, and environmental security—without increasing the foreign aid budget.

6

The Old Order Collapses and the Old Order Continues

A mature great power will make measured and limited use of its power. It will eschew the theory of a global and universal duty which not only commits it to unending wars of intervention but intoxicates its thinking with the illusion that it is a crusader for righteousness, that each war is a war to end all war. Since in this generation we have become a great power, I am in favor of learning to behave like a great power, of getting rid of the globalism which would not only entangle us everywhere but is based on the totally vain notion that if we do not set the world in order, no matter what the price, we cannot live in the world safely. If we examine this idea thoroughly, we shall see that it is nothing but the old isolationism of our innocence in a new form. Then we thought we had to preserve our purity by withdrawal from the ugliness of great power politics. Now we sometimes talk as if we could preserve our purity only by policing the globe.

—Walter Lippmann, 1965

America can't afford to serve as the world's policeman. A police force is supported by annual operating expenses—salaries, uniforms, weapons, and the like—that are paid for by those whose security it guarantees. In the Persian Gulf War, America recouped only the one-time costs of the war; we alone pay the annual $300 billion operating costs of the United States military. Those who promote the role of Uncle Sam as global cop are urging Americans to forgo funds that might be spent educating our children or researching new civilian technologies. Spending huge sums to maintain a military larger than we need for our own security is the road to impoverishment. The United States can afford to be the world's policeman only on the day Germany and Japan together pay us $150 billion a year.

Until then, America is more like the world's toughest private detective, as played by Humphrey Bogart: Working out of a seedy building, we struggle to pay the rent and find the next meal. Occasionally, a rich client asks us to find out who is trying to kill him or her.

In this chapter, I will discuss the flaws in the arguments commonly offered for continuing a military-oriented approach to our national security, which in turn requires a high level of military spending.

Because America's national security after World War II was not based on traditional notions of territorial integrity, the concept of security was stretched to cover different fears. Even if our freedom and borders were not directly threatened by the Soviet Union, the idea of permitting a Soviet takeover of Western Europe was unacceptable to most Americans. Moreover, communism was seen as an inexorably spreading cancer that had to be vigilantly fought everywhere if the world—including America— was to survive. These fears were the logic behind America's postwar national security burden. The burden was extensive and expensive.

The primary threat was a massive military attack by the Warsaw Pact on Western Europe with only a few days' warning, and that required huge military forces permanently tied down in Europe. Since NATO's conventional forces might not prevail, a variety of nuclear weapons were needed to deter attack, including thousands of battlefield and theater nuclear weapons. A global war against the Warsaw Pact would have included major sea battles in the Atlantic and Pacific oceans as well as epic air and land battles between NATO and the Warsaw Pact in central, northern, and southern Europe. Since we saw communism as a global threat, we had to prepare to fight all wars simultaneously. Thus did America require large standing military forces and constantly high defense spending.

All those scenarios are now defunct. Even before the disintegration of the Soviet Union, the Soviet empire collapsed and with it the threat of a global war with the west. The Berlin Wall has fallen, East Germany is reunited with West Germany, the Warsaw Pact has folded, and the

178

Soviet military has long since withdrawn all its troops from Hungary and Czechoslovakia. Russia has asked to join NATO. Should hardliners seize power in what used to be the Soviet Union, they could not reassert hegemony in Eastern European countries, let alone convince those countries to support a tank invasion of Western Europe. Similarly, whether or not a dictator arises who applies military force inside one of the new republics is irrelevant to the larger strategic issue of the demise of the Warsaw Pact.

After the dissolution of the Soviet empire came the disintegration of the Soviet Union. Turmoil in the new republics may be a fertile source of prodefense political rhetoric, but no amount of turmoil will affect the fundamental military calculation—we no longer need plan for a global war with the Warsaw Pact. As a February 1992, draft Pentagon report on post-cold war strategy stated, "It is improbable that a global conventional challenge to U.S. and Western security will reemerge from the Eurasian heartland for many years to come."[1]

The possibility of a tank invasion of Western Europe coupled with a global war in the Atlantic and Pacific oceans has vanished. The battles America will fight in the future will be isolated incidents, like Panama, Libya, Grenada and Iraq. (The multifront "war" we need fear today is economic; and in this arena, the number of combatants the United States faces simultaneously is growing rapidly.) American security no longer requires vast and costly conventional and nuclear forces permanently dedicated to the defense of Europe.

Although the old Warsaw Pact conventional forces pose no danger to us or our allies, it has been argued that their nuclear weapons threaten United States national security. The new threat is that the breakup of the Soviet Union will accelerate the spread of nuclear weapons and related technology. As explained in the section below on weapons proliferation, and in the Appendix, that threat cannot be mitigated by increasing the size or capability of the United States' immense nuclear arsenal, or by spending tens of billions of dollars on Star Wars weapons. It can be greatly reduced, however, through effective diplomacy and assistance to ensure that nuclear weapons remain under tight control, that thousands of weapons are quickly disabled and dismantled, and that all new states emerging from the former Soviet Union join the Nuclear Nonproliferation Treaty and put in place effective export controls.

179

The old threat posed by nuclear weapons is that of a large-scale nuclear attack against the United States or its allies. It is against that danger that we still justify more than $50 billion of our annual defense budget. The collapse of the Soviet empire and the Soviet Union makes decades of nuclear strategy, nuclear planning, and nuclear weapons budgets obsolete.

Throughout the cold war, the United States always had more long-range nuclear weapons than the Soviet Union, as well as more advanced technology: more accurate missiles, quieter submarines, and superior bombers and cruise missiles. In the late 1970s, some Americans worried that the Soviet numerical advantage in one category of weapons—land-based missiles (ICBMs)—might pose a threat to our security, a threat called the "window of vulnerability." To address this question, President Reagan assembled a Commission on Strategic Forces led by Brent Scowcroft (now President Bush's national security adviser). The Scowcroft commission "closed" the window of vulnerability in 1983 when it concluded that our other strategic forces (bombers and submarines) were adequate to deter a Soviet nuclear attack.[2] Nevertheless, the commission argued that an ambitious nuclear modernization program was needed because United States nuclear weapons have a larger function than deterring a Soviet nuclear attack on the United States:

> If comparative military trends were to point toward their [the Soviets] becoming superior to the West in each of a number of military areas, they might consider themselves able to raise the risks in a crisis in a manner that could not be matched.
> *In a world in which the balance of strategic nuclear forces could be isolated and kept distinctly set apart from all other calculations about relations between nations and the credibility of conventional military power, a nuclear imbalance would have little importance unless it were so massive as to tempt an aggressor to launch nuclear war.* But the world in which we must live with the Soviets is, sadly, one in which their own assessments of these trends, and hence their calculations of overall advantage, influence heavily the vigor with which they exercise their power [emphasis added].[3]

The commission did not imagine that within a few years of their report, the world they had hypothesized would be born. Even before the disintegration, the Soviet Union had lost whatever ideological and economic

180

power it had in relations with other nations. Were the Soviet Union Humpty-Dumpty put back together again, nuclear weapons could not restore that loss. The collapse of the Warsaw Pact as a conventional military power has left its strategic nuclear forces rather like disconnected muscles without bones. The nuclear balance no longer has much importance—the possibility of the other side achieving a massive advantage is of vanishingly low probability. Indeed, it is no longer clear who the other side is: Russia is a hollow superpower and "balance" is no longer the relationship.

The Strategic Arms Reduction Talks (START) treaty in particular will slash the ICBM force of the former Soviet Union in half and codify a United States nuclear warhead advantage of 9,000 to 7,000. This numerical edge, coupled with the nuclear modernization program of the 1980s (the MX missile, B-1 bomber, Trident submarine) is much more than adequate.[4] For at least the next generation, America's security cannot be enhanced by designing, testing, or building new nuclear warheads, missiles, and bombers. Richard Perle, assistant defense secretary during the Reagan administration, said in early 1990, before the Soviet breakup, "For the foreseeable future, I believe we can safely reduce the investment we make in protecting against a massive surprise Soviet nuclear attack." This reduced investment "may mean skipping the next generation of weapons systems on the grounds that the increased risk in the near term of 'making do' with the current generation of equipment is manageable while the future is murky."[5] President Bush's post-cold war nuclear strategy for America, outlined in a September 1991 speech to the nation, makes several useful changes, including deep cuts in short-range nuclear weapons. But as I will discuss in the next chapter, his strategy would continue the development of many systems that in turn would require *increases* in defense spending in the late 1990s.

Even the defense cuts announced by President Bush in his 1992 State of the Union address will leave the United States spending above $50 billion *a year* on nuclear programs throughout the decade.[6]

In the last cold war military budget, that of fiscal year 1990, America spent $200 billion—more than 60 percent of overall defense spending—on the Soviet and Warsaw Pact threat.[7] The national security paradigm that was used to justify this mammoth spending collapsed in 1989 with the Berlin Wall and was swept away by the break-up of the Soviet Union

181

at the end of 1991. America should be able to divert most of that money—$150 billion (50 percent of the defense budget)—to nonmilitary uses.

Nevertheless, the October 1990 budget summit agreement left national defense spending in 1996 only 22 percent lower than for 1990. National defense spending was to be cut so slowly that 1996 spending would be $293 billion (in 1996 dollars) compared with 1991 spending of $299 billion (in 1991 dollars). That is, the cut in spending is achieved through the effect inflation has on purchasing power: $293 billion in 1996 is the equivalent of $253 billion in 1991. Even President Bush's January 1992 five-year plan would leave defense spending in 1997 at $289 billion (in 1997 dollars). Put another way, from 1993 through 1997, America will spend nearly $1.5 *trillion* on defense!

Military spending remains high for reasons that have little to do with security. As I will discuss in the next chapter, Pentagon misplanning in the 1980s has made cutting the defense budget an especially painful process, and Congress has a vested interest in hanging on to pork-barrel military projects. Moreover, as I have argued throughout, there has been no coherent alternative national security paradigm with the power to convince policymakers to change the status quo and reorient priorities. In the absence of a wholly new worldview, we have seen the pasting together of a new military security paradigm that suggests endless military commitments for the United States.

The Third World Threat

This emerging doctrine might be called the Third World threat.[8] As commonly stated, it combines a variety of concerns, all related in some way to the Third World: the threat of terrorism, the liberation of Grenada and Panama, the proliferation of weapons of mass destruction, the drug trade and narcogangsters, and the threat to the Persian Gulf shipping lanes.[9] Yet, when this new formulation is examined in detail, it fails to justify a national security worldview based on military security.

Strong rhetoric is inevitable when discussing national security threats, but the useful questions that must be answered are these: What specific danger is posed to the well-being of Americans by a particular threat, and what is the appropriate response? Which is to ask, are the principal threats to America's well-being military in nature, and do they require a military response?

Terrorism is an excellent whipping boy. In nearly all cases, however, responses to terrorist attacks are likely to remain extremely limited because we can rarely identify any group or any country to retaliate against. In the rare cases when we know precisely who is responsible for a terrorist attack and where they are based, a small military strike may be warranted. The impact of terrorist activity on military force planning and the defense budget is negligible.

Similarly, individual "liberations" such as Grenada and Panama are small-scale operations, not requiring massive military forces. Panama, for instance, was (until the Gulf war) the biggest American military operation since Vietnam, but used only 25,000 troops. Moreover, America's large annual budget deficits have significantly impaired our capacity for long-term follow-through in the form of foreign aid to liberated countries such as Panama, or for that matter, Nicaragua and the Philippines. In other words, quick military victories can easily be eviscerated by our continuing economic insecurity.

The end of the cold war should help diminish rather than encourage the United States to focus on the Third World as a source of conflict. After all, much of America's strategic interest in the developing world was due to our competition with the Soviet Union. As Samuel Huntington, director of Harvard University's Institute for Strategic Studies, has written: "Without the Cold War it is hard to see how much interest the United States will have in who governs Afghanistan or whether India or Pakistan controls Kashmir. South Asia is simply not an American strategic priority. The same is true for many parts of Southeast Asia and for most of Africa."[10]

America need no longer worry about deterring a "global war." Only the existence of the Warsaw Pact made a global war possible. The United States may have to deal with occasional minor skirmishes, and perhaps a rare medium-size battle, but gone is the possibility of one major land war simultaneously with two major ocean wars, the scenario that drove our military planning and spending for decades. The other three problems invariably listed as part of the "Third World threat"—weapons proliferation, drug trafficking, and dependence on Persian Gulf oil—require more consideration.

Weapons Proliferation and National Security

The spread of weapons of mass destruction is another handy whipping boy. Everyone is against it. But the key questions are: What is the threat to United States security from proliferation? What new military forces and hardware are needed in response?

As the Gulf war showed, the United States can devastate the most heavily armed Third World country without resort to chemical weapons, nuclear weapons, or ballistic missiles. Saddam Hussein's ballistic missiles had more terror value than military value. Had he been able to deliver chemical weapons, the terror value (and Allied casualties) would have risen, but the military outcome would have remained unchanged.

The ability of another country to deliver nuclear weapons into the United States is the clearest military security threat to the United States. Moreover, the apparent success of the ground-based Patriot antimissile system against Hussein's short-range SCUD missiles has led some to call for renewed funding for the Strategic Defense Initiative (SDI), also known as Star Wars, to build space-based defenses against long-range missiles. The flaws in such reasoning are numerous.

First, Patriots are designed to shoot down tactical ballistic missiles, which have a short range, are the size of a large truck, and travel about two kilometers per second. These short-range missiles are relatively easy targets, and, as the Gulf war shows, we know how to hit parts of those missiles in midair. But the Patriot was apparently not very good at hitting the SCUD's warhead, and it is the warhead that must be destroyed if ground damage is to be avoided. An Israeli Reserve Air Force officer told Congress in April 1992 that the official Israeli Air Force team that examined the Patriot's performance in Israel concluded the Patriot destroyed *at most one warhead.* A Congressional Research Service analyst who examined the Army's classified data concluded that applying the Army's own methodology and using the Army's own data, there was strong evidence for the destruction of *only one SCUD warhead.*[11] Analysis has further shown that there is no evidence that the Patriot defense in Israel reduced the amount of ground damage.[12] Thus, the Patriot demonstrated little ability to defend populated areas from sustaining casualties, the primary mission of Star Wars.[13]

Intercontinental ballistic missile (ICBM) warheads, however, are only the size of a human being, travel five times faster than tactical missiles, are usually accompanied by up to nine other warheads, and may be easily hidden among hundreds of decoys. After spending countless billions in the 1960s and 1970s, and another $24 billion from 1983 through 1991, we still have no idea how to shoot down ICBM warheads. One former Pentagon weapons analyst told Congress in April 1991, "In summary, the Gulf War experience with Patriot has revealed no new realistic strategic defense choices for the U.S. and its allies. We have still not solved any of the fundamental problems that have always confronted strategic missile defenses."[14] (The scientific problems with space-based defenses—and other problems with the SDI program—are discussed at length in the Appendix.)

However great our concern about weapons proliferation may be, it does not justify increased spending on offensive or defensive weapons because we get almost nothing for our money. Moreover, Army spokesman Major Peter M. Keating has explained, Patriot and SDI "are not even a spinoff of each other."[15] Therefore, the performance of the Patriot does not justify increased funding for SDI, which is a poorly run program. *The General Accounting Office concluded in 1991 that much of the $24 billion spent by the SDI office may have been wasted because of poor planning, pressure to field unproven technology, and overly optimistic budget requests.*[16] Expanding research and development on ground-based defenses may be worthwhile, but that money should come from funds now devoted to impractical space-based SDI defenses.

The second reason the SDI program should be scaled back: The security problem for the United States is not nuclear warheads on ICBMs per se, but rather the possibility that some enemy's nuclear bomb would be detonated in this country. Neither space-based nor ground-based defenses can stop a bomb from being brought into the country on a fishing trawler or smuggled in by land. In this regard, missile defenses do little more than provide $120 billion of false security; worse still, they actually undermine our security by taking money away from military and nonmilitary projects that would otherwise increase our security.

Long-range ballistic missiles are notoriously unreliable until tested ten or twenty times. A sizable fraction of our most advanced missiles and space launch vehicles routinely blow up shortly after launch. In the event a Hussein or other dictator ever obtained a nuclear bomb, it seems exceedingly unlikely he would risk putting it on anything as prone to self-destruction as an ICBM. A Congressional Research Service expert told

185

Congress in October 1991 that no Third World country is expected to acquire an ICBM this next decade.[17] Other experts testified that it is much harder to build an ICBM than either a tactical ballistic missile or an intermediate-range ballistic missile and that any ICBM program would be very visible to outside countries.[18] So even if missile defenses were useful, there would be no need to deploy them in the near term. Americans rightly worry about nuclear proliferation, but SDI, or Star Wars, affords not a scintilla of security.

Third, if America were serious about proliferation, it would not have a nonproliferation strategy aimed at shooting down enemy weapons *after* they had been built. It would focus on the ounce of prevention, rather than the megaton of cure. The United States is currently the principal roadblock to the negotiation of a comprehensive ban on the testing of all nuclear weapons. With twenty-thousand nuclear weapons, the United States has not had a compelling argument for continuing to develop new types of nuclear bombs for quite some time. The collapse of the Warsaw Pact and Soviet Union means that we are no longer in a race with another superpower to develop new and improved types of nuclear weapons. Ending nuclear testing therefore would not reduce United States military security. Quite the reverse, it would increase our security. A comprehensive test ban (CTB) makes it harder for a potential new nuclear power to have confidence that any nuclear weapon under development would actually work, making it less likely that country would use such a weapon. The 1990 Review Conference for the Nuclear Nonproliferation Treaty was unable to reach a consensus statement, in large part because developing nations (those without nuclear weapons) felt the superpowers were not doing enough to achieve a CTB. The United States refused to accept language sought by Mexico declaring: "The continued testing of nuclear weapons by the nuclear-weapon State Parties to this Treaty would put the future of the Non-Proliferation Treaty beyond 1995 in grave doubt."[19] The Nonproliferation Treaty is up for renewal in 1995, and it may collapse in the absence of a CTB. That would be a tragedy. It would end the international trade restrictions and monitoring provisions that have helped restrain global nuclear proliferation for the past two decades.

The CTB is by no means a cure-all; nations can still try to skirt the Nonproliferation Treaty and covertly assemble all the parts necessary for a bomb. But they could not test those weapons without violating the CTB. In this way, the CTB reinforces the global taboo against the production of nuclear weapons and will assuredly intercept more nuclear bombs than Star Wars. Once a CTB is achieved, restrictions on the testing of long-range ballistic missiles should be pursued. The next chapter will discuss more ambitious measures to stop weapons proliferation, such as creating a collective security regime in which states that export or import weapons of mass destruction are made to suffer economically.

Drug Policy and National Security

America's drug problem is serious. America is the world's largest consumer of illegal drugs, with United States users spending an estimated $28 billion a year on cocaine, $68 billion on marijuana, and $10 billion to $12 billion on heroin. Imports account for 80 percent of all illegal drugs and 100 percent of cocaine and heroin consumed in the United States.[20] The domestic toll of drug use by perhaps thirty million users, of the rapid rise in drug-related violent crimes in our nation's inner cities, and of the soaring health care costs, including the accelerated spread of AIDS, is beyond calculation.

In 1986, President Reagan signed a secret directive identifying the illegal traffic of narcotics as a national security threat and authorizing the Department of Defense to engage in antidrug operations, including surveillance of suspected drug traffickers and search-and-destroy missions against drug laboratories in foreign countries. Previously, both United States law and policy blocked the use of our military for what are essentially law enforcement actions aimed at stopping criminal activity. Many in the Pentagon had initially expressed reluctance about waging the drug war, arguing that the Pentagon cannot act as a surrogate police force and fearing a prolonged "war" with steady casualties but few results. Secretary of Defense Frank Carlucci said in 1988: "That is not the function of the military. We are not the frontline agency in the war on drugs." But in September 1989, Secretary of Defense Dick Cheney issued a directive stating: "Detecting and countering the production and trafficking of illegal drugs is a high priority national security mission." Cheney's guidelines asserted: "The Department of Defense will assist in the attack on production of illegal drugs at the source."[21]

The total cost of Defense Department interdiction activities rose from about $5 million in fiscal year (FY) 1982 to about $400 million in FY

1987 to $888 million in FY 1990 to $1.2 billion for FY 1991. The Pentagon now has hundreds of soldiers on antidrug operations on the ground in Central and South America, and flew more than 37,000 hours on drug missions in 1991.[22] The drug war has thus become one component of our national security strategy in its traditional sense of providing direction for military activity.

While the justification for this military-oriented approach may be rhetorically persuasive, the military approach itself simply does not work. President Bush said in 1990, "Then there are narcogangsters that concern us all, already a threat to our national health and spirit," which presents a frightening link from narcogangsters to America's drug problem to a threat to our national health and spirit.[23] The link, however, is flawed. Narcogangsters are monstrous, and our drug problem is monstrous, but the threat to America's national health and spirit is domestic drug use; the problem is one of demand and not supply. Moreover, even as we crush the Colombian drug cartel, the supply remains largely unaffected. After two years of intense United States antidrug efforts in South America, the State Department and White House estimate that cocaine production is stuck on a high plateau of at least 700 metric tons (and may actually be rising), while American consumption is 500 metric tons (European and Asian consumption make up the difference). At the end of 1991, the same number of people used cocaine weekly in the United States as did in 1989. A variety of recent studies by the General Accounting Office, the State Department, and the Pentagon have concluded that United States counternarcotics programs in Central and South America have not been effective.[24]

The director of the Center of International Studies at the Universidad de los Andes in Bogotá, Colombia, Juan Tokatlian, wrote of United States policy in 1988:

> Drug use is considered a malignant phenomenon whose nature is best explained by external factors and variables. This malady—perverse and polymorphous—comes from abroad, whether or not as the result of a conspiracy to undermine the foundations of US society. . . . This has led to the emergence of a sociological language of drugs which is truly new, and in which certain words are given special importance. . . . Such is the case with the term *drug trafficking*, which suggests the external dimension of the issue: i.e., that the core of

188

the problem is the *traffic in* and transport of drugs, rather than their consumption.[25]

The concept of a "war on drugs," as it has come to be called, implies a military-oriented solution based on coercion, repression, and supply interdiction. Such a "solution" generates a variety of problems. A United States military interventionist policy creates dangers for the national sovereignty and national security of other countries.[26] The United States support may actually be *helping* the drug cartels, by providing American military training to Bolivian recruits who will end up working in the drug industry.[27]

The United States military strategy is not only ineffective but is strikingly inappropriate for a problem that is criminal in nature and social in origin.[28] Theodore Moran believes the supply-side approach will not work:

> The profitability of the current system is so great that even dramatically improved success in supply-side enforcement (interdiction of production and distribution) will only marginally offset the incentive for generating new sources. The prospect of providing alternative economic opportunities to woo Peruvian, Colombian, and Bolivian peasants away from coca production appears dim when one considers that marijuana has come to be the largest cash crop of California's rich, fertile and irrigated agricultural regions, where alternative opportunities are abundant.[29]

How can America eradicate the coca crop when there is virtually unlimited land suitable for growing it in the Andes? How can we destroy even enough crop to raise the domestic price when it costs only $350 for the five hundred pounds of Peruvian leaf that are needed to make one pound of pure cocaine, whose street price in United States cities is $45,000?[30] And there is always another producer; cocaine refining is now spreading beyond Colombia to rural Peru, Bolivia, and the remote jungles of Brazil and Venezuela. We also see the rise of United States-manufactured "designer" drugs.

We must be careful to avoid a national security doctrine that always looks beyond our borders as the source of our problems. In this sense, our drug policy resembles our energy policy—we focus on supply rather than demand, on symptoms rather than root causes. Carlton Turner,

President Reagan's director of drug abuse policy, said, "You can spend the country into bankruptcy and never stop the drugs coming in." Yet, in the 1991 antidrug budget, about 70 percent is targeted toward reducing supply (both foreign and domestic) and only about 30 percent is targeted at reducing demand.[31] These funding priorities should be reversed. We should spend more money on demand-reduction programs, such as drug treatment and drug education.

The main conclusions: (1) the Pentagon should have at most a very limited role in tackling America's drug problem; (2) we need to concentrate our antidrug efforts at home, rather than in foreign countries; and (3) the drug problem does not need more taxpayer dollars but rather a reallocation of the dollars currently being spent.

The Persian Gulf

The last element of the so-called "Third World threat" is America's energy insecurity. Our growing dependence on Persian Gulf oil and the region's historical instability have combined to motivate our strategic interest in the region for decades. The question to be examined next is, Do America's energy insecurity in general, and the Gulf war in particular, justify spending *more* money on defense and continuing a worldview that overemphasizes military security at the expense of efforts aimed at nonmilitary solutions to our nation's problems?[32] Here are four reasons I believe the answer is no.

First, America cannot permit the Gulf victory to make us complacent about our domestic problems since we do not tackle those problems as intelligently as we did the military side of the Gulf war. America is standing tall again militarily because we invested heavily in a highly trained force and advanced technology, and we applied John Boyd's systems approach to our Gulf strategy. America is having trouble competing economically because we fail to invest in a highly trained work force; to devote adequate resources to advanced civilian technology; or to take a systematic approach to our economic strategy, such as having a manufacturing industrial policy.

Second, no matter how just or successful the war with Iraq was, it does not represent either a new world order or a new military security paradigm. It is the same old world order of force begetting force, the rule of the jungle. Tomahawk missiles and F-15Es do not represent a new world order, merely the old world order with new weapons. If President Bush had committed America to stopping aggression wherever it occurs, that might well be a new military security paradigm, but he has not. During the Gulf crisis period alone, we allowed Libya to use aggression to take Chad, we allowed Syria to use aggression to solidify its control of Lebanon, and we allowed the Soviet Union to use aggression to stop democratization in the Baltics. If the new world order means that the United States is the world's policeman, then we are at best only a part-time global cop.

Even in the Gulf war, the United States sent a mixed message about its goal of thwarting aggression. President Bush seriously undercut that stated objective when he urged the Iraqi people to rise up against Hussein, used CIA funds to further rouse the Iraqis, but then failed to support the Kurdish rebellion as the war ended, even reneging on his promise to stop Hussein from using military aircraft against a rebellion. If the United States would not thwart aggression against a group it supported, in a country it was at war with and partly occupying, where would we act? And who will count on us in the future?

We were defending neither Saudi Arabia nor Kuwait for our traditional mission of promoting democracy or self-determination. It remains to be seen whether Kuwait will move significantly toward democracy. The mess we left in Iraq combined with the continuation of Kuwait's absolute monarchy undercuts the notion that we had a plan to promote democracy or regional stability through our actions during and after the war. We were successful in smashing Hussein's military capability, but even there we let too much of his army escape.

Moreover, this hardly represents a triumph of United States planning, given that we were in years past a key supplier of weaponry to Iraq; that the Pentagon and Department of Energy assisted the Iraqi nuclear weapons program; that the CIA may have helped the Iraqis acquire technology for cluster-bombs and fuel-air explosives; and that as late as a month before the war began, the administration was opposing trade sanctions against Iraq.[33] Shortly after the war's conclusion, the administration announced it was continuing the policy of providing weapons to whichever Middle East countries were then our allies. America may well find itself in the region being shot at with its own weapons some time in the next decade.

The one aspect of a new world order the Gulf war has strengthened is the United Nations' role in maintaining world peace. Indeed, a multinational response to Iraq was necessary for an effective economic blockade and for legitimizing the use of military force. That the United States led the way in bringing about an international response supports the argument that we can change our military security policy. The United States need not base its military posture on the ability to stand alone against all aggression.

The third reason the Gulf war fails to justify high levels of defense spending for a new military security paradigm: Unusual circumstances made Iraq a unique case. Iraq had the fourth largest army in the world (in terms of main battle tanks), it was replete with a vast chemical weapons arsenal, and by invading Kuwait, it threatened to control much of one of the few strategic assets most nations cannot easily replace— oil. (A nonstrategic reason we sent so much military power is that the end of the cold war had made the equipment available. In retrospect, whether we actually needed it all is uncertain.[34]) Even so, we sent only about 30 percent of our total military force to Saudi Arabia.

It is difficult to see what other enemy could justify such a force mobilization. The next two largest tank armies are Germany and Israel. As Joint Chiefs of Staff Chairman Colin Powell said in April 1991: *"I would be very surprised if another Iraq occurred. . . . Think hard about it, I'm running out of demons. I'm running out of villains. . . . I'm down to Castro and Kim Il Sung"* (emphasis added). And even those two "villains" may not survive long as their nations' economic woes mount. In any case, a March 1991 Congressional Budget Office study showed that after the Pentagon reduces its force size by 25 percent, our ground forces and especially our air forces would still have massive superiority over North Korea and Cuba. Against North Korea we would have an 8-to-1 advantage in tactical air forces and against Cuba, 15-to-1. We apparently overestimated the military capability of Iraq and crushed it with stunningly few Allied casualties, largely because our rapidly established air superiority allowed us to devastate enemy forces, supply lines, command and control, and war-fighting infrastructure and—most essential—to implement a maneuver-oriented strategy.[35]

The argument that the unique case of Iraq shows that the world remains a dangerous place and that this sound bite represents a new security paradigm is without basis in fact. The world is far less dangerous

192

to us since the Warsaw Pact collapsed, and even less dangerous now that we have smashed the mighty Iraqi military machine.

Finally, the notion that instability in the Middle East demands sizable new defense expenditures is also unsupportable. Even before the Iraqi crisis, the Pentagon had allocated significant annual funding to Persian Gulf contingencies: about $64 billion in 1990.[36] The war with Iraq increased our fiscal year 1991 Persian Gulf expenditures, but even here, our allies underwrote much of the one-time expense. In the future, we will have more equipment prepositioned, reducing the time and cost needed to respond to any regional crisis. And as I will discuss in the next chapter, a different arms transfer policy and foreign aid program, including a multibillion dollar Middle East peace fund, should help return the focus of United States policy to avoiding such crises in the first place. We can plan for any new Gulf war contingency and still drastically reduce the $200 billion a year we now spend on the old Soviet and Warsaw Pact threat. Even with a much-reduced military, we could handle another major Gulf crisis—especially since we have smashed the biggest regional war machine for some time to come, and since we could once again count on the support of other nations.

So the Gulf war calls for no new military security paradigm. On the contrary, it raises useful questions about our military-oriented approach to our dependency on foreign oil. The dollars and cents of the matter point to a wholly different approach. We must question the wisdom of increasing military expenditures for the Persian Gulf when the total value of American oil imports from the region in 1989 was only about $10 billion (representing about one fifth of all oil imports) and the United States could easily reduce its dependence on that oil.

Persian Gulf Oil

The region's oil may not be the sole reason we are interested in the Gulf, but it is surely the primary reason. If there were no oil in the Gulf, why would Iraq's aggression against Kuwait be more important to us than Libya's aggression against Chad, or Syria's against Lebanon, or Israel's aggression against Lebanon in the early 1980s? After the invasion, President Bush said, "Our jobs, our way of life, our own freedom and the freedom of friendly countries around the world would all suffer if control of the world's great oil reserves fell into the hands of Saddam

Hussein."[37] Later, Secretary of State James Baker said the "simple" explanation for why we were in the Gulf was "jobs."

Now that we have secured the Saudi and Kuwaiti oil fields from Iraqi aggression, this question must be asked: What is the best way to secure oil for America in the future? If we continue with the military-oriented national security worldview of the 1980s, we will continue without a sensible domestic energy policy, and we will instead increase our defense expenditures for Persian Gulf force planning. The flaws in such a policy are profound.

First, while Germany and Japan were induced to help subsidize the Gulf war, they do not reimburse us for our annual Persian Gulf defense expenditures and they are not likely to in the future. *Since their economies are more dependent on imported oil than ours, our policy in effect heavily subsidizes the economies of our two major trading competitors.*

Second, defense costs to maintain access to petroleum supplies are not reflected in the price of gasoline. In 1985, America paid more than $200 a barrel imported from the Gulf to keep the shipping lanes open— more than seven times the price we paid for the oil itself. The "military insurance costs for Persian Gulf oil" from 1986 to the first half of 1990 have been estimated at between $196 to $266 a barrel.[38] Such mispricing leads us to overuse the fuel, with negative economic and environmental consequences. Our misguided domestic energy policy since 1980 has caused our reliance on Persian Gulf oil to rise 500 percent from 1985 to 1989. About half of our $100 billion trade deficit is due to oil. How many jobs are lost because America's profligate use of oil leads to such a high capital outflow? As explained in Chapter 4, continuation of current policy will, in the long run, lead only to greater dependency on foreign oil and greater capital outflow, and greater subsidies for our competitor's energy.

The danger posed by Saddam's threat to oil fields was qualitatively different from the Soviet threat. Communism's threat to freedom was real, as the post-World War II history of Eastern Europe made evident. Saddam Hussein's threat to our "freedom" was, if anything, a threat to our freedom to overuse cheap oil. Communism may have threatened the American way of life, and the possibility of a Warsaw Pact tank invasion threatened the Western European way of life. Saddam Hussein at most imperiled not the American way of life but the American life-style, which allows 5 percent of the world's population to use 25 percent of the world's

194

petroleum, a life-style that quite obviously cannot be emulated by the rest of the world. Moreover, once we and our allies had placed defensive forces in Saudi Arabia, the Saudi fields were secure, and the necessary world supply was ensured; only the price remained high. This high price was viewed by some as endangering American jobs.

In the post-cold war world, military security threats are much more nearly coequal with, for instance, economic security threats or energy security threats. If our drug problem deserves to be labeled a "national security" problem, then it is a national security problem with a social and economic cause. Since we justified removing General Manuel Noriega from Panama largely on the basis of his role in drug trafficking, the invasion of Panama was, in some sense, a war fought because of United States domestic failings, rather than military necessity. It may, therefore, be the first post-cold war conflict (in contrast to the liberation of Grenada, which was justified as removing a potential communist outpost in the Caribbean). The Panama invasion apparently had little long-term effect. A 1991 General Accounting Office report indicated that the flow of drugs and drug profits from Panama had increased dramatically since the December 1989 invasion.[39]

Even more than the events leading to our invasion of Panama, Iraq's invasion of Kuwait posed a United States national security problem with a domestic social and economic cause—our unwillingness to control our thirst for oil. Secretary of State James Baker told the House Foreign Relations Committee in February 1991, "We should view security not just in military terms." Secretary Baker also spoke of five post-Gulf war challenges. Four were regional: greater regional security, arms control, economic reconstruction, and Arab-Israeli peace. "And a fifth and final challenge, Mr. Chairman, concerns the United States. We simply must do more to reduce our energy dependence." Baker said an American energy strategy "should involve energy conservation and efficiency."[40] But when President Bush addressed Congress a month later, he said, "Tonight let me outline *four* key challenges to be met" (emphasis added). *The fifth challenge—to reduce energy dependence—had vanished; energy conservation and efficiency were no longer a necessary response to the Gulf war.*

While Bush's military approach to our energy insecurity did maintain access to oil supplies in the short run, his postwar National Energy

195

Strategy would increase United States dependence on Middle East oil. As detailed in Chapter 4, an energy policy based instead on demand-reduction would not only reduce United States vulnerability to the vagaries of Persian Gulf politics; it would dramatically increase American economic and environmental security. It is the *absence* of a wise domestic energy policy that threatens American jobs.

The Persian Gulf War was a *tactical* success because we had a brilliant tactical game-plan or orientation—fast-cycle manuever warfare. The war was a *strategic* muddle because we lacked a coherent vision at the strategic level. We have no long-term plan for solving either the regional problems that lead to military conflict or the domestic problems that lead us to seek foreign solutions.

The Third World threat, the new world order, the world's policeman—none of these provides a new military security paradigm that can justify the kind of narrow national security paradigm that the cold war did. Quite the reverse. America by its own choice (and in part to pay for the military buildup of the 1980s) has borrowed itself into an era of constrained budget choices. Pouring money into approaches that attack symptoms, rather than root causes, is no longer practical. Moreover, the Third World should be seen as an opportunity, not a threat. Insofar as narcogangsters and Persian Gulf instability are threats to United States national security, nonmilitary approaches will be superior. By halving military forces and spending, we can free funds for nonmilitary solutions without jeopardizing military security. By reorienting foreign aid away from its military focus, we can increase economic, energy, environmental, and military security.

196

7

The End of Military Security

*I would be very surprised if another Iraq
occurred.... Think hard about it, I'm running out of
demons. I'm running out of villains.... I'm down to
Castro and Kim Il Sung.*

—Colin Powell, Chairman of the
Joint Chiefs of Staff, April 1991

Military spending must be *decreased* so that overall national security, broadly defined, can *increase.* But cutting defense dollars will be more difficult than it should be, thanks to Pentagon misplanning, congressional negligence, and White House intransigence. Nevertheless, large defense savings—the long-awaited peace dividend—will be assured if cuts are made wisely. But there is another peace dividend: A dramatic increase in the world's security when the United States leads the way toward cooperative security.

The ballooning national debt led to real declines in defense spending beginning in the late 1980s. The deepening economic problems in the United States coupled with the collapse of the Warsaw Pact led to a budget agreement in October 1990 that will cut defense spending 22 percent during the first half of the 1990s. In early 1991, the Pentagon submitted a plan to Congress to achieve these cuts, including a 25-percent reduction in the overall size of our military forces. Yet that plan, drastic as it was, falls far short of achieving the spending cuts required through 1996. Moreover, the plan defers production of many new weapons systems, instead of canceling them outright, relying on the fervent wish that military spending will start increasing again in the second half of the 1990s. But the alarming growth of the national debt, coupled with the greater urgency of economic, environmental, and energy security needs, makes further cuts inevitable. Increases in defense spending are improbable, and President Bush has already announced slightly deeper cuts in his 1992 State of the Union address.

The bottom line is simple but stark: It will be increasingly difficult for the United States to maintain armed forces larger than half their present size. Furthermore, unless the government quickly cancels virtually all of the next generation of weapons, America's armed forces in the early twenty-first century will not only be under half the size they are today, but they will probably also be short of equipment, ammunition, spare parts, and adequate training—a return to the so-called "hollow forces" of the 1970s.

We do have an alternative. As we scale back our defense spending, we can preserve the effectiveness of our military and our ability to project power worldwide, if we acknowledge that the end of the cold war dramatically reduces the need for most new weapons systems, and if we apply two of the early lessons of the Persian Gulf War. First, many of our existing weapons are very effective. Second, many older weapons that have been upgraded are also effective. The key to sustaining America's military strength as defense spending is cut is to pursue a policy of canceling or freezing the development of most *new* weapons, and instead buying and occasionally upgrading *existing* weapons. This chapter will examine the long history of the Pentagon's planning problems and the alternatives facing the country.

Unilateral Disarmament

The first comprehensive analysis of the flaws in our weapons acquisition policy was written during the Nixon administration by Norman Augustine, now chief executive officer of Martin Marietta. In a 1971 paper that was originally classified, Augustine used historical data to show that "the cost of new military hardware is determined simply by calendar time." Every ten years, tanks double in cost and aircraft quadruple in cost, which led him to note that if trends were not reversed, the Air Force would consist of one plane by the middle of the twenty-first century.

In 1990, Augustine wrote that "the trend thus far continues unchecked," and therefore he "noted only partially facetiously," that if someday the entire United States defense budget were used to purchase a bomber, "it will be the B-4 that produces this singular event and *the year will be 2020*" (emphasis added).[1]

Franklin Spinney, a Pentagon staff analyst, warned the House Appropriations Committee in his 1983 "Plans/Reality mismatch" briefing: "Costs are going up much faster than your budgets. The net result is lower rates of modernization and ultimately shrinking forces." The consequences of this policy were explained to the Armed Services Committee in December 1986 by General Bernard Rogers, the commander of our NATO forces for eight years: "I am less than encouraged in what has happened over the past 7½ years. . . . *We are practicing unilateral disarmament* when, with the increasing cost of new systems, we are replacing older systems with fewer numbers of new systems, even though the new systems may be more capable" (emphasis added).[2]

In a time of vast Reagan military spending increases, what did General Rogers mean by unilateral disarmament? The numbers tell the story. We spent 75 percent more on aircraft from 1982 to 1985 than we did between 1977 and 1980, but we produced only 8 percent more aircraft. We spent 91 percent more on missiles, but increased our missile inventory only 6 percent. We spent 147 percent more on tanks and other armored vehicles, but ended up with only 30 percent more weapons.[3]

We can and should pay more for higher quality weapons. Moreover, the Gulf war shows that the United States has many capable weapons, most based on technology that was begun in the 1970s. The rapid increase in defense spending in the early 1980s made it possible for us to buy that generation of expensive weapons. Between 1980 and 1985, the budget for weapons procurement more than doubled, so the Pentagon could afford to buy weapons even twice as expensive as previous models without reducing force size.

By fiscal year 1986, three years before the Berlin Wall came down, the national debt, then $2 trillion, combined with the Gramm-Rudman budget balancing law, forced the start of a steady decline in defense funding. But the cost of new weapons kept skyrocketing so that a shrinking military became inevitable, as long as the Pentagon insisted on buying yet another *new* generation of weapons in the 1990s.

And the Pentagon insisted. Its own internal Future-Years Defense

Program (FYDP) continued to project steady *increases* in defense spending.[4] Although every year, from 1986 onward, the Pentagon saw its budget lowered, it assumed in its FYDP each year that, starting in the very next year, the defense budget would start growing again—and continue growing for five straight years. In 1986, the FYDP projected a 1990 defense budget of more than $450 billion.[5] In 1988, the Defense Department lowered its projected growth rate, but still anticipated a 1992 defense budget of more than $400 billion (the actual figure was under $300 billion). Even in April 1989, after five consecutive years of budget *cuts* averaging 2.8 percent a year, the Pentagon's FYDP still projected an inflation-adjusted annual rate of *growth* averaging 1.7 percent.[6]

Thus, throughout the second half of the 1980s, the Defense Department was continuing to research and develop far more weapons than it would ever get money to build: the Navy's new Seawolf submarine, Aegis destroyer, Trident II missile, and A-12 attack aircraft; the Air Force's advanced tactical fighter, C-17 airlift, the MX rail-garrison, Midgetman missile, and B-2 Stealth bomber; the Army's light helicopter family and replacements for the M-1 tank and Bradley infantry fighting vehicle; the Marines' V-22 tilt-rotor aircraft; and whatever strategic defense system might finally result from the R&D effort of SDI—Star Wars. The full list is even longer.[7]

The central point of this analysis bears repeating. These weapons will invariably be much more expensive than the weapons they are designed to replace. To buy these next-generation weapons in the same quantity as we bought the current generation, the defense budget will have to *rise* drastically in the second half of the 1990s. Therefore, most of these new weapons must be canceled or deferred merely to stop defense spending from rising in the late 1990s; such is the inevitable result of trying to squeeze a $400 billion defense plan into a $300 billion budget.

Canceling a few will not do the job. Politicians are often quoted as saying that the cancelation of a particular weapon would save the taxpayer $10 to $20 billion. But there is so much spending growth built into the Pentagon budget that canceling a single new system by itself, such as the B-2 Stealth bomber, while funding another, such as Star Wars, cannot be said to save the taxpayers any money. It is as if a family had dreamed of replacing its two-door hatchback and its station wagon with a Porsche and a Mercedes, then decided to buy only the Porsche, and concluded that it had saved tens of thousands of dollars.

The business-as-usual defense planning that kept so many new programs going stems from two causes and one fatally flawed premise. First, research and development funds for a new system are a fraction of production costs, so it is possible to begin the development of a variety of weapons cheaply. Some, like the Stealth bomber, begin as so-called "black" programs, where funds are allocated to classified programs before details are provided to Congress. Second, once a significant amount of money has been allocated, and the weapon nears development, it becomes difficult to kill in Congress, in part because a constituency will have mobilized to support it, and in part because Congress is loath to cancel weapons "after so much money has already been spent on them."[8] The flawed premise: The entire edifice of annual Pentagon planning in the late 1980s was made shaky by its shaky premise—that sometime very soon the budget would finally stop shrinking and would return to the rapid growth of the early 1980s, making the new weapons affordable. The ballooning national debt rendered this assumption false.

The Shrinking Pentagon

In the fall of 1990, the Congress and the White House worked out a five-year budget deal that would reduce defense spending about 22 percent. The President had agreed to multiyear defense budgets with steady declines in funding; it would no longer be possible to act as if decreasing defense budgets would suddenly turn into growing defense budgets. From 1990 to 1997, the total gap between what the Pentagon had been planning to get and what the president now agreed the Pentagon would get was to be $500 to $600 billion.[9] In other words, the Defense Department would have to cut more than half a trillion dollars from its long-term plans, no easy task.

By 1991, the Pentagon had specified a plan that did not make up for even half of the shortfall, but nevertheless called for a surprisingly deep 25-percent cut in overall military force structure.[10] Between 1990 and 1995, the Army would be reduced from 28 divisions (18 active) to 18 (12 active). During that period, the Air Force would be reduced from 36 tactical fighter wings (24 active) to 26 wings (15 active), a reduction of some 700 fighters; strategic bombers would be reduced from 268 to 181. The Navy would be reduced from a 545-ship fleet to 451, and lose one aircraft carrier, leaving it with 12 carriers.[11]

The major next-generation program canceled in the 1991 Pentagon plan was the Navy's A-12 naval attack plane.[12] More surprising was the termination of a host of weapons used successfully in the Persian Gulf: the F-14D Tomcat, the F-16 Falcon, the Bradley infantry fighting vehicle, the M-1 tank, the AH-64 Apache helicopter, and the F-15 Eagle.[13] These effective existing weapons were cut in anticipation of their more expensive replacements coming on-line within the next ten years. This unjustifiable assumption leads to misspending and misplanning. It weakens America's military security.

The Pentagon's problem through 1996 is how to meet the budget summit targets. They will require further cuts of hundreds of billions of dollars.[14] On top of those cuts, the Pentagon must slash another $50 billion through 1996 to meet the new targets set by President Bush in his 1992 State of the Union address. Several painful choices lie ahead.

If reductions in force size well beyond 25 percent are to be avoided, many more systems must follow the path of the A-12. The A-12 was to be the successor to the aircraft-carrier-based A-6 attack plane, and would have incorporated the latest stealth technology. In 1987, the Defense Department decided against modernizing the A-6 and instead opted to replace it during the 1990s with some 620 A-12s at a cost of $57 billion, nearly $100 million each. Designing and building the A-12 proved far more difficult than the builders, McDonnell Douglas and General Dynamics, expected. Mismanagement and cost overruns led to increased price estimates that the planes would cost more than $150 million each. At that price, twenty-five A-12s would cost as much as an aircraft carrier. On the day he announced his decision to cancel the plane, Defense Secretary Cheney said, "No one can tell me exactly how much more it will cost to keep this program going."[15]

The decision surprised many, in part because it was the largest weapons program ever canceled by the Pentagon, and in part because outright cancelation has not been the preferred method for handling troubled programs. The normal approach has been to "stretch out" a program, buying weapons at a slower rate and often reducing their number. Unfortunately, stretching out the next generation of weapons lowers production efficiency, inevitably leading to higher unit costs. Money is seldom saved.[16] Therefore, many of the new programs are now beginning to collapse of their own weight.

Consider the B-2 Stealth bomber. Originally, we were to buy 132 planes for $75 billion. In April 1991, trying to adapt to budget realities, Cheney reduced the planned buy to 75 planes, a 43-percent reduction in force size. Yet the total cost was reduced only 19 percent, to $61 billion. And in January 1992, President Bush drastically curtailed the program, to 20 Stealth bombers, pushing the per-plane cost over $2 billion, and bringing us a giant step closer to Augustine's nightmare of a 1-plane Air Force in the twenty-first century.

In April 1991, Cheney also reduced the C-17 order from 210 to 120, predictably increasing the projected cost from $200 million to $250 million each. He deferred peak production until the mid-1990s. The Air Force's stealthy Advanced Tactical Fighter (ATF) program has also been stretched out, so that most of them will be built after 1996. The projected cost is $95 billion for 650 planes, nearly $150 million per plane.

The Navy had originally been hoping to buy as many as four Seawolf submarines a year at a cost of about $1.5 billion each. By 1991, the Navy could afford to buy only one at a time, and the price had jumped to $2.4 billion for a single sub. By January 1992, the Seawolf program had collapsed. With ballooning costs, serious construction problems, and no mission, the President pulled the plug on this cold war relic, and proposed building only one sub.

Another budget buster is the Strategic Defense Initiative: Star Wars. The SDI budget for 1992 was increased to $4.1 billion in the aftermath of the Gulf war, but even this funding level is wholly inadequate to satisfy SDI's needs. In May 1991, the director of the SDI program, Henry F. Cooper, told Congress that the SDI program would cost $120 billion through 2005.[17] To "fully fund" Star Wars, as President Bush called for in September 1991, the SDI budget would have to more than double by the mid-1990s, reaching $10 billion a year in the next century, to pay for the several major systems to be developed—hundreds of Brilliant Pebbles satellites, dozens of surveillance and tracking satellites, as well as countless ground-based strategic interceptors, antitactical ballistic missiles, and sensors.[18] Even this may not be enough, if history is any guide. Studies suggest that the final cost of weapons systems is typically more than twice the cost estimated at the early stages of their development. Moreover, most major weapons systems have one or more serious hardware flaws that become apparent only after deployment. What would happen if we launched one thousand "Brilliant Pebble" satellites into space, and then discovered a flaw that required fixing? Would we send the Space Shuttle to each one? Would we turn the system off and replace it? Either way, the extra cost would be astronomical.

In late 1991, Congress approved a plan to go forward with deployment of an SDI system. As I will argue in the Appendix, SDI offers little hope of being an effective or useful weapon. It crowds out scarce defense dollars needed for potent weapons. In an age of constrained budgets, that is a very real threat to overall United States military security. All of these systems—Star Wars, the ATF, the C-17—are viable only with vast increases in Pentagon spending, which is exceedingly unlikely to happen.

The Late 1990s Budget Squeeze

Even assuming the Defense Department is able to meet the current budget targets with deferments, stretchouts, cancelations, and further cuts in force size, it faces a still tougher challenge starting in the second half of the decade. The Pentagon must avoid repeating its worst error of the late 1980s: basing R&D and procurement decisions on long-term plans that are viable only if sometime soon—in this case fiscal year 1997—the defense budget starts rising again. So far, the Pentagon has not gotten the message.

In March 1991, the Congressional Budget Office told the House Armed Services Committee: "In the long run, substantial real increases in the U.S. defense budget would be required to modernize fully remaining U.S. forces with the new weapons now planned. To avoid budget increases, the Congress will have to be highly selective in choosing new weapons to be bought." Three months later, the nonpartisan Defense Budget Project came to the same conclusion.[19]

In September 1991, the Brookings Institution released a study showing that if all the next generation weapons are put into production and begin deployment, Pentagon spending must start rising in 1997 at a rate of roughly 8 percent ($20 billion) a year, and continue rising at that rate until spending reaches $350 billion in 2001—*surpassing the highest level of defense spending reached in the 1980s and equaling the peak spending of the wars in Korea and Vietnam* (in inflation-adjusted dollars). Total Pentagon spending between 1992 and 2001 would be $2.8 trillion![20]

Although the Brookings Institution, the Congressional Budget Office, the Defense Budget Project, and leading analysts such as Norman Augustine and Franklin Spinney warn of the impending budget squeeze in exquisite detail, key government officials seem entirely unaware of it. President Bush's September 1991 speech called for eliminating most tactical nuclear weapons, mobile land-based missiles, and other nuclear programs, but endorsed the Stealth bomber and full funding for the Strategic Defense Initiative. After the speech, National Security Adviser Brent Scowcroft said, "Five years out, I think there will be a peace dividend." Defense Secretary Richard Cheney said, "The most recent initiatives will produce long-term savings."[21] Both assessments are mistaken. Without far more significant program cuts, defense spending must rise.

What will happen to our military security when the defense budget does not rise in the second half of the 1990s? That depends on how the Defense Department, the White House, and Congress respond to the major defense choice they face in the early 1990s—force size versus modernization.

The issue may be framed as follows: In the 1980s, the budget for military hardware doubled, but so did the unit cost of the weapons bought. As a result, the military ended the 1980s with roughly the *same* number of weapons that it started the decade with. The defense budget in the 1990s has already been cut 25 percent. If in the 1990s the Defense Department buys the same weapons it did in the 1980s, it will be able to field only 75 percent of the force it had in the 1980s. If, on the other hand, this scaled-down budget is used to buy the *next generation* of weapons, which cost roughly twice as much as their predecessors, then the military will be able to field forces perhaps only 50 percent as big as in the 1980s. This is my own calculation, supported in part by a March 1991 analysis by the Congressional Budget Office that concluded: (1) Replacing aging equipment with the *current generation* of weapons would require procurement funding to average $67 billion a year—roughly the amount planned for 1995; (2) but sustaining the proposed 1995 force size with the *next generation* of weapons would require, over the long

205

run, an average annual procurement cost of $109 billion (in 1991) dollars.[22]

The calculation shows that if, as seems likely and prudent, the defense budget is cut even more than 25 percent, the only way to avoid very deep cuts in force size (below 50 percent of 1990 levels) is to defer for five years or cancel outright *most* of the following weapons: The Trident II missile, ATF fighter, C-17 transport, LH helicopter, and Star Wars. These are harsh choices made necessary by earlier extensive misplanning and blue sky assumptions.

No one can say what defense spending will be five to ten years from now. It almost certainly will decline, to help balance the budget, and ought to decline for reasons of national security as redefined.

The defense budget began its decline in fiscal year 1986 because of the $2 trillion national debt, which made reductions inevitable, not because of changes in the Warsaw Pact; those were still a few years away. The Pentagon had begun considering *significant* cuts in force size by 1988—a year before the Berlin Wall collapsed. In 1990, the end of the cold war made it easier to accept the five-year cuts in defense spending required by the budget agreement, but again it was the national debt, which had ballooned to $3 trillion, that made such cuts necessary. Yet even those cuts could not stop the overall debt from growing even more. The deficit for fiscal year 1992 will exceed the defense budget for the first time in decades. *By 1996, the national debt will reach $5 trillion: The interest on the national debt may well exceed the defense budget.* Under those remarkable circumstances, a prudent military planner should anticipate that further annual cuts in the 3-percent to 4-percent range may well be necessary. Those are the fiscal arguments for cutting the defense budget.

The military argument for even deeper cuts—to 50 percent of 1990 levels—was stated succinctly by the Office of Technology Assessment, in July 1991:

> If one believes that the pre-World War II spending levels and the postwar peacetime minimum are more appropriate to the current security environment, then a 25-percent cut would merely return us to "normal" cold-war levels, while a further 25-percent cut may be a justifiable response to the end of the cold war.[23]

Stopping at a 25-percent defense cut means remaining stuck in cold war thinking. A 50-percent cut would reflect a genuine reorientation to changing circumstances.

In the last cold war national defense budget (fiscal year 1990), some 60 percent of spending—roughly $200 billion—was devoted to the Soviet and Warsaw Pact threat. As discussed in the last chapter, on military security grounds we can save most of that money because we are running out of enemies. Even deep spending cuts leave us with significant military superiority over likely adversaries. On overall national security grounds, we desperately need the money for economic, energy, and environmental security. The 1990 budget agreement left defense spending in 1996 only $70 billion below the 1990 level (in inflation-adjusted dollars).

Defense spending can and will be cut much more deeply. The absence of a comprehensive and realistic long-term defense plan not only means that we will probably end up with a deeper cut in force size than is necessary; it also means that we will probably short-change funds for readiness and sustainability, repeating the mistakes of the 1970s that led to "hollow forces."[24] In 1988 congressional testimony, defense analyst William Kaufmann explained why cuts in military readiness and sustainability—personnel, spare parts, ammunition, training, and maintenance—are called "attack of the termites": "In effect, what happens as a consequence is that the defense house looks from the outside to be in excellent order while all the parts on the inside that make it function are progressively eaten away. . . ."

These cuts are as devastating to the underlying vitality of the military as the 1980s' cuts in education, R&D, and infrastructure have been to the underlying vitality of the American economy. Just as the nation requires a systematic, long-term plan to restore economic security as resources are shifted from defense to civilian needs, we need at the same time a comprehensive long-term plan to maintain our military security. Otherwise there will be a haphazard battle between those who want to preserve weapons systems, those who want to preserve force size, and those who want to preserve readiness and sustainability.[25] The result of such chaos would be a far smaller and less potent military than this nation could otherwise afford. We must do better.

A More Prudent Defense Plan

Defense analysts William Kaufmann and John Steinbruner have put forth a detailed, long-term plan in their September 1991 Brookings Institution study, *Decisions for Defense, Prospects for a New Order.* Their comprehensive ten-year program would reduce the Pentagon budget to $225 billion in fiscal year 1996 ($20 billion less than the 1991 Pentagon plan) and to $169 billion in 2001 (all in 1992 dollars).[26]

The Brookings program (they refer to it as the "low plan") reduces the Army to 11 divisions (7 active) in 2001; it reduces the Navy to 6 aircraft carrier battle groups and a total of 259 ships; and keeps the same number of Air Force fighter wings as the 1991 Pentagon plan. This option would provide the same United States resources as used during Operation Desert Storm with one exception: only 4 carrier battle groups instead of 6. Naval forces, however, were not the decisive element of the Allied success. As the authors note, "It is hard to argue that 6 carrier battle groups were essential to the success of the campaign."[27]

Moreover, the Navy is beginning to have severe problems fully equipping its aircraft carriers. Vice Admiral Richard Dunleavy, chief of naval aviation, told *Defense News* in March 1991, "We are in a *death spiral* and that is pretty bad analysis. Unless we change the way we do business, how to make less expensive aircraft and how to employ them, we are going to have a crisis on our hands as to where naval aviation is going" (emphasis added).[28] Reducing the number of carriers to six in the year 2001 will help alleviate the naval aviation problem and give the Navy a decade to solve the problem of building affordable aircraft.

The Brookings "low plan" meets the test of Desert Storm while saving the country nearly $75 billion a year. Under this option, the United States could not fight another battle as large as Desert Storm *and* simultaneously fight a second war elsewhere in the world. In the post-cold war era, however, the likelihood of two such huge attacks at the same time is low (no such simultaneous attacks occurred during the forty-five years of the cold war), especially now that the United States has demonstrated to the world how effectively it can destroy even a large, modern, well-dug-in army. Moreover, as the authors note, "It may well be the case that the United States committed larger forces to the [Desert Storm] campaign than were necessary to achieve the same outcome."[29]

It should also be pointed out that attacking is not the only option available to the United States. Had we, for example, been engaged in another military operation during the Gulf crisis, we could have extended the embargo against Iraq until the first operation was completed, thus avoiding two simultaneous battles.

Finally, it is not easy to find potential enemies for the United States (and its allies) that approach the magnitude of Iraq's armed forces. As noted above, Joint Chiefs of Staff Chairman Colin Powell said he'd be "very surprised if another Iraq occurred." And that for "villains," we're "down to Castro and Kim Il Sung." Tactical air forces were decisive in the Persian Gulf War, and the Brookings "low plan" allows the United States more than a five-to-one advantage in air power over North Korea (about the same as we had against Iraq) and more than a ten-to-one advantage in air power over Cuba.

To achieve their defense savings without cutting force structure even more deeply, Kaufmann and Steinbruner stop the production of the B-2 at 15 aircraft, scale back SDI, continue upgrading current generation combat aircraft but defer *all* next-generation successors, postpone the Army's new systems, cancel the SSN-21 Seawolf attack sub, terminate the C-17 and extend the life of the C-141 airlift aircraft.[30] Since most of these next-generation weapons were designed with the Soviet and Warsaw Pact threat in mind, their cancelation will not jeopardize United States security, especially since such changes increase security by preserving force size and readiness.

We do need more airlift, for rapid deployment of our forces in a crisis. Sadly, the C-17 does not look like the solution. It costs more than $350 million per plane at current production rates and will only decline significantly in cost if we build 24 planes a year in the mid-1990s. Kaufmann and Steinbruner note that the C-17 will not significantly change the "weight and speed" of a deployment comparable to Desert Shield in the future. The C-17's capability has been scaled back; it has been plagued with technical and manufacturing problems; McDonnell Douglas has been accused of trying to cover up serious defects in the plane's wings; it is a billion dollars over its development budget; and McDonnell Douglas still has "a good way to go" to solve chronic cost problems, according to the Air Force. The Air Force should consider reopening the production line for the C-5 cargo plane.[31]

In an era of tight budgets, tough choices must be made. Upgrading weapons that have proved effective in the Gulf war is superior to terminating them and going forward instead with untested and expensive new weapons. Our military security cannot benefit if we wake up in the year 2000—only a few years hence—with rusty and cobwebbed production lines for our best battle-tested weapons, and with inadequate money for their uncertain replacements.

The ten-year reduction plan allows many years to reverse policy decisions should events warrant, such as the rise of a new global military threat. But a major military foe is unlikely to rise in the next decade. Who can match the awesome power unleashed by the United States in the Gulf war? Kaufmann and Steinbruner describe the "precise tactical air operation that for now is unique in the world": "It would not be easy to duplicate the combination of functions on which such operations are based: the *rapid* gathering, processing and dissemination of necessary information; the *immediate* translation of that information into operational plans; and the *effective* implementation of those plans by people and equipment" (emphasis added).[32] In John Boyd's terms, America has the fastest, most effective military time-cycle in the world, and it is the only nation with the trained people and superior weapons necessary to make such a fast tempo possible. The unusual synthesis of special training, strategy, and weapons is a formidable achievement. Moreover, many key aspects of United States military superiority—satellites, aircraft carriers, a large high-tech air force—cannot be developed either quickly or in secret. America would have many years' warning of another nation's attempt to match our military might.

In February 1992, Secretary of Defense Richard Cheney described to the Senate the remarkable state of America's military security:

> Today we have no global challenger, except with respect to strategic nuclear forces. No country is our match in conventional military technology or the ability to apply it. There are no significant alliances hostile to US interest.
>
> To the contrary, the strongest and most capable countries in the world are our friends. No region in the world critical to our interest is under hostile, nondemocratic domination. . . .
>
> Threats to our security have become more distant, not only physically, but in time as well. A challenge to our security would have to overcome our formidable alliances, and their qualitative advantages that we displayed so impressively during Desert Storm. The events of the last four years have provided America with strategic depth in

which to defend our national interest that we have lacked for decades.[33]

Deeper Cuts Possible Through Cooperative Security

The "low option" provides a great deal of effective military security for $169 billion. On the other hand, it is far from the absolute minimum that can be spent while still maintaining a potent defense. For instance, the Brookings plan includes no reductions in national intelligence spending. The $30 billion spent in that arena is another relic of the cold war and should be cut proportionally with defense spending, saving another $10 billion to $15 billion per year.

It is likely that new cooperative security arrangements with allies around the globe will be established in the 1990s. They will further reduce—rather than increase—pressure on United States military spending. For the foreseeable future, the United States would have both better military security and increased national security if, instead of squandering resources and effort on larger forces and ever more sophisticated weapons, we attempted to create a true "new world order" based on preventing aggressions from rising in the first place. The United States would work with other major powers—Russia, the United Kingdom, France, Germany, Japan, China, Brazil, and India—to establish a worldwide security standard based on restrictions on offensive military capability. These limitations on force size and weapons mix could be informally negotiated based on a nation's size and population.

The first enforcement mechanism would be the court of world opinion, which has become powerful by the spread of rapid, global communications networks—CNN, faxes, and the like—and has made coups and clandestine military buildups exceedingly difficult to achieve. Second, for serious violations, economic sanctions could be started. As the Gulf crisis showed, skillful diplomats can quickly organize comprehensive boycotts, and the United Nations can be an effective vehicle for international economic response. With global commerce becoming ever more competitive, few nations could risk the imposition of even marginally effective sanctions. The final resort, to be used only against direct acts of territorial aggression, would be war—with the burden shared by a coalition military

211

response. Again, the Gulf war showed that the United Nations can play a key role in thwarting global aggression.

The key to true military security is *prevention* of weapons proliferation and war. One crucial measure would be strong global controls of weapons export. All weapons transfers would be licensed and fully disclosed. End-use would be strictly monitored to prevent weapons buildup programs or diversions of weapons to Third World countries.[34] Such an export control plan would have short-term costs. We would have to forgo billions of dollars in arms deals, which in the long run would save us billions more. A well-enforced global export policy would slow the spread of the technology and weapons that could eventually undermine America's overwhelming military advantage. Such a policy would minimize the likelihood that the United States would ever face its own advanced weapons technology, as it did in the Gulf. Above all, such a global watchdog program would bring America long-term military security benefits.

Kaufmann and Steinbruner, in addition to their "low plan," have proposed a "Cooperative Security" defense plan. This one projects that the defense budget could decline to $155 billion in 1998, which is $85 billion *a year* below the Pentagon's currently planned 1997 budget. Since the new Cooperative Security six-year budget does not significantly differ from their "low option" until 1995, there is no near-term risk to the nation of working toward this new world order.[35]

This new world, and the recommended defense cuts, are mutually reinforcing. A world based on cooperative security would be attainable only if every member were demilitarizing. The United States would have the necessary credibility to help lead such a world only if we were perceived as part of the solution—cutting our forces in half and curtailing arms exports. And in such a world, the United States would not need high levels of defense spending.

The claims politicians and others make about their multiyear programs for defense cuts are often misleading. Cumulative savings sound impressive—$50 billion over five years—but that amount of total savings can be achieved by a permanent $10 billion spending cut in the very first year (and spending $290 billion a year for five years instead of $300 billion a year). By way of comparison, the Cooperative Security plan would provide $210 billion in cumulative savings through 1997, *and another $430 billion by 2002, and $85 billion per year thereafter.* Here is a genuine peace dividend for a nation that desperately needs to increase funding for nonmilitary security.

The criterion for judging defense-reduction programs should be: What is the final level of defense spending achieved? Proposals that leave annual defense spending significantly above $200 billion by the end of the decade are not serious attempts to address this nation's problems, and such proposals do not reflect an understanding of the remarkable changes that have occurred in the world over the last few years. The defense budget can be cut in half by the year 2001 while preserving our military security. Moreover, we can not only envision a world where defense spending can be reduced more rapidly, we can take steps to bring such a world about.

Rethinking Foreign Aid

The most effective way for the United States and the world community to create a new order based on cooperative security is neither with export controls nor with the threat of a coalition military response. Rather it is with the promise of a new path: a richer life linked to demilitarization. Japan and Germany remain the most celebrated success stories of such a policy.

The United States and other nations should encourage demilitarization by cutting their own military budgets and by tying foreign aid and economic assistance to a nation's willingness to abide by the global security standards. A carrot-and-stick approach is needed. The World Bank and International Monetary Fund should deny foreign aid and loans to nations that refuse to join cooperative security coalitions or that spend more than a certain percentage of GNP on the military. On the other hand, nations should be rewarded with loans, grants, or debt relief when they reduce arms spending and arms imports.[36]

Moving to a cooperative security regime requires much more than a military hardware policy. We must completely rethink foreign aid. As I have discussed in Chapters 1 and 5, much Third World conflict has its roots in environmental and resource problems. Those problems become ours—dangers such as global warming and deforestation pose a direct security threat to the United States. We must abandon the traditional

213

foreign aid budget (such as Bush's 1992 request), which is roughly half military-oriented security assistance and half development and humanitarian assistance. Although United States foreign aid as a percent of GNP is the lowest of the industrialized countries, and although Japan has now matched us in total dollars of foreign aid, America does not need to spend a dollar more on foreign aid. The $16 billion budgeted for 1992 is enough money. What we need is to reorient priorities. To fund the program described below, we should move toward a foreign aid budget that is 20 percent military security assistance and 80 percent development and humanitarian assistance.

A new foreign aid program should focus on three goals: promoting sustainable development, preventing global warming, and boosting United States exports. One such program was proposed by John W. Sewell and Peter M. Storm of the Overseas Development Council in a 1991 study, *United States Budget for a New World Order*.[37] Their suggestions include a Sustainable Development Fund "to address the interlinked global challenges of environment, poverty, and population growth"; more direct loans from the U.S. Export-Import Bank tied to the purchase of American goods; a Multilateral Reconstruction Fund "to catalyze global efforts to reconstruct and develop areas where major regional conflicts are moving toward resolution"; a Middle East Peace Account for "specifically identified programs associated with the Middle East peace effort"; increased debt relief; a special Development Fund for Africa; and increased funding for refugee assistance.

No new spending would be required. Where would the money come from for such ambitious plans? From reductions in old cold war programs. There are the Base Rights Programs, which were part of the cold war containment strategy of circling the Soviet Union with a ring of bases. There is Foreign Military Financing, which contributes to regional arms races and not stability, and also derives from the cold war era of "national security as military security."

The Middle East Peace Account would be funded at an annual level of $5 billion. One early strong candidate would be money for promoting regional solutions to impending fresh water shortages.

Sewell and Storm note that before the Third World debt crisis, developing countries were major markets for United States exports. The loss of these customers has been disastrous: "In the second half of the

1980s, the debt crisis resulted in a loss of more than $60 billion of potential U.S. exports each year, causing the loss of an estimated 1.5 million jobs by the end of the decade. Growth in non-OECD export markets, therefore, will be important to narrowing the U.S. trade deficit and maintaining U.S. international economic strength."[38] They propose $6 billion in funding for debt relief over the next five years (as compared with the Bush request of $714 million over three years). The authors do not propose doing so, but such debt relief should be given preferentially to those countries that agree to reduce military expenditures, to accept strict export/import controls on weapons transfers, and to abide by other global security standards as they are developed.

The Sustainable Development Fund would become the centerpiece of United States foreign aid, reaching a funding level of only $5 billion in 1996. As Sewell and Storm explain, "A focus on energy use would be particularly important. Developing countries will need assistance to use energy more effectively, to identify patterns of industrialization which have less damaging effects on the global environment, and to develop new energy sources for the rural and urban poor."[39]

Promoting exports through foreign credits and subsidized loans will help us remain competitive with the Japanese, who are masters of the technique. I would recommend that the United States link export credits to efforts to combat global warming, giving a boost to emerging United States suppliers of energy efficiency and renewable energy, and helping to ensure that we do not lose this market to Japan and Germany.

The United States has a unique opportunity to help Eastern Europe and the former Soviet republics become economically stable democracies, to help ensure that they never again become our military adversaries. Those who believe America is powerless to help these countries should consider energy aid. Most of these countries are environmental nightmares, heavily dependent on coal. Like the Third World, they cannot hope to prosper without cleaner, more efficient energy systems. Saved energy also frees both domestic investment *and* oil and gas exportable for hard currency to buy more technologies for modernizing industry and agriculture. The cleaner-burning gas, in turn, can displace global warming from European coal.

A variety of approaches would help.[40] Energy-saving equipment

215

should be the target of credits by international lenders, joint ventures, foreign technical advice, and public education. New housing to alleviate shortages should have superwindows and superinsulation. Western expertise should assist in development of oil and especially cleaner-burning natural gas. Improving the efficiency of natural gas pipelines in Eastern Europe and the former Soviet Union is particularly important; those leaky pipelines not only waste a significant amount of energy, but they also are a major contributor to global warming since natural gas is a powerful greenhouse gas.[41] Russian aeroturbine makers could make advanced gas-saving power plants that could quickly displace unsafe nuclear reactors. A fund should be established to keep former Soviet weapons scientists busy on these and other sustainable energy projects. Creating an effective and efficient transportation infrastructure should be an early project for the former Soviet republics, which lose much of their harvest because it is not delivered to market on time. An additional benefit of such energy aid is that it would allow Russia to expand oil exports, further reducing the importance of Persian Gulf oil.

Such aid would help Russia's economic, and hence political, reforms succeed, which would diminish the possibility that that country would return to its expansionist policies, which could in turn provide a justification for increasing the United States defense budget later in the decade.

One final note about Pentagon spending will bring the analysis full circle to the discussion of fast-cycle manufacturing in the Introduction. This chapter has focused on how defense spending might be reduced by canceling weapons systems and shrinking force structure, rather than by improving program management and eliminating waste. Pentagon procurement policies are a morass that hundreds of studies, blue-ribbon commissions, and the like have not been able to clean up. What is required is not trimming fat around the edges but a lean-production revolution in the defense industry.

Weapons contractors need to adopt flexible manufacturing. As J. Fred Bucy, the former president of Texas Instruments, wrote in 1990, the adoption of fast-cycle manufacturing by the Defense Department "should allow the United States to have the most modern armed forces in the world at *half* the current $300 billion budget" (emphasis in original).[42] That would represent a complete reorientation of an industry well known

216

for perhaps the slowest of all production cycles. Some weapons appear more than a decade after they are conceived.

Flexible manufacturing allows production lines to rapidly switch from one product to another, a key advantage in a world of vanishing weapons production lines. The Pentagon's Manufacturing Technology Program was intended to promote multipurpose defense assembly lines, but the Bush administration has proposed that the 1992 budget for this program be cut by 70 percent.[43]

Another advantage to the country would be a more rapid response time of our defense industrial base. Right now there is no global threat on the horizon, and America can safely cut its military forces and budget in half. Some are concerned that this build-down would be difficult to reverse if a new threat arose. As noted above, achieving the awesome power America demonstrated in Desert Storm would take many years of highly visible effort by a nation or group of nations. Therefore, the United States would have time to respond if we were unable to use diplomatic and economic measures to stem the threat. If the United States defense industry were to develop the ability to do research, development, and production of weapons in half the current time, we could respond to any new threat very quickly—far quicker than the threat itself could develop. Indeed, the ability to rapidly build up our military would be almost as great a deterrent to a potential enemy as the overwhelming firepower we demonstrated in the Persian Gulf War.

Achieving fast-cycle manufacturing for weapons is an important national goal and will require a new, cooperative approach by Congress, the Pentagon, the White House, and defense contractors. Such a reorientation should not be impossible for a military that so successfully applied the fast-cycle approach in the Persian Gulf War.

The United States can unilaterally and significantly reduce its planned spending on defense, intelligence, and military-nuclear programs over the next ten years with no loss of military security. At the same time we stand to gain in overall national security if the savings are transferred to a variety of environmental, energy, and economic security measures, including deficit reduction. Similarly, a refocused foreign aid program can increase our military security while increasing our economic and environmental security, by attacking the root causes of regional conflict and encouraging demilitarization. Even deeper defense cuts are possible through the creation of a wholly new global security arrangement based on cooperation and prevention. Such an arrangement will require a new vision of the future, where the Third World is seen as a partner in global sustainable development, not as a military threat, a vision based on an understanding that the era of national security as military security is over.

8

Conclusion: The End of Isolationism

Although I am fully convinced of the truths of the views given in this volume . . . , I by no means expect to convince experienced naturalists whose minds are stocked with a multitude of facts all viewed, during a long course of years, from a point of view directly opposite to mine. . . . [B]ut I look with confidence to the future—to young and rising naturalists, who will be able to view both sides of the question with impartiality.

—Charles Darwin, *The Origin of Species*

With models of remarkable economic growth and social change around the planet, why does this country remain stuck with failing policies? Why are the nation's leaders unable to see the urgent need for change? One reason may be that they have not experienced the problems facing the 80 percent of Americans whose incomes have stagnated or declined since the early 1970s.

A $62,000 total annual income will put a family in the upper class— the richest 20 percent of Americans, whose incomes grew rapidly in the last decade and a half. An $80,000 income puts a family in the top 10 percent, where income growth was even higher, and a $100,000 income puts a family in the top 5 percent, where income growth exceeded 50 percent.

Change would require that those who run the country *observe* America's problems, *reorient* their thinking, *decide* what new policies are needed, and then *act*. But most of those in positions of power and influence—the politicians, the business leaders, the media, the academics, the public policy experts—are in the top 20 percent. They are among the fifty million Americans who have thrived since the mid-1970s. They can afford to own their own homes, send their children to good schools, see the best doctors, and in general avoid or minimize most economic, social, and environmental troubles that afflict their fellow citizens. They have become disconnected. The fortunate fifth of Americans observe only a rosy world.

If I have been more critical of the Republicans than the Democrats on these pages, it is primarily because the Republicans control the White House and only the President can articulate and put in place a new, coherent strategy for the country. The modern Republican party remains oblivious to most of the problems that afflict the bottom 80 percent of Americans, perhaps because it has traditionally been the party that believes that enriching the top 20 percent is the way to help the other 80 percent. Further, the principles that dominate countries like Japan— that government has a role in solving a nation's economic and environmental problems, and that national security is more than military security—has historically been difficult for the Republican party to accept.

In theory, the Democratic party is the party of the middle class and the poor, and as such is supposedly more sensitive to the stagnation most Americans have been experiencing. For the Democrats it is not so much a failure of observation, although that is part of the problem, but rather a failure of orientation. They have become the party of the status quo, defenders of the old big government programs, many of which are no longer relevant to the problems facing this country. Popular proposals such as extended unemployment insurance and tax cuts may make the pain easier for the middle class to bear in the short term, but they offer no long-term hope.

The nation faces two paths.

The first path is a continuation of current policies. Perhaps military spending is cut a little faster; perhaps a few innovative programs to boost manufacturing are put in place. But no comprehensive or systematic approach is taken, funding is meager, and the executive branch undercuts those programs. Our energy and environmental policies remain largely unchanged.

The vibrant economy, abundant energy supply, and clean environment that since 1945 we had taken for granted, almost as a birthright, continue

220

to disappear. We enter a long period of slow growth, where the bottom four fifths of Americans will have stagnating or declining living standards, where home ownership, higher education, adequate health care, and high-paying jobs are becoming increasingly difficult to attain. The aging population strains the social security and medical systems.

This downward path is self-reinforcing. Personal savings do not increase significantly, as Americans struggle to maintain their life-styles. The federal deficit does not shrink, as slow growth leads to increased failures of businesses and savings institutions, which in turn causes even slower growth in revenues but increased expenditures. Deficits grow for state governments, which are increasingly forced to solve problems ignored by the federal government. The infrastructure and educational systems do not receive needed improvements. Our competitiveness in the global market declines further.

The two parties do not work together. Vitriolic partisan squabbling continues to foster a domestic policy logjam. The politics of hate and division grow. Already we can see, in the growing white middle-class resentment toward affirmative action and the rise of hate-preaching fringe politics, the mistaken belief that good jobs are hard to get because minorities and women have taken them, when in fact it is a dozen years of slow-growth or no-growth policies that have wiped out those good jobs by the millions.

America doubled its prison population in the 1980s, surpassing the former Soviet Union in the total number of prisoners and South Africa in prisoners per capita. The slow-growth policies of the 1980s saw the poor get poorer; the no-growth policies of the 1990s, coupled with tightened state and federal budgets and declining middle-class generosity, will not reverse the increasing poverty or imprisonment rates of the poor. Nor will antidrug policies that focus on drug supply rather than demand. Our cities will continue to sicken, and tragedies such as the spring 1992 riots in Los Angeles will become more common.

Just as narrow-vision politicians drive a wedge between the middle class and the poor, they drive a wedge between the middle-class and the environment, arguing—again mistakenly—that protecting the environment is antijobs. The politics of obfuscation and delay triumph, and we lose a crucial decade in the struggle against global warming, overpopulation, and other major problems facing the planet. For the majority of

221

Americans whose quality of life is already hanging by a thread, each environmental insult—urban smog and asthma, ozone depletion and cancer, global warming and drought—is particularly devastating.

The absence of a strong civilian industrial policy means that so-called free trade will further depress Americans' livings standards. That likelihood, coupled with slow growth relative to Japan, leads to a broad array of protectionist measures by the United States, matched by a united Europe's growing fear of both America and Asia. America's domestic political bickering is mirrored by the growth of international trade disputes and the crystallization of three distinct trading blocs. Japan's high-investment policies allow it to surpass the United States in total GNP by 2010—only a few years away. Japan's regional industrial policy turns Asia into the most powerful bloc in terms of manufacturing and high technology. With its stronger history of government intervention in the economic market, the European bloc, led by a united Germany, forges ahead of the United States into second place behind the Japanese-led Asian bloc. America trails, a poor third.

Failure to achieve international agreements on the environment, coupled with America's declining international generosity (caused in part by the slow growth and ballooning debt), hinders Third World efforts to achieve sustainable development. The Third World splits into two groups: a minority who achieves fossil fuel-based growth at the expense of the environment, and the majority who wallow in poverty and overpopulation, which also leads to environmental degradation through deforestation, unsustainable agriculture, and water pollution. Global warming accelerates, environmental refugees flee by the millions, and regional instability increases.

There is an alternative to that grim script.

Here is a road map to a better tomorrow: We reallocate our energy budget to emphasize energy efficiency and renewable power, while terminating billions of dollars in wasteful subsidies. We reduce the defense and intelligence budget by $100 billion a year more than currently planned. These savings go toward (1) deficit reduction; (2) the development of critical technologies, including pollution minimization, advanced materials, information and communications, biotechnology, resource-efficient technologies, advanced low-fuel transportation technologies, and state-of-the-art manufacturing techniques; (3) low-cost capital, loans, and tax breaks to foster the spread of these technologies into businesses; (4) public funding ranging from prenatal care and Head Start to worker training and retraining required to create a twenty-first-century labor force; and (5) infrastructure needed to support high-technology industry, employment, and worker training, with special emphasis on mass transit as well as schools, government buildings, and low-income housing, all highly energy efficient. (A deeper dent in the deficit could be made by a moderate tax increase on the wealthiest 10 percent of Americans.)

The energy policies alone stand to put $100 billion to $200 billion a year back into American households, businesses, and schools, while minimizing environmental degradation. The economic policies should succeed in fostering high-paying jobs in construction, manufacturing, science, and engineering, and a host of related service jobs, including environmental control, transportation, retail trade, education, and the many white-collar jobs associated with thriving industries. The ultimate goal must be the evolution of an industrial ecosystem, a "clean" production system that increases living standards while reducing energy use and preserving or improving the environment.

The United States redirects its foreign aid budget to emphasize sustainable development and reduction of global environment problems. A new international order based on collective security, demilitarization, and environmentally sustainable development permits deep reductions in United States military spending in the second half of the decade and increased American exports to the developing world, which, with our help, leap-frogs directly into growth based on energy and resource efficiency. Global climate change will be minimized in the short run, providing breathing room for the transition to a system based on renewable energy.

This path is also self-reinforcing. The increase in investment by the government, coupled with deficit reduction, leads to rising incomes, increased growth, and rising federal and state revenues, which in turn leads to even higher levels of investment. Steady growth and declining federal deficits make a trade war less likely, while increasing the political and budgetary prospects for both domestic and global efforts aimed at protecting the environment.

America must adopt this path if it is to be a superpower in the fullest sense of the word.

*   *   *

The policies I recommend do not require sudden, drastic change; they are evolutionary. The defense cuts are spread over five to ten years, the improvements in energy efficiency, carbon dioxide emissions, manufacturing, and worker training will also take place over many years. The transition to renewable power, the industrial ecosystem, and sustainable development may take twenty to forty years. The model for change is flexible manufacturing: steady, incremental improvements in efficiency. Nevertheless, redirecting our current path may be extremely difficult because, while the changes themselves are evolutionary, the shift in thinking required to make those changes is revolutionary.

Although our current downward path is based on an increasingly outmoded and ineffective approach to the nation's major problems, that approach is in some respects also a systematic one. The idea of national security as military security and the military-oriented industrial policy are a legacy of the successful battle to win the cold war. As I have argued throughout this book, it was systematic in the sense that almost every aspect of American policy was devoted to its success. Our energy policy is not systematic, but it is a coherent supply-side industrial policy based on fossil fuels and nuclear power. It is a legacy of our now-fading resource abundance and an archaic definition of energy security. Our environmental policy, though neither systematic nor coherent, is hostage to our misguided energy and economic policies.

Worthwhile or not, our current set of national security policies represents a paradigm—a worldview, a common orientation. In the absence of a new worldview, the status quo will endure. It is difficult enough to change horses in midstream, but it is impossible if there is no horse to change to.

The other key force thwarting change is the very nature of policy-making. A new set of national security policies can be created and put in place only by the executive branch. Congress, by its very committee structure, appoaches problems piecemeal. And even if the Congress enacted a comprehensive set of policies in one area, say a civilian industrial policy, the executive branch could always undercut its intent through lax enforcement or implementation. No systematic approach can work if the people responsible for making it work oppose it philosophically. As the earlier discussion of the Persian Gulf victory and flexible manufacturing make clear, it is the nature of a systematic approach that every element

224

of the system must work together smoothly, so that the positive aspects are reinforced and the negative ones minimized. All of those involved in creating the new system must have a common orientation, and by this I do not mean rigidly identical views, but rather a common perspective on the key national goals. The Congress can no more impose a new national security paradigm on the White House than the production-line workers of a company can impose flexible manufacturing on the managers. If everyone is not moving in the same direction, the only result will be chaos.

Congress shares the blame for the nation's problems; in the absence of an alternative vision for America's economic security, military spending has become a jobs program for congressional politicians of both parties. Nevertheless, America's national security policies—the energy, environmental, economic, and military security agendas of the nation— are embodied in the President. Without radically different presidential leadership, we will continue down the grim path.

Focusing on economic, energy, and environmental security while reducing the emphasis on military security is often labeled a return to isolationism, as if the term must be linked solely to our global military capabilities. But in a broader sense we have already become isolationist. Consider, as one example, our response to one of the major global security issues of the twenty-first century, global warming. Instead of leading the way in global efforts to solve the problem, we weaken international treaties, and short-change our own domestic funding for the energy technologies that can solve the problem.

America is the largest source of most pollutants—toxic waste, greenhouse gases. We use more energy than any other country. Our overuse of resources makes them scarcer and more expensive for Third World countries. Nations are inspired by our democratic values, but we are no development model for them. The rest of the world cannot possibly adopt our life-style without destroying the planet, but we do not seem to notice.

Our economic problems, particularly our budget deficit, make us stingy with countless nations that deserve our help—Eastern Europe, the former Soviet republics, Panama, and the like. Another Marshall Plan—$100 billion in today's dollars—is inconceivable. We give the lowest amount of overseas development assistance as a percentage of GNP of any industrialized country.

225

Is this how a superpower leads the world?

Our overemphasis on military solutions to problems such as drugs and energy, our military-oriented foreign aid, the myth of the Third World military threat—all these hinder efforts to promote environmentally sustainable development and to deal with the root causes of Third World problems. If we cling to the view that global problems can be solved only militarily and only *after* they erupt into regional conflict, we will remain isolated from the world's real problems of poverty, overpopulation, environmental degradation, and unsustainable development, much like an upper-class suburban family that believes the security problems of the inner city can be solved by hiring more cops.

In redefining security, we redefine isolationism and leadership. Our current downward path is the isolationist one. The upward path of collective global security, demilitarization, reoriented foreign aid, and resource-efficient global growth can end our isolationism and restore our leadership position.

National security issues are those problems that take precedence over all others. Former Soviet Foreign Minister Eduard Shevardnadze offered one of the most sensible and succinct descriptions of those problems in 1988:

> The struggle between two opposing systems is no longer a determining tendency of the present-day era. At the modern stage, the ability to build up material wealth at an accelerated rate on the basis of front-ranking science and high-level techniques and technology, and to distribute it fairly, and through joint efforts to restore and protect the resources necessary for mankind's survival acquires decisive importance.[1]

That is a statement from a Russian that could not have been imagined even three years earlier. If such a rigid, inefficient, and despotic society can even ponder so profound a paradigm shift, surely our own more flexible, pragmatic, and democratic society can make the necessary changes.

Here is where security lies.

Appendix

Pseudoscience and SDI

*There is no defense in science against the weapons
which can destroy civilization.*

—Albert Einstein, 1946

Scientists and technical experts inside and outside the military have repeatedly examined the latest idea for defending this country against long-range missiles and found it to be unworkable. Then, within a few years, a new idea, invariably a copy of an earlier, failed proposal, rises from the dead. Yet, after thirty-five years of research, development, testing and retesting, and tens of billions of taxpayer dollars, the basic technical problems remain unsolved, and the principal rationale for missile defense—defending against a Soviet nuclear attack—has vanished.

Nevertheless, the nation is once again poised to let strategic defenses suck scarce dollars from the national security budget: In his September 27, 1991, address to the nation on post-cold war defense policy, President Bush said America must "fully fund" the Strategic Defense Initiative (SDI) and deploy a defensive system; that would cost the nation $120 billion over the next fifteen years. By the end of 1991, Congress had signed on to plans for deploying a ground-based system and left the door open for deploying the entire system.

This Appendix examines the technical problems besetting so-called Star Wars weapons, and why currently proposed defenses (for instance, space-based rocket interceptors called Brilliant Pebbles) are no more

227

promising than the earlier incarnations. In previous chapters, I explained some of the reasons America underinvests in civilian technologies vital to the nation's security, such as energy efficiency, renewable technology, flexible manufacturing, and industrial development. It is equally important to understand how America came to overinvest scarce research and development dollars in a program rejected by most scientists and engineers as incapable of contributing to the nation's security. It is a cautionary tale of inflexible thinking.

Consider an April 1989 comment on the classic Star Wars weapon—lasers—by Major General Eugene Fox, then acting deputy director of the SDI Organization:

> The trail to prove the military worth of the directed energy weapons is longer than I had anticipated. I don't know whether I would call lasers a disappointment, but they have not come along as fast as I thought they would.[1]

That assessment, an unusually candid departure from the persistently optimistic SDI progress reports, would have come as no surprise if the normal methods and processes of science had not been abandoned in the selling of SDI. The scientific consensus on such weapons has always been pessimistic. The very day of President Reagan's SDI speech in 1983, two Air Force generals directing laser weapon programs had warned Congress of the gigantic technical obstacles to achieving a laser missile defense; one of them specifically recommended against an acceleration of the laser program.[2]

But their cautions were brushed aside when President Reagan announced his quest for an impenetrable strategic shield. As enthusiasts rallied to the cause, politics eclipsed science. Strongly pushed by the president, SDI advanced with the cheerleading of executive branch science advisers, the evasion of critical reviews, and the stifling of internal dissent. SDI capitalized on a generally scientifically uninformed public, favorable media images, and the hesitations of policymakers confronted with what appeared to be confusing scientific claims. While some good science and engineering has been done under the aegis of the SDI program, overall SDI has been pseudoscience at its worst.

228

Science and Pseudoscience

Science philosopher Karl Popper distinguished science from pseudoscience in part by the methods each employs. Pseudoscience, he said,
advances a theory, then searches for positive examples to corroborate
the hypothesis. The scientific method does the opposite. It seeks out any
proof that the theory is wrong. If we are genuinely searching for the
truth, we should subject our theories to the most relentless criticism, in
the hope that if it is false it will reveal itself to be false.[3] According to
Popper:

> The point is that whenever we try to propose a solution to a problem,
> we ought to try as hard as we can to overthrow our solution, rather
> than defend it. Few of us, unfortunately, practise this precept; but
> other people, fortunately, will supply the criticism for us if we fail to
> supply it ourselves. Yet criticism will be fruitful only if we state our
> problem as clearly as we can and put our solution in a sufficiently
> definite form—a form in which it can be critically discussed.[4]

By this criterion, SDI has not produced good science. The SDI Organization has relentlessly focused only on blue skies, never on obstacles.
Worse, it has attempted to discredit critics rather than carefully test its
hypotheses against their critiques. Moreover, it has failed to state clearly
the problems SDI is supposed to address. In most cases it has also failed
to put its proposals in a "sufficiently definite form," to use Popper's
phrase, keeping the design of future defenses so nebulous that any criticism can be countered with a brief assertion that the problem is going
to be solved by future breakthroughs.

SDI differs with strategic defense proposals advanced prior to 1983.
Those earlier proposed "solutions" were put in the definite form of specific defense designs and underwent a critical review within the defense
community. And as a result of that scrutiny they were roundly rejected.

The Past as Prologue

Over the past thirty-five years, strategic defense proponents have
often based their proposals on exaggerated or even false scientific claims.

They have trumpeted numerous systems; each was to be a major technological breakthrough, each could be built quickly and cheaply. Each would keep us safe from enemy missiles. At every turn, the scientific and military establishments were accused of obstructing progress. They were labeled nay-sayers, afraid to leap to a new world of strategic defense against the terrifying ballistic missiles. A "Luddite mentality," Vice President Dan Quayle called it in a 1989 speech.[5] But until 1983, those so-called "Luddite" scientists and soldiers critical of missile defenses held the upper hand.

Before SDI, the Army organization now known as the Strategic Defense Command was the main focus of ballistic missile defense development. While the Army was frequently enthusiastic about its latest program, civilian scientists and engineers within the Defense Department provided a critical perspective. And antidefense countermeasures were regularly flight-tested against the Army systems, providing an essential sanity check on claims for the capabilities of defense.

As a result, in the 1960s and 1970s, technical arguments eventually prevailed over political enthusiasm for ground-based defenses. SDI supporters now acknowledge that the missile defenses then proposed could have been readily overwhelmed or blinded by attack on their large and vulnerable radars. Congress funded a system of one hundred nuclear-tipped interceptors at Grand Forks, North Dakota, during the early 1970s for political reasons: Congress did not want to undermine President Richard Nixon's negotiating position in the Strategic Arms Limitation Talks then under way, and the Soviets had deployed a limited system of their own around Moscow. However, by 1975 all agreed that it was not worth keeping the expensive system operating.

At the same time, more exotic space-based defenses, similar to some of those now under development in the SDI program, were being examined. The BAMBI (ballistic missile boost intercept) program was envisioned as a network of hundreds of rocket interceptors based on satellites, each equipped with an infrared sensor to home in on Soviet missiles in the boost phase—essentially the same idea as current "space-based interceptor" or "Brilliant Pebbles" concepts.

BAMBI was abandoned in 1962. According to Dr. Robert Cooper, former Reagan administration director of DARPA, BAMBI was rejected when "it was decided that the expense and the vulnerability of that system to direct attack was too high" and that "the probability of BAMBI ever being a cost-effective system" was low. On the survivability issue, Cooper told Congress in 1987 that even today, "in the judgment of a vast majority of conservative engineering opinion, there is just no way to deal with it."[6]

Space-based defenses resurfaced in the first few years of the Reagan administration, but they were again dismissed on technical grounds. Retired General Daniel Graham promised that by using "off-the-shelf" technology, our nation could build a BAMBI-like network of several hundred satellites called the High Frontier. But a 1982 Air Force Space Division analysis concluded that the High Frontier "has no technical merit and should be rejected. . . . No alternate configuration supported a favorable conclusion." Another Defense Department analysis stated: "It is the unanimous opinion of the Air Force technical community that the High Frontier proposals are unrealistic regarding state of technology, cost and schedule."[7]

Another possible defensive system, space-based chemical lasers, was also judged to be unpromising.[8] General Bernard Randolph warned a House committee on March 23, 1983, that a laser weapons system would require many megawatts of power, would need a precision mirror much larger than any yet manufactured, would weigh 150,000 pounds, and would cost "many, many billions of dollars." He explained that to point the system at a target would be like pointing "from the Washington Monument to a baseball on the top of the Empire State Building and hold it there while both of you are moving. . . . As a technologist, I view the whole thing with a fair amount of trepidation."[9]

Presidential Science

With SDI, the Reagan administration took a different approach. Part of the change was a reflection of President Reagan himself. Reagan came to office with no scientific or technical background, with enormous faith in American science and technology, and with a strong will to believe that there must be some way to protect the United States from Soviet nuclear attack other than relying on the threat of retaliation.

Reagan's technological optimism and will to believe in defense made him vulnerable to the urgings of missile-defense enthusiasts, particularly Edward Teller. From 1981 to 1983, Teller repeatedly briefed the President and his key advisers on what he saw as the enormous promise of the nuclear-pumped X-ray laser, called Excalibur, being researched at Lawrence Livermore National Laboratory.[10]

Some of Teller's specific claims for the X-ray laser, made after Reagan's Star Wars speech, have since been declassified. In 1984, Teller wrote: "A single X-ray laser module the size of an executive desk which applied this technology could potentially shoot down the entire Soviet land-based missile force." In fact, there was and is no scientific evidence to support that statement. Dr. Roy Woodruff, then director of Livermore's Defense Systems programs, warned that Teller's claims were "overly optimistic" and "technically inaccurate," and eventually resigned in protest. Livermore senior scientist Dr. George Maenchen was more direct. "All these claims are totally false," he said. "They lie in the realm of pure fantasy." But that is not what Reagan heard. Teller and others had convinced him that strategic defense could work and work soon.[11]

Preparation of Reagan's Star Wars proposal, like the Iran-contra effort, was held within a small inner circle of staff, bypassing the normal channels of review that might have pointed out potential problems.[12] The secretaries of state and defense heard of the "surprise" proposal only days before it was to be made, and both Secretary of State George Shultz and Assistant Secretary of Defense Richard Perle made strenuous efforts to stop or alter the speech. While Reagan had discussed the idea of missile defense with the Joint Chiefs of Staff, they were reportedly appalled by the President's leap from their cautious support for additional research to his vision of an all-encompassing shield. Top Pentagon technical experts, such as DARPA director Robert Cooper and director of defensive systems John Gardner, said they were not consulted about Reagan's initiative.[13]

Unfortunately, the White House office where the President should have been able to turn for objective science opinion—the Office of the Science Adviser to the President—was compromised. Reagan's science adviser, George Keyworth, was one of the few administration scientists consulted before the March 23 speech, but even he did not see the document that provided the basis for the speech until March 19. Keyworth did not discuss the new initiative with his own advisory body, the White House Science Council (WHSC). Keyworth did not think his job was to represent the views of the scientific community. As the *National Journal* wrote in November 1985: "Within the White House, Keyworth functions more as a promoter of the president's policies than as an adviser with frequent access to the Oval Office." Responding to these charges in a *Physics Today* interview, Keyworth acknowledged that "the criticism is just." Earlier, he had said that the WHSC "is a tool of the president, not a tool of the scientific community. This is the president's home and we are guests here. The WHSC members behave like very dedicated and responsible guests."[14]

Had Keyworth felt it his job to give the President the considered judgment of the scientific community, his advice on the feasibility of a space shield would surely have been negative, for outside the power cocoon that shielded the President from objective advice, the scientific community was almost unanimously skeptical of SDI. An October 1986 survey of the National Academy of Sciences showed that 98 percent of its members in disciplines most relevant to SDI research thought SDI would never provide an effective defense of American cities. Similarly, a 1986 poll of the nation's physicists found that 87 percent believed that even if a system could be designed against today's threat, it was either "very likely" or "somewhat likely" that the Soviet Union could soon develop effective countermeasures. Most of "the vast middle class of engineers working in strategic defense today" are similarly skeptical according to former DARPA director Cooper.[15]

But Keyworth was not about to present these critical scientific views to the President. Not only did he see his role as supporting the President's programs, but he also was a Teller protégé, recommended by Teller for the science adviser job.[16] Keyworth immediately became a strong public advocate of SDI and, two years later, repeated Teller's most extravagant X-ray-laser claims in a speech at Livermore. From the outset, SDI received no serious scientific review within the White House. Unfortunately, the other normal channels of technical and military review within the executive branch were bypassed as well.

Evading Pentagon Review

Reagan's 1983 speech presented the Defense Department with a presidential call for a new program, but no clear road map for carrying it out. In response, the Defense Technologies Study Team, better known as the Fletcher Commission, was created. But here again, the methods of pseudoscience prevailed: The Fletcher Commission's mandate was not so much to examine *whether* the President's vision could be accomplished, but to determine *how* it could be, and the commission was staffed with an overwhelming majority of strong supporters of missile defenses. Even Gerold Yonas, chief scientist for the SDI program, noted that the process that led to the decision to develop space-based defense "would have been less disturbing had the studies been carried out quietly before the President made his specific program request in public."[17] The commission eventually completed a several-volume report on the technologies of missile defense, recommending a five-year, $26 billion research program. According to one former Pentagon weapons analyst: "If you read volume seven [the classified concluding section of the Fletcher report], you wouldn't bother reading the rest of the report. It presents an overwhelming case against the possibility of a hope of mounting something useful. It quite unambiguously indicates the problem was insolvable unless certain things were solved that no one even knew how to address."[18] But the full report remains classified: Only a brief optimistic summary was ever released to the public.

With the Fletcher Commission's recommendations in hand, the Strategic Defense Initiative Organization (SDIO) was inaugurated in 1984 under the leadership of Lieutenant General James Abrahamson. Abrahamson soon became known for a style of intense and adversarial advocacy, unusual even in the Defense Department.

The establishment of the SDIO was a watershed, for by taking overall control of missile-defense efforts away from the military services, the program was exempted from all the normal processes of military and technical review, critical or otherwise, within the Pentagon. Under normal circumstances, any program has to compete for resources against other military programs, with the military services and field commanders playing a strong role in deciding the outcome. A new development program is undertaken when a military requirement for a new weapon is approved by the Joint Chiefs of Staff, and the program is then regularly reviewed by the Defense Acquisition Board (DAB), which can call on the Defense Science Board for technical advice. This system often does not produce the best weapons at the lowest cost, but it is certainly better than going forward with no review at all, which was the approach taken with SDI. With Reagan's support, SDI instantly became exempt from the rough-and-tumble of Pentagon budget battles. And until 1987, SDI was managed entirely outside the normal weapons-acquisition process, with no Joint Chiefs of Staff requirement, no DAB review, and no consideration by the Defense Science Board, the Pentagon's primary technical advisers.

SDI was shifted into the normal acquisition process for the first time in 1987, as SDI supporters hoped for greater legitimacy within the Defense Department and more support from the uniformed services. But the result was the opposite: External reviews immediately began to cast the cold light of truth and reality on the program's major technical and military flaws.

First, the Joint Chiefs of Staff created a "requirement" for the system, and the SDIO came up with a "Phase I" architecture intended to meet that requirement. For the first time, reviewers had something specific to address—a proposal in "definite form," in Popper's terms—and it did not look good. The Joint Chiefs of Staff requirement reportedly called for a defense that could stop only 30 percent of a limited "first wave" Soviet attack, leaving 70 percent of the Soviet missile warheads untouched, and providing no protection at all for American cities. When this specific goal became well known, SDIO's claim that defenses would protect the American people from nuclear war became even more difficult to sustain.

Just as important, the specific "architecture" for a first-phase defense that the SDIO proposed simply could not stand up to scrutiny. In 1987, when the Defense Science Board was finally called upon to review the program—years after the Board should have been consulted—it issued a devastating report: The Board listed as "missing technology" such basic items as the ability to protect the space battle stations from attack, the space-based interceptors' ability to find and hit Soviet missiles, the sensors' ability to discriminate warheads from decoys, and the possibility of producing the necessary sensors in the first place. The science panel's report recommended against approving the Phase I system for the next phase of development, since there was yet "no way of confidently assessing" its performance, its cost, or its schedule.[19]

But SDI was the President's program, and could not be denied. The science panel's chairman, Robert Everett, reportedly under political pressure, removed the key recommendation against approval from the panel's report to the Defense Acquisition Board. The board then decided to approve SDI's request for an accelerated schedule.

Despite this censoring of the Defense Department's first serious technical review of SDI, the program's troubles were far from over. Over the next year, other analysts, including scientists from the Livermore and the Sandia weapons laboratories and the Congressional Office of Technology Assessment, pointed out simple and inexpensive Soviet countermeasures that could defeat SDI's proposed Phase I architecture.[20]

In addition, the Joint Chiefs of Staff became increasingly concerned about the effect SDI's huge cost would have on other weapons programs.[21] At a second DAB review in June 1988, Abrahamson was told that the projected costs of the Phase I system were too high, and that the amounts of money SDI was planning on spending over the next few years were not going to be available. The SDIO went back to the drawing board, and by the third DAB review in October 1988, virtually every aspect of the system had been redesigned. The SDIO claimed that its new design would cut the cost of the Phase I system by $46 billion, nearly in half. But early in 1989, as soon as analysts began focusing on the weaknesses of this new plan, the SDIO changed it again, announcing a new emphasis on so-called "Brilliant Pebbles," thousands of interceptor rockets circling the earth, programmed to shoot enemy missiles. BAMBI and High Frontier reborn.[22]

SDI's success in evading the negative impact of these reviews, particularly the censoring of the science panel's report, reflected a more widespread phenomenon. With the President so personally tied to the vision of a space shield, support for SDI became a litmus test for loyalty to the administration, the most devastating blow yet to the scientific method. Internal criticism was muted or absent; criticism of the program was viewed as unpatriotic. Hedrick Smith notes that the policy style adopted for SDI "handed great power to a small staff inclined to bow to Reagan's impulses and to filter out dissent."[23]

Unfortunately, this attitude trickled down into the technical program itself, as the case of Teller's critic, Dr. Roy Woodruff, shows: Woodruff's dissent earned him a quick demotion by Livermore director Roger Batzel, and banishment to a windowless office that Woodruff's friends dubbed Gorky West, in reference to the exile of Soviet physicist Andrei Sakharov. That Woodruff's scientific judgment was accurate didn't seem to matter. By allowing Teller's mistakes and misstatements to go uncorrected, the laboratory undermined its own scientific credibility. In 1986, then Undersecretary of Defense Donald Hicks tried to put forward this suppression of internal dissent as official policy, saying that he would advocate cutting off funding to any scientist who showed "disloyalty" by questioning

SDI. "It's a free country," Hicks said, but "freedom works both ways. They're free to keep their mouths shut . . . [and] I'm also free not to give the money."[24] While the Defense Department soon disavowed Hicks's remarks, they were emblematic of the Reagan administration's pseudoscientific approach.

Pseudoscience Comes to Capitol Hill

Congress was a source of outside review for SDI that could not be avoided, since it provided the budget for the program. As in the executive branch, however, attempts to bring a dose of realism to the program were described as playing into Soviet hands, and critics were often branded as unpatriotic. The Congress faced the oft-repeated threat of presidential vetoes if SDI was not adequately funded. Perhaps most important, few in Congress had the technical background to analyze the claims of SDI supporters, and the SDIO did its best to confuse the issue with showy "demonstrations" of dramatic progress and attempts to discredit outside critics.

Those "demonstrations" were a classic example of the self-validation methods of pseudoscience. In 1985, for example, SDI workers shot a laser beam at a Titan missile anchored to the ground at close range; the missile quickly exploded. The SDIO labeled it a successful test, even though a high-powered rifle would also have blown up the thin-skinned missile. Since then, the film of the explosion has been shown hundreds of times on television, generating little meaningful scientific data but much media coverage. Nevertheless, the then director of SDI, General Abrahamson, called this photo opportunity a "world-class breakthrough."[25]

Another 1985 example involved a low-intensity laser, which was bounced off a reflector placed on the space shuttle *Discovery*. Special mirrors adjusted the low-power laser for the distortions of the atmosphere, a feat that had been accomplished in a variety of ground tests in the past. But Defense Secretary Caspar Weinberger called it a "breakthrough" and said, "The barriers that we thought would be high have crumbled. For example, we can now apparently remove the various disintegrating effects of the atmosphere on a laser beam."[26]

In a remarkable attempt to deceive Congress, Weinberger told a congressional committee that "this disposes of the favored sneer of those opposed to strategic defense, that it will only work in good weather," and asserted under questioning that the weather at the time had been "heavy overcast and rain. . . . It was also obscured by smoke from a volcano." Later, when the committee was preparing to publish the transcript of the hearing, the Defense Department notified the committee that *"further research revealed that [the weather] was actually clear"* (emphasis added).[27] In fact, the test had nothing to do with the "bad weather" problem, which is still unsolved. The test contributed little to our understanding of the many serious problems that must be overcome before a high-powered ground-based laser could become a viable weapons system.

Scientists from across the political spectrum have pointed out that such early technology demonstrations do more to slow progress than to enhance it, freezing in technology prematurely and draining funds from more promising approaches. Even Brent Scowcroft, now President Bush's national security adviser, concluded in 1988 that the SDIO's emphasis on such demonstrations is "driven significantly by political considerations—that is, sustaining political support for the program."[28] It remains a serious problem that SDI tests are planned, conducted, interpreted, and publicized by the SDI Organization, which apparently is more committed to promoting the weapons than analyzing them.

Selling SDI to Congress required not only providing plenty of showy demonstrations, but discrediting those who attempted to present a more balanced view, in particular, Congress's own scientific experts at the Office of Technology Assessment (OTA). In 1984, the OTA issued a balanced but pessimistic background paper on directed-energy weapons, concluding among other things that President Reagan's dream was "so remote that it should not serve as the basis of public expectation or national policy about ballistic missile defense." The SDIO immediately swung into action with a stinging reply, accusing the OTA of myriad "fundamental errors." But even Major General John Toomay, a leading member of the Fletcher Commission and a strong supporter of missile defenses, felt compelled to defend the OTA. He charged that the SDIO's attack was "not a competent document," and contained "falsehoods, irrelevancies, and misinterpretations."[29]

By 1988, the SDIO's approach was little changed. When the OTA came to similarly pessimistic conclusions about space-based interceptors (after an extensive study with complete access to classified information), SDIO officials tried to thwart the study by dragging out the declassification process for more than a year after the study's completion. The worst blow for scientific scrutiny came when officials classified all the chapters on potential countermeasures to SDI. Countermeasure studies, undertaken by "red teams" within the SDI program, had long been given short shrift. Here, again, rather than actively seeking out the possible flaws in their system, officials censored the critical study, suppressing the bad news. And when the rest of the study was released, the SDIO still responded with a statement deriding the conclusions as based on "opinions" rather than the SDIO's "empirical data."[30]

The SDIO's treatment of analysts outside the government was even more scurrilous. In 1987, when a prestigious panel assembled by the nonpolitical American Physical Society concluded that we were at least a decade away from knowing whether beam weapons (such as lasers) could ever provide a survivable and cost-effective defense, the SDIO circulated to Congress a package of wild criticisms from SDI supporters, including a statement by one scientist comparing the society's publication of the report to the decline of German science under the Nazis. This ever more extreme effort to discredit any outside review reached its comical height in 1987, when Livermore's Strategic Defenses Systems Studies Group issued a report that made clear how space-based interceptors were weapons of limited capability vulnerable to inexpensive countermeasures. A Defense Department spokesman described the report— from one of the nation's largest SDI contractors—as "just another of those reports by people who, for one reason or the other, don't want us to proceed with defenses against ballistic missiles."[31] *To accept only positive evidence and to attempt to discredit all challenges is the very definition of pseudoscience.*[32]

Science Lessons

The SDI debate took place when numerous studies showed America falling behind most of the West in the basic understanding of science. A survey by the National Science Foundation, for example, found that only 6 percent of Americans could be termed "scientifically literate." Three hundred years after Copernicus, 20 percent of the American public, according to another poll, believed that the sun orbits the earth, while another 7 percent didn't know. Secretary of Education Lauro F. Cavazos asked at the time, "How many times must this nation be reminded of its educational deficit?"[33]

The science gap extends to policymakers. Columnist David Broder notes that "the gap in expertise between the scientists and the politicians is awesome and intimidating." Former Republican Congresswoman Claudine Schneider adds, "Quite honestly, there's a limited participation by most members of Congress on most science issues. There are no experts up here, so rather parochial interests tend to predominate."[34]

SDI entered into this science gap with a "gee whiz" enthusiasm that capitalized on Americans' historic optimism about technological fixes. Americans wanted to believe that the unthinkable horrors of nuclear war, dramatized during the nuclear freeze campaign, could be eliminated by new technology and American scientific power. For the public and policymakers alike, a poor science background made for hesitancy and compromise. Confronted with competing claims about SDI, the public and congressional response was to give SDI some rope—to see whether the program would either yield a true breakthrough or hang itself.

The media played in with a barrage of exciting and favorable images of "Star Wars." The stories were keyed to impressive graphics and computer simulations provided by the SDIO. Lasers blasting missiles in space dominated the coverage (complete with sound effects impossible in the vacuum of space). Even if a reporter's commentary was skeptical of SDI claims, the visuals tended to overwhelm the narrative, leaving an impression of weapons that either existed or soon could exist. SDI proponents used television's limitations to their advantage. The airwaves were full of sound bites: "Destroy weapons not people," "Make nuclear weapons impotent and obsolete," "SDI will work." Sound bites take seconds to assert, but several minutes to rebut. Science came in second to showmanship.

Print journalists as well, with tight schedules and competing stories, often find it easier to run the SDI press release with a few quotes from critics tacked on at the end than to do a deeper, longer, and less dramatic piece about why such systems won't protect America or where all the money has gone. At press conferences on SDI experiments, some journalists have pressed SDI scientists for words like "dramatic progress" or "breakthrough," to make a juicier story.[35]

Moreover, reporters and congressional committees usually confused equal time with balance. Debates or panel presentations typically gave equal time to scientists on both sides, despite the overwhelming scientific consensus skeptical of the program. Thus, a year-long study by a distinguished, independent panel of the American Physical Society would be given the same weight in news stories or congressional hearings as the assertions of a single SDI scientist. Indeed, congressional hearings with any outside perspective at all were a relative rarity: most discussions of SDI featured only officials of the SDIO. Another advantage SDI had over critical organizations in the battle for media attention was enormous public resources.[36]

All of these factors help explain why it took so long for SDI to be exposed as an emperor with no clothes. But above all else, the SDI program was finally doomed by the administration's own pseudoscientific approach: shunning criticism and loyally rallying around whatever proposal was current.

Science is a systematic process. Observations are made. The data are analyzed and then synthesized to create a hypothesis or theory. Finally a test is designed and run. The test provides new observations, which are then compared with those predicted by the theory to see if the theory needs modifications. This process of observation-hypothesis-test is analogous to Boyd's observe-orient-decide-act loop, discussed earlier.[37] Both are dynamic, *self-correcting* processes. In Boyd's framework, constant reorientation is needed because the enemy and the external world are constantly changing. In the scientific method, Nature's physical laws do not change, but the hypothesis is constantly modified and improved as better instruments become available and new data are gathered. In developing new weapons, improvements in enemy technology and possible enemy countermeasures must continually be integrated into the design and testing process. Just as those with a rigid worldview (orientation) are doomed to fail, so, too, are those with an unshakable hypothesis, one impervious to real-world tests.

In 1989, after six years of SDI, and thirty years of strategic defense research, technical progress had been made in areas such as miniaturization, data collection, and sensor fabrication, but it had not been accompanied by the half-dozen or so major breakthroughs necessary to achieve a worthwhile strategic defense. As James Schlesinger, Nixon's defense secretary, said in 1989:

241

SDI remains, at best, a collection of hopes and technical experiments. . . . The TV networks can present the animations or animated cartoons (which they mislabel "news") showing laser beams zapping Soviet missiles during the boost phase. For the moment, that all remains the gleam in the eyes of some technologists—a combination of Buck Rogers and P. T. Barnum.[38]

The absence of breakthroughs, the accumulation of critical reviews, and the Gramm-Rudman budget limits finally took their toll. In 1989, for the first time, Congress reduced SDI's budget from the previous year's funding.[39]

Like a vampire, pseudoscience can survive only if shrouded in the darkness of classified research, secret tests, and see-no-evil analyses. In the light of day—open scientific criticism—it recoils in horror and turns to dust. As Popper said, if we fail to provide the criticism ourselves, others will eventually do it for us.

In 1990, Congress slashed the SDI budget by 25 percent. Even pseudoscience succeeds for only so long—or so it seemed. But with pseudoscience, as with vampires, you must drive the stake through the heart. Anything else is just temporary.

Star Wars has once again been revitalized. The latest reincarnation is called GPALS (global protection against limited strikes), which would rely on hundreds of Brilliant Pebbles, orbiting interceptor rockets. What reawakened Star Wars was the exciting images of the Patriot missile apparently intercepting virtually every Iraqi SCUD missile launched. These images were worth $1 billion in added funding for the program in 1992, as Congress became convinced that effective missile defenses were not only possible, but available. Yet, as discussed in Chapter 6, the images of success were just that—images. The Patriot may have been able to hit debris from parts of the SCUD, such as the fuselage, that broke up during midflight, but an Israeli study reportedly found no evidence that the Patriot actually intercepted and destroyed the warheads, which do the damage. Further analysis has found no evidence that the Patriots reduced ground damage.

Even if the Patriot had been successful, its performance is wholly irrelevant to the reality of SDI's continuous technical failure since 1983. As former Defense Secretary Harold Brown wrote in 1991:

Neither the technology of Patriot nor the task it had to perform bears any close relation to SDI. Patriot was originally built as an air defense system, using technology conceived in the 1960s. In the 1980s, improvements in its software and warheads gave it a limited capability to defend against primitive short-range missiles such as the Iraqi Scuds. None of this involved either funding, technology or management from the SDI program. Nor did it give the Patriot any capability whatever against long-range missiles that might threaten the United States. Even the Scuds, if armed with thermonuclear weapons—whose explosive power is a million times greater than that of conventional explosives—would have posed an insurmountable problem for Patriot.[40]

Using the Patriot's performance in the Persian Gulf War to justify increased funding for the SDI program would be more pseudoscience. But that's just what Congress did.

Politics triumphed over science. Images overcame thoughtful analysis. Patriot became an American success story—and SDI adroitly hitched itself to this rising star.

Led by Sam Nunn and John Warner, chairman and ranking minority member of the Senate Armed Services Committee, and Les Aspin, chairman of the House Armed Services Committee, Congress approved the Missile Defense Act of 1991—authorizing the deployment of a ground-based system at Grand Forks. The dead had risen. This ill-conceived legislation

1. Called for deploying defenses by 1996, faster than even the administration's optimistic schedule;
2. Increased the SDI budget by $1 billion without even the pretense of a cost analysis;
3. Ignored expert testimony that there isn't a threat serious enough to warrant this crash program; and
4. Instead of "redirecting" the SDI program toward ground-based systems, as its authors claimed, gave space-based systems a new lease on life, allowing SDI to justify its existing plans.

Indeed, in December 1991, the director of SDI wrote a remarkable memo to the undersecretary of defense for acquisition about documentation that the SDI Organization was preparing on its space-based GPALS system. The memo stated: "This documentation supports an initial deployment for GPALS toward the end of the decade according to last year's report to Congress—not 1996 as recently called for by Congress." The SDI Organization was already reinterpreting Congress's support of a ground-based system as support for SDI's space-based programs.[41]

Brilliant Mistakes

The SDI office has learned no science lessons. Its current proposal, Brilliant Pebbles, is once again more hype than science. In 1988, proponents claimed each interceptor would weigh only five pounds; carry a miniaturized supercomputer, revolutionary sensors, high-power rockets for maneuverability, and shielding from Soviet attack; and still cost a mere $50,000. As any Pentagon watcher might have predicted, the weight and cost estimates skyrocketed by a factor of 10 within a year. By 1991, the estimated cost per interceptor had reached $1.5 million (30 times the original estimate)—but even that figure is strikingly low compared to the cheapest satellite the Air Force has, the NAVSTAR system, which costs nearly $50 million per satellite, while possessing none of the remarkable capabilities the "Brilliant Pebbles" will require.[42]

The Pebbles have the same problems that have plagued space-based defenses for decades. Studies suggest the Pebbles might not work in a nuclear war environment,[43] they can be shot down by ground-launched antisatellite rockets that cost only one fortieth as much as the Pebbles themselves,[44] and could be underflown by short- and medium-range missiles.[45] Finally, the Pebbles can be bypassed altogether by nuclear weapons delivered into this country on ships sailed into our major harbors or in packing crates smuggled across our borders. Thus, they provide no defense for either ourselves or our allies.

It bears repeating that stopping intercontinental ballistic missiles from entering this country is not the primary proliferation concern facing the United States. Stopping nuclear bombs from entering this country is. Deploying space-based defenses would not protect us from terrorists or fanatical dictators with nuclear bombs, who are unlikely to use ballistic missiles to carry such bombs.

The breakup of the Soviet Union has raised concerns about its nuclear weapons, but CIA director Robert Gates told Congress in 1992 that the intelligence community was "not concerned" about the possibility of an unauthorized launch of strategic or tactical nuclear weapons from the former Soviet Union.[46] Thus, those weapons provide no justification for building strategic defenses. The best way to prevent non-Russian republics from retaining control of nuclear weapons is through effective diplomacy and assistance in order to ensure that all weapons are quickly dismantled and disabled and that all republics join the Nuclear Nonproliferation Treaty.[47]

Such an approach offers far more likelihood of defending this country from unauthorized or accidental nuclear launch than building a defensive system.[48] Our national security does not require that we build every weapons system we can imagine; as *Aviation Week and Space Technology* warned in an editorial: "Strategy has been confused with high technology." Finally, the United States cannot afford space-based defenses.

Pseudo-accounting

The death blow to Star Wars will not be dealt by its critics, but by its budget. The SDI budget for 1992 was increased to more than $4 billion in the aftermath of the Gulf war, but even that funding level is wholly inadequate to satisfy SDI's demands. In May 1991, the director of the SDI program, Henry F. Cooper, told Congress that the SDI program would cost $120 billion through 2005.[49] To "fully fund" this program, as the President called for in September 1991, the SDI budget would have to more than double by the mid-1990s, reaching $10 billion per year in the next century, in order to pay for hundreds of Brilliant Pebbles satellites, dozens of surveillance and tracking satellites, as well as countless ground-based strategic interceptors, antitactical ballistic missiles, and sensors. As discussed in Chapter 7, even this amount is not likely to be enough, since weapons systems invariably grow in cost over time and since any failure of the system after launch would prove very expensive to fix.

Even if the SDI program were a well run weapons program, and even if independent scientific analysis proved that a space-based system could be effective, the budget deficit and the planned cuts in the defense budget mean there is no money to maintain the current funding level, let alone increase it dramatically. But for a program that has been incompetently managed and that is more pseudoscience than science, it is worse than foolish to contemplate doubling or tripling its budget; it is a threat to our national security.

For SDI to rise from 1 percent of the defense budget today to 3 percent in a decade would force the Pentagon to curtail or cancel nuclear and conventional weapons systems that could actually contribute to our nation's military security. Moreover, insofar as plans for components of the proposed SDI system are made based on unrealistic expectations of phenomenal funding growth, more money will be wasted as those plans are cut back. The General Accounting Office noted that the history of the SDI program has been to waste money in such a fashion—"making plans and starting projects on the basis of unrealistic and overly optimistic funding requests and schedules," which in turn repeatedly forced costly adjustments to fit budget constraints.[50] Such self-delusionary planning might be called pseudo-accounting, to match the SDI program's pseudoscience, except that, as discussed in Chapter 7, such accounting has become the Pentagon norm.

Funding for strategic defense research and development should be reduced to under $2 billion a year. Half the money should go to Army programs aimed at defending against tactical ballistic missiles, follow-ons to the Patriot. The other half of the money should go to long-term research on promising new technologies, especially directed energy weapons such as the free-electron laser. Such funding would help protect against military or technological surprises harmful to United States security. Since we know how to defeat space-based chemical rocket systems such as Brilliant Pebbles, there is little point in pursuing their development. The Army should devote a fraction of its funding, say 10 percent, to "red team" research and analysis aimed at countering SDI programs, to serve as a sanity check on such research. The SDIO should perform a similar function for Army programs.

At this funding level, strategic defense would cost America under $30 billion over the next fifteen years, rather than $120 billion as SDIO plans. Our military security would benefit because SDI would not crowd out increasingly scarce defense dollars needed for potent weapons rather than pseudoscience—a particularly serious concern because, as explained earlier, the Pentagon is now putting into the pipeline several other weapons that will require increased funding in the late 1990s. Our national security would benefit because tens of billions of dollars could be shifted from SDI research and development toward either deficit reduction, or, even better, R&D into a host of critical civilian technologies.

Notes

INTRODUCTION: WHY AMERICA BEAT IRAQ BUT LOSES TO JAPAN

1. Boyce Rensberger, "Nerve Cells Redo Wiring," *Washington Post*, June 10, 1985, p. A5; quoted in John Boyd, "The Strategic Game of Interaction and Isolation," unpublished lecture notes, June 1987, p. 16. The article noted: "The research was on adult mice, but since all mammalian nervous systems appear to behave in similar ways, the researchers assume that the findings also apply to human beings."

2. Gunther Blumentritt, "Experience Gained from the History of War on the Subject of Command Technique," January 27, 1947; quoted in John Boyd, "Patterns of Conflict," unpublished lecture notes, December 1986, p. 79.

3. Quoted in Edward Luttwak, *The Pentagon and the Art of War* (New York: Simon and Schuster, 1984), p. 266.

4. James Fallows, *National Defense* (New York: Random House, 1981), p. 28.

5. George Stalk and Thomas Hout, *Competing Against Time* (New York: The Free Press, 1990), p. 109.

6. Ibid., pp. 111–114.

7. Carl von Clausewitz, *On War*, ed. and trans. Howard and Paret (Princeton, N.J.: Princeton University Press, 1976), pp. 119–121.

8. A key breakthrough that made the blitzkrieg possible was General Heinz

249

Guderian's simple decision to put a radio and radio operator in every tank, an innovation that was a major reason the Germans, with fewer tanks, were able to defeat the French and British at the start of World War II. See Fallows, op. cit., p. 28.

9. Tom Peters explains the fast-cycle nature of CNN in his 1991 PBS special, "Speed Is Life."

10. George Stalk, "Time—The Next Source of Competitive Advantage," *Harvard Business Review*, July–August 1988, p. 45.

11. The figures are from Richard Rosecrance, "Too Many Bosses, Too Few Workers," *New York Times*, July 15, 1990, p. F11. The white-collar layoffs announced by many of these companies since Rosecrance wrote his article may have reduced these alarming figures somewhat.

12. Quoted in Boyd, "Patterns of Conflict," op. cit., p. 74. It is ironic that in one of history's most despotic regimes, success came by giving the military freedom.

13. Ibid.

14. Joseph Bower and Thomas Hout, "Fast-Cycle Capability for Competitive Power," *Harvard Business Review*, November–December 1988, p. 111.

15. James Womack et. al., *The Machine That Changed the World* (New York: Macmillan, 1990), pp. 118–119.

16. See U.S. News & World Report, *Triumph Without Victory* (Times Books: New York, 1992), Chapter 10, "The Jedi Knights," pp. 150–172, and "Revenge of the 'Jedi'," *Army Times*, April 22, 1991, pp. 12–14.

17. Luttwak, op. cit., pp. 44–45.

18. Sun Tzu, *The Art of War*, trans. Samuel B. Griffith (London: Oxford University Press, 1971).

19. Stalk (1988), op cit., p. 47.

20. See Peter Drucker, "The Big Three Miss Japan's Crucial Lesson," *Wall Street Journal*, June 18, 1991, and "Nissan's Flexible, 'Thinking' Line for Auto Body Assembly," *New York Times*, August 25, 1991, p. F11.

21. John Boyd, "Patterns of Conflict," op. cit., p. 62.

22. Fallows, op. cit., p. 32.

23. "A Very Old General May Hit the Beach with the Marines," *Wall Street Journal*, January 9, 1991.

24. Quoted in Fred Kaplan, "The Force Was with Them: Army's Jedi Knights Forged Gulf War Strategy," *Boston Globe*, March 17, 1991, p. A23.

25. John Boyd, "The Strategic Game of Interaction and Isolation," op. cit., p. 47.

26. Quoted in U.S. News & World Report, *Triumph Without Victory*, op. cit., p. 263.

27. Quoted in *The New York Times*, February 28, 1991.

28. A good discussion of the maneuver warfare strategy used in the Gulf is G.I. Wilson, "The Gulf War, Maneuver Warfare, and the Operational Art," *Marine Corps Gazette*, June 1991, pp. 23–24.

29. John Boyd, "Patterns of Conflict," p. 86.

30.   Stalk (1988), op. cit., p. 50.

31.   The phrase is from Philip R. Thomas, *Competitiveness Through Total Cycle Time* (New York: McGraw-Hill, 1990), p. 9. Faster cycle time means "increased opportunities to learn from the feedback of experience, which I call Cycles of Learning. Conscientious use of such feedback will, in turn, accelerate results."

32.   The phrase is borrowed from Tom Peters, *Thriving on Chaos* (New York: Harper and Row, 1988), p. 195. The "variety war" is described in Stalk (1988), op. cit.

33.   *New York Times National Edition*, February 25, 1992, p. A16. The advertisement demonstrates that Chrysler understands the importance of fast-cycle manufacturing. That the company has actually put in place the changes needed to achieve a faster product cycle is the subject of the lead article in the March 3, 1992, *The Wall Street Journal*, "Chrysler Is Making Solid Progress in Spite of Executive Turmoil," pp. A1, A10.

34.   Stalk and Hout, op. cit., pp. 32–34.

35.   "U.S. Garment Makers Come Home," *New York Times National Edition*, October 8, 1991, pp. C1, C17. For a more detailed discussion of how faster, more advanced manufacturing helps bring jobs back to America, see "U.S. Companies Come Back Home," *Fortune*, December 30, 1991, pp. 106–112.

36.   See, for instance, Stephen Cohen and John Zysman, *Manufacturing Matters* (New York: Basic Books, 1987), pp. 21–24. The book is devoted to demonstrating the many benefits a nation derives from successful manufacturing. I will discuss these issues at greater length in Chapter 2.

37.   I have concentrated on the importance of Boyd's *strategy* in the Gulf war, because virtually all other analyses have focused on the other key factors, the performance of our highly trained, all-volunteer army and especially our superior surveillance and weapons technology. I tend to agree with General Schwarzkopf's remarks to David Frost, that we would have won had the Iraqis had our weapons and we theirs. Without Boyd's guiding strategy, America's investment in technology and people would not have paid off so remarkably. Another key component of the Gulf victory deserves mention—our investment in military infrastructure. The bases we had built in Saudi Arabia, and the satellite-based reconnaissance and telecommunications network we had put in place were very important in supporting our Gulf strategy. Unfortunately, as I discuss in Chapter 2, another reason for our waning economic vitality is that we have neglected our investment in civilian infrastructure.

38.   Edward Luttwak, "From Geopolitics to Geo-Economics," *The National Interest*, Summer 1990, p. 20.

39.   Thomas Kuhn, *The Structure of Scientific Revolutions*, 2nd ed. (Chicago: University of Chicago Press, 1970), p. 77.

40.   In achieving an updated and unifying definition of "security," there is one specific meaning of the term that is illuminating. The general meaning of the word "security" is "freedom from danger"—from "se-" ("without") and "cure" ("care"). One particular definition of "secure" is "to make firm or fast, by attaching: *to secure a rope.*" To be secure one must be interconnected. Insecurity

derives from disconnection and isolation. Colonel Boyd titles one of his briefings "The Strategic Game of Interaction and Isolation," because an army must maximize both its own interconnections and its adversary's isolation. That is the essence of the strategy the Allies inflicted on Iraq. In the larger sense, achieving national security requires seeing the crucial interactions among economic, energy, environmental, and military policies.

CHAPTER 1: NATIONAL SECURITY, AN EVOLVING IDEA

1. W. W. Rostow, *How It All Began: Origins of the Modern Economy* (New York: McGraw-Hill, 1975), p. 191.
2. Drew McCoy, *The Elusive Republic* (New York: W.W. Norton, 1980), p. 148.
3. Quoted in Rostow, op. cit., pp. 191–192.
4. Quoted in Ralph K. Andrist, ed., *The Founding Fathers, George Washington, A Biography in His Own Words* (New York: Newsweek, 1972). The address was never delivered but was published widely in the 1790s.
5. C. Vann Woodward, "The Age of Reinterpretation," *The American Historical Review,* October 1960, pp. 2–3.
6. Robert Wiebe, *The Search for Order 1877–1920* (New York: Hill and Wang, 1967), p. 248. Chapter 9, "The Emergence of Foreign Policy" (pp. 224–255), discusses the importance of trade and economics to United States foreign policy.
7. Frank Freidel and Alan Brinkley, *America in the Twentieth Century,* 5th ed. (New York: Alfred A. Knopf, 1982), pp. 81–82.
8. Albert Hirschman, *National Power and the Structure of Foreign Trade* (Berkeley, Calif.: University of California Press, 1945; expanded ed., 1980), p. 54.
9. Friedel and Brinkley, op. cit., pp. 280–281.
10. Nicholas J. Spykman, *America's Strategy in World Politics: The United States and the Balance of Power* (New York: Harcourt, Brace, & Co., 1942). See also Hirschman, op. cit.
11. Quoted in Daniel Yergin, *Shattered Peace: The Origins of the Cold War and the National Security State* (Boston: Houghton Mifflin Co., 1977), p. 194.
12. In their discussion of the development of the concept of national security for their entry in the *International Encyclopedia of the Social Sciences,* Morton Berkowitz and P.G. Bock give Walter Lippmann the credit as the person "who first defined national security explicitly" (see below). Berkowitz and Bock, "National Security," in David L. Sills, ed., *International Encyclopedia of the Social Sciences,* Vol. 11 (New York: Macmillan, 1968), pp. 40–45.
13. Robert Post "National Security and the Amended Freedom of Information Act," *Yale Law Journal,* Vol. 85 (January 1976), p. 410.
14. Yergin (1977), op. cit., p. 5.
15. The historian John Lewis Gaddis has noted the federal government's "key decision to rely on the economic rather than the military instruments of containment in the late 1940s." *American Historical Review Forum,* April 1984, p. 383.

16. An excellent discussion of the myriad ways that American cold war export controls have hurt United States competitiveness can be found in Robert Kuttner, *The End of Laissez-Faire* (New York: Alfred A. Knopf, 1991), pp. 197–209.

17. The report also stated that "the Soviet Union, unlike previous aspirants to hegemony, is animated by a new fanatic faith, antithetical to our own, and seeks to impose its absolute authority over the rest of the world," and "the cold war is in fact a real war in which the survival of the free world is at stake."

18. NSC 68 spells out four possible courses of action: continuing current policies, isolation, war, and "a rapid build-up of political, economic and military strength in the free world." The first course, however, leads to the second (as described in the text), and the third course is rejected as "repugnant to many Americans," and unlikely to be effective in achieving victory "in the fundamental ideological conflict."

19. Amos A. Jordan and William J. Taylor, Jr., *American National Security* (Baltimore: Johns Hopkins University Press, 1981), p. 64.

20. Merlo Pusey, *Eisenhower the President* (New York: Macmillan, 1956), pp. 246–247.

21. Quoted in Ernest May, "National Security in American History," Chapter 3 of Graham Allison and Gregory Treverton, eds., *Rethinking America's Security* (New York: Norton, 1992), pp. 104–105.

22. Douglas Kinnard, *President Eisenhower and Strategy Management* (Lexington, Ky.: University Press of Kentucky, 1977), pp. 127, 128, 135.

23. The fact that the cold war may have been used for political purposes to assist the passage of these bills does not detract from the point that the post-World War II security paradigm was setting the terms of the debate and driving policy.

24. Both quotations are from Jeffrey Rayport, "DARPA" Case Study, Harvard Business School, February 14, 1990. In the first, Rayport quotes from Defense Department documents; in the second, from *Barron's*, November 6, 1989.

25. Ibid, p. 7.

26. Ibid, pp. 5, 8. In 1989, DARPA employed just 160 people to manage its $1.3 billion budget.

27. As far back as 1953, Senator Mike Mansfield reported to the Senate upon returning from an Asian trip, "The security of the United States is no less involved in Indochina than in Korea"; quoted in Barbara W. Tuchman, *The March of Folly* (New York: Ballantine Books, 1985), p. 259. Interestingly, Tuchman writes of the newly elected Kennedy administration: "As far as the record shows, they held no session devoted to re-examination of the engagement they had inherited in Vietnam, nor did they ask themselves to what extent the United States was committed or what was the degree of national interest involved" (p. 283). See also May, op. cit., pp. 100–102.

28. Maxwell D. Taylor, "The Legitimate Claims of National Security," *Foreign Affairs*, Vol. 52, No. 3 (April 1974), pp. 592–594.

29. Daniel Yergin, *The Prize* (New York: Simon and Schuster, 1991), p. 662. The oil import numbers are also from Yergin (p. 567).

30. Quoted in Ralph Cavanagh et al., "National Energy Policy," *World Policy Journal,* Spring 1989, p. 242.

31. Quoted in Thomas McNaugher, *Arms and Oil* (Washington, D.C.: Brookings Institution, 1985), p. 3.

32. The energy statistics are from Arthur H. Rosenfeld, "Energy Options: Technological Solutions and Limits," January 23, 1992, presentation, University of California, Berkeley, and Daniel Yergin, "Energy Security in the 1990s," *Foreign Affairs,* Fall 1988, p. 115. The payoff of federal energy efficiency investments is from Arthur H. Rosenfeld, "The Role of Federal Research and Development in Advancing Energy Efficiency," testimony before the subcommittee on Environment of the House Committee on Science, Space, and Technology, April 17, 1991.

33. Yergin (1991), op. cit., 765–766.

34. U.S. Department of Energy, *National Energy Strategy* (Washington, D.C.: U.S. Government Printing Office, February 1991), p. 3.

35. Franklin P. Huddle, "The Evolving National Policy for Materials," *Science,* February 20, 1976; quoted in Lester Brown, *Redefining National Security,* Washington, D.C.: Worldwatch Paper #14, October 1977, p. 41.

36. Brown (1977), op. cit., p. 38.

37. Jessica Tuchman Mathews, "Redefining Security," *Foreign Affairs,* Spring 1989, p. 168.

38. Earthscan, *Environment and Conflict,* Earthscan briefing document 40, Washington, D.C., November 1984, pp. 22–23.

39. Robert Rotberg, "Haiti's Past Mortgages Its Future," *Foreign Affairs,* Fall 1988, pp. 97–98.

40. Earthscan, op. cit., p. 14.

41. Hobart Rowen, "Global Overpopulation," *Washington Post,* February 17, 1985, pp. E1, E7. Rowen also quotes a 1974 National Security Study Memorandum prepared by President Ford's national security adviser, Brent Scowcroft, which concluded that achieving political stability in the third world "will require that the president and the secretary of state treat the subject of population growth control as a matter of paramount importance."

42. Theodore Moran, "International Economics and National Security," *Foreign Affairs,* Winter 1990/91, p. 74.

43. Mathews (1989), op. cit., p. 162. Mathews served on the National Security Council from 1977 to 1979 as director of the Office of Global Issues.

44. Harold D. Lasswell, *National Security and Individual Freedom* (New York: McGraw-Hill, 1950), p. 75.

45. Arnold Wolfers, *Discord and Collaboration* (Baltimore: Johns Hopkins University Press, 1962), p. 147. (The original version of this essay dates from 1952.)

46. Barry Buzan, *People, States, and Fear: The National Security Problem in International Relations* (Chapel Hill, N.C.: University of North Carolina Press, 1983), pp. 4, 9. A particularly frank admission of this danger was made by Lyndon Johnson, who told Eric Sevareid, "I can arouse a great mass of people with a very simple kind of appeal. I can wrap the flag around this policy, and use patriotism as a club to silence the critics." Quoted in Jordan and Taylor, op. cit., p. 45.

254

47.   Robert Post "National Security and the Amended Freedom of Information Act," op. cit., pp. 406, 408.

48.   Walter Lippmann, *U.S. Foreign Policy: Shield of the Republic* (Boston: Little Brown, 1954), quoted in Berkowitz and Bock, op. cit., p. 40. National Security Council's "working definition" is given in Peter Peterson and James Sebenius, "Rethinking America's Security: The Primacy of the Domestic Agenda," Chapter 2 (in Graham Allison and Gregory Treverton, eds., op. cit., p. 57). Wolfers, op. cit., p. 150. *International Encyclopedia of the Social Sciences*, op. cit., p. 40. Bellany is quoted in Buzan, op. cit., p. 217. Jordan and Taylor, op. cit., p. 3. Charles Maier, "Peace and Security Studies for the 1990s," unpublished paper for MacArthur SSRC Fellowship Program, June 12, 1990, p. 12.

Buzan (pp. 216–217) cites a variety of other definitions of national security: "National security is that part of government policy having as its objective the creation of national and international political conditions favourable to the protection or extension of vital national values against existing and potential adversaries" (Frank Trager and F.N. Simonie, 1973). National security includes traditional defense policy and also "the non-military actions of a state to ensure its total capacity to survive as a political entity in order to exert influence and to carry out its internal and international objectives" (Michael H. H. Louw, 1978). Security is "the *relative freedom* from harmful threats," (John E. Mroz, 1980; emphasis in original.).

49.   Richard Ullman, "Redefining Security," *International Security*, Vol. 8, No. 1 (Summer 1983), p. 134. One of the most important formal justifications for United States cold war policy, NSC-68, was concerned with the possibility of a direct Soviet attack on the United States—in the longer term. But, as noted earlier, the immediate Soviet threat to American national security was framed more as severe restriction of choices for American policymakers: Either increase defense spending substantially now or face dire consequences (and even more restricted and unpleasant choices) in the future.

50.   Ibid.

51.   Ibid., p. 133.

52.   Robert Hormats, "The Roots of American Power," *Foreign Affairs*, Summer 1991, p. 133.

53.   Lasswell, op. cit., p. 55.

CHAPTER 2: RESTORING ECONOMIC SECURITY

1.   The American Assembly report was the product of a group of economists, politicians, civil servants, businessmen, and policy analysts who gathered in 1953 at the third American Assembly Conference, "Economic Security for Americans." See American Assembly, *Economic Security for Americans* (Ann Arbor, Mich.: University Microfilms International, 1954), p. 9.

2.   Robert Reich, "Who Champions the Working Class," *New York Times*, May 26, 1991.

3. Arthur Kennickell and Janice Shack-Marquez, "Changes in Family Finances from 1983 to 1989: Evidence from the Survey of Consumer Finances," *Federal Reserve Bulletin*, January 1992, and U.S. Bureau of the Census, *Money Income of Households, Families, and Persons in the United States 1990* (Washington, D.C.: U.S. Government Printing Office, August 1991), p. 202. Family income data is usually divided into five groups (quintiles) based on income. The quintile income-growth figures can vary from source to source depending on factors such as the year the figures are calculated from, whether before- or after-tax income is used, and whether "household" income or "family" is used. Most sources, however, show the same trend, which is what matters. According to the Census Bureau, the mean before-tax inflation-adjusted income of the middle 20 percent of American families was $35,322 in 1990, $35,267 in 1979, and $35,151 in 1973. See also, Lawrence Mishel and David M. Frankel, *The State of Working America 1990–91* (Armonk, N.Y.: M. E. Sharpe, 1991), p. 24. For an opposing view, see Richard B. McKenzie, "The 'Fortunate Fifth' Fallacy," *Wall Street Journal*, January 28, 1992.

4. U.S. Bureau of the Census, *Poverty in the United States: 1990* (Washington, D.C.: U.S. Government Printing Office, August 1991), pp. 1–2, 24. According to the Census Bureau report, the average poverty threshold for a family of four in 1990 was $13,359. Furthermore, "Of all poor persons, 38.5 percent or 12.9 million persons were in families (or were unrelated individuals) whose total income in 1990 was *below one-half* of their respective poverty threshold" (emphasis added), p. 9.

5. Juliet Schor, *The Overworked American* (New York: Basic Books, 1991), p. 81. Schor notes that while Europeans have been gaining vacation time, Americans have been losing it. "In the last decade, U.S. workers have gotten *less* paid time off—on the order of three and a half fewer days each year of vacation time, holidays, sick pay, and other paid absences" (p. 32). She also calculates that "leisure time has fallen by 47 hours a year" (p. 36). See also Lawrence Mishel and David M. Frankel, *The State of Working America 1990–91*, op. cit., p. xi.

6. "For Some Two-Paycheck Families, the Economics Don't Add Up," *New York Times*, April 21, 1991, and "Families on a Treadmill: Work and Income in the 1980s," Staff Study for the Joint Economic Committee, U.S. Congress, January 17, 1992, p. 18.

7. For instance, *The Wall Street Journal*, in one of its "Asides" (December 12, 1991, p. A14), states, "What is laughingly referred to in news stories as the 'nonpartisan' Congressional Budget Office has just announced that the years of Ronald Reagan's presidency produced mainly declines in the real incomes of most Americans. And no doubt the reason so many Americans felt they were living in the midst of a dynamic and growing economy is that this clever old man with the rosy cheeks bamboozled them for eight years." Many Americans did live in the midst of a dynamic and growing economy. The top 20 percent who did very well in the 1980s represent some 50 million Americans and include most of the readers and staff of *The Wall Street Journal*.

8.   U.S. Bureau of the Census, *Household Wealth and Asset Ownership: 1988* (Washington, D.C.: U.S. Government Printing Office, December 1990). The "wealth" or "net worth" of families used in the report "is based on the sum of the market value of assets owned by every member of the household minus liabilities (secured or unsecured) owed by household members." The "median net worth is the amount which divides the net worth distribution into two equal groups, one having household net worth less than that amount and the other having net worth above that amount." Declines in net worth for the bottom 80 percent are not statistically significant at the 90 percent level, and so in the strict sense, one should say that the net worth for 80 percent of Americans stagnated. The declines for the upper-middle class and the lowest class are, however, significant at the 68 percent level. Moreover, these declines in wealth are very likely to grow the next time the figures are reported, given that the Census Bureau figures cited above predate the recession and the remarkable decline in total real net worth of households in 1990. See also Arthur Kennickell and R. Louise Woodburn, "Estimation of Household Net Worth Using Model-Based and Design-Based Weights," report to the Federal Reserve Board and Internal Revenue Service, April 1992.

9.   "Foundations of Homeownership Crack," *Wall Street Journal*, June 14, 1991, p. A5D. "Now You Can Get into the College of Your Choice," *Washington Post Weekly*, April 1–7, 1991. The article cites data from the U.S. Department of Education. Jane Bryant Quinn, "How to Save for College," *Newsweek*, October 21, 1991, pp. 52–54. Quinn estimates you would need to save $906 a month for the ten-year-old and $591 a month for the four-year-old. If you planned to send them to a public university in your state, you would still need to start saving more than $700 a month. Recent studies have revealed that the nation's elite universities are taking an increasing percentage of their students from the richest families, those making over $100,000 a year. The middle class is being squeezed out: Families making between $40,000 and $75,000 a year accounted for 39 percent of the student body of the nation's top universities in 1978 but only 31 percent by 1989. See "The Rich Get Richer and the Poor Get Rejection Letters," *Washington Post Weekly*, May 4–10, 1991, p. 32. According to the article, an increasing number of elite universities are moving toward "a long-taboo policy of considering a potential student's wealth when choosing its freshman class."

10.   Office of Technology Assessment, *Making Things Better: Competing in Manufacturing*, OTA-ITE-443 (Washington, D.C.: U.S. Government Printing Office, February 1990), p. 3. It is possible for both oil *and* manufactured goods to make up more than half the trade deficit in a given year because the United States is a net exporter of some other goods. In a year with a $100 billion trade deficit, the United States could run a $55 billion deficit in oil and $55 billion deficit in manufactured goods *if* in that year we had a net surplus of $10 billion in agricultural products.

11.   William Serrin, "A Great American Job Machine?" *The Nation*, September 18, 1989, p. 270.

12. "Manufacturing Revival Undercut by Revisions," *New York Times National Edition*, April 24, 1992, pp. C1–C6. The earlier miscalculation that showed a rebound in manufacturing's share of GNP was caused primarily by using constant 1982 prices for manufactured goods. This significantly overestimated the value of computers, which fell steadily in price throughout the 1980s. See also *Employment and Earnings*, Bureau of Labor Statistics, June 1992.

13. Mishel and Frankel, op. cit., pp. 258–259.

14. Serrin, op. cit., p. 270. For a good discussion of the loss of high-paying jobs, pensions, and health care benefits, see Donald Barlett and James Steele, *America: What Went Wrong?* (Kansas City: Andrews and McMeel, 1992).

15. *Balance Sheets for the U.S. Economy, 1949–90* (Washington, D.C.: Federal Reserve Board, September 1991). See also "Heavy lifting, How America's Debt Burden Threatens the Economic Recovery," *U.S. News & World Report*, May 6, 1991, p. 55. In the single year from the end of 1989 to the end of 1990, household net worth fell 4.3 percent. See also "Not Getting Ahead? Better Get Used to It," *New York Times*, December 16, 1990, pp. E1, E6.

16. "White-collar Lay-offs in America: A Lot More Than You Would Think," *The Economist*, February 2, 1991, p. 66.

17. "The New Executive Unemployed," *Fortune*, April 8, 1991, p. 37. See also "Unlike Past Recessions, This One Is Battering White-collar Workers," *Wall Street Journal*, November 29, 1991, pp. A1, A2, and "Is Your Job Safe?" *U.S. News & World Report*, January 13, 1992, pp. 42–48, which notes that unlike the two previous recessions (1973–74 and 1981–82), white-collar jobs *decreased* rather than *increased*.

18. Richard Rosecrance, "Too Many Bosses, Too Few Workers," *New York Times*, July 15, 1990, p. F11.

19. Had the borrowed money been used for investment in the future (education, worker training, civilian R & D, infrastructure, and the like), it would eventually have paid for itself in future growth. Unfortunately, such investment declined in the 1980s. Much of the borrowed money went to increasing the military budget.

20. *Gaining New Ground: Technology Priorities for America's Future* (Washington, D.C.: Council on Competitiveness, 1991). The Council on Competitiveness cited throughout this book is a nonprofit, nonpartisan organization of leaders from business, higher education, and organized labor working toward improving the competitiveness of American companies and workers. It has no connection with the White House Council on Competitiveness, chaired by Vice President Dan Quayle. The Quayle council's primary mission is to weaken environmental regulations, based on the belief that such regulations undercut competitiveness, a common misconception that is discussed in Chapter 5.

21. "By 1989, the U.S. was able to regain its 1972 share of world exports, but only because its manufactures were made extraordinarily cheap by a dollar worth radically less than its 1972 exchange value. Even then, the 1972 trade surplus produced by superior U.S. export performance had been replaced by 1989's $113 billion deficit. Any country can have balanced trade; the question is at what real exchange rate and at what real income. The trick is to maintain that trade balance

with high and rising real income." Michael Borrus and John Zysman, "The Highest Stakes: Industrial Competitiveness and National Security," BRIE Working Paper 39, April 1991 (to appear as a chapter in Wayne Sandholtz et al., *The Highest Stakes: Technology, Economy and Security Policy* [New York: Oxford University Press, 1992], p. 9).

22.   "The Global Economy, Can You Compete?" a *Business Week* Special Report, December 17, 1990, p. 70.

23.   *The Economist*, June 22, 1991, p. 35.

24.   Supporting the less fortunate has traditionally been a central component of American economic security. The "four major hazards to economic security" considered by the 1953 American assembly conference were "old age, unemployment, sickness and disability, and the possible death of a breadwinner." Forty years ago, economic security meant social security, not competitiveness. See *Economic Security for Americans*, op. cit., p. 17.

25.   The figures cited here are the average from 1980 to 1987. Michael Kidron and Ronald Segal, *The New State of the World Atlas*, 4th ed. (New York: Simon and Schuster, 1991), p. 36. Income distribution in the United States has become more *inequitable* in recent years. In 1989, for instance, the ratio of income received by the richest fifth of Americans to that of the poorest fifth was 9.7. In contrast, in the late 1960s and early 1970s, income distribution was more equitable and the ratio was about 7.4. See Mishel and Frankel, op. cit., p. 20.

26.   As used here, economic security is similar to "competitiveness" as defined by the President's Commission on Industrial Competitiveness: "A nation's competitiveness is the degree to which it can, under free and fair market conditions, produce goods and services that meet the test of international markets while simultaneously expanding the real incomes of its citizens. International competitiveness at the national level is based on superior productivity performance and the economy's ability to shift output to high productivity activities, which in turn can generate high levels of real wages. Competitiveness is associated with rising living standards, expanding employment opportunities, and the ability of a nation to maintain its international obligations. It is not just a measure of the nation's ability to sell abroad, and to maintain a trade equilibrium. The very poorest countries in the world are often able to do that quite well. Rather, it is the nation's ability to stay ahead technologically and commercially in those commodities and services likely to constitute a larger share of world consumption and value-added in the future." Quoted in Borrus and Zysman, op. cit., pp. 47–48.

27.   For a discussion of the ebbs and flows of this debate in American history, see Samuel Huntington, "The U.S.—Decline or Renewal," *Foreign Affairs*, Vol. 67, No. 2 (Winter 1988/89), pp. 76–96.

28.   Joseph S. Nye, Jr., *Bound to Lead: The Changing Nature of American Power* (New York: Basic Books, Inc., 1990), pp. 179, 228.

29.   C. Fred Bergsten, "The World Economy After the Cold War," *Foreign Affairs*, Vol. 69, No. 3 (Summer 1990), pp. 96–97. Bergsten is director of the Institute for International Affairs.

30. Huntington (1988/1989), op. cit., pp. 84, 92. The first quote, in full, is "In short, if 'hegemony' means having 40 percent or more of world economic activity (a percentage Britain never remotely approximated during its hegemonic years), American hegemony disappeared long ago. If hegemony means producing 20 to 25 percent of the world product and twice as much as any other individual country, American hegemony looks quite secure."

31. Samuel Huntington, "America's Changing Strategic Interests," *Survival,* Vol. XXXIII, No. 1 (January/February 1991), p. 16. Huntington here offers a broad definition of the American national interest: "The promotion of U.S. strategic interests will involve not only foreign and defense policy but also domestic policy on the budget, taxes, subsidies, industrial policy, science and technology, child care, education, and other topics."

32. See Theodore C. Sorensen, "Rethinking National Security," *Foreign Affairs,* Vol. 69, No. 3 (Summer 1990), pp. 1–18.

33. Harold D. Lasswell, *National Security and Individual Freedom* (New York: McGraw-Hill, 1950), p. 51.

34. This is a modification of Richard Ullman's definition given in Chapter 1. I have eliminated his phrase "over a relatively brief span of time" because I believe that many of the most serious threats to a nation, such as environmental and competitiveness problems, occur over a long time period. I have eliminated his reference to "private nongovernmental entities" primarily to highlight the distinction between the two components—economic security and economic independence.

35. These statistics are from U.S. General Accounting Office, "International Trade" (Washington, D.C.: GAO/NSIAD-91-278, September 1991), p. 9; "The Big Split," *Fortune,* May 6, 1991, pp. 41–42; "Computers: Japan Comes on Strong," *Business Week,* October 23, 1989, p. 104; and OTA, *Making Things Better,* op. cit., p. 16.

36. "The U.S. Achilles' Heel in Desert Storm," *Washington Post National Weekly Edition,* April 1–7, 1991, p. 11, and *60 Minutes,* April 21, 1991.

37. Quoted in "A Japan That Can Take Credit," *Newsweek,* July 15, 1991, p. 27.

38. This is the phrase Jeffrey Rayport cites as, punctuating "discussions about economic or defense issues in the summer and fall of 1989." Jeffrey Rayport, "DARPA" Case Study, Harvard Business School, February 14, 1990, p. 15. One of the most comprehensive historical analyses on America's aversion to industrial policy is in William S. Dietrich, *In the Shadow of the Rising Sun* (University Park, Pa.: Pennsylvania State University Press, 1991), especially Part Three, "The Political Roots of American Economic Decline," and Part Four, "Economic Policy and the Industrial Policy Debate in America."

39. OTA, *Making Things Better,* op. cit., pp. 74–75.

40. Ibid., p. 75. The OTA notes that the 707 was "such a clone of the KC-135 refueling tanker that Boeing made for the Air Force that the first prototype 707 wheeled out of the Seattle plant had no windows in the fuselage."

41. See Office of Technology Assessment, *Competing Economies: America, Europe, and the Pacific Rim,* OTA-ITE-498 (Washington, D.C.: U.S. Government

Printing Office, October 1991), Chapter 8, "Government Support of the Large Commercial Aircraft Industries of Japan, Europe, and the United States," pp. 341–362; "There's No Stopping Europe's Airbus Now," *New York Times*, June 23, 1991, Section 3, pp. 1, 6; "The Wild Blue Yonder of Aerospace Alliances," *Wall Street Journal*, June 24, 1991, p. A11; and "The Sincerest Form of Flattery," *The Economist*, November 11, 1989, pp. 79–81. As many of these sources make clear, the Japanese are also trying to break into the commercial-aircraft market. See also, "Asia Bids for a Stake in Aerospace," *The Economist*, November 23, 1991.

42. Kevin L. Kearns, "Behind Those Shrinking Trade Deficit Numbers," *Wall Street Journal*, July 25, 1991, p. A9. The others are meat products, corn, logs and wood, cigarettes, fish, and aluminum.

43. Gavin Wright, "The Origins of American Industrial Success, 1879–1940," *American Economic Review*, September 1990, pp. 651, 661, 662.

44. Ibid., p. 665.

45. C. Vann Woodward, "The Age of Reinterpretation," *American Historical Review*, Vol. 66, No. 1 (October 1960), pp. 5, 8.

46. I will cite only one unusual story that suggests the extent to which some people take economic security for granted. In the October 8, 1991, issue of the supermarket tabloid *Weekly World News* is the following headline: "Young Americans Doomed to Be Paupers, Says Expert." The story reads as follows: "America's young adults will never be as successful or earn as much money as their parents because wages have fallen steadily for the past 10 years and will continue to fall in the future, a leading economist warns. Lawrence Mishel, research director of the Economic Policy Institute in Washington, says a shift in employment toward low-wage industries and a deterioration of wages in the face of inflation are to blame for the bad forecast." What is remarkable about the story is not Mishel's work, which I have cited earlier, but the fact that it is reported alongside such stories as "Man Electrocuted by Lightning Bugs," "Photo of Elvis Cured My Gout!" and "Ghost of Richard Burton Vows: I'll Wreck Liz's Wedding!" as if America's long-term economic decline were just another amazing, unbelievable occurrence.

47. See "In the Realm of Technology, Japan Seizes a Greater Role," *New York Times*, May 28, 1991, pp. C1, C8. The president of the research company that conducted the patent study said, "It's scary. The Japanese are continuing to expand in virtually every area of technology. Anybody who believes that the Japanese increase is just in autos and electronics is totally oblivious of the facts. Their performance is impressive across the board, *in virtually every field*" (emphasis added).

48. See, for instance, *Gaining New Ground*, op. cit., p. 21, and Robert Kuttner, *The End of Laissez-Faire: National Purpose and the Global Economy After the Cold War* (New York: Alfred A. Knopf, 1991), pp. 192–228.

49. "Report Card on Bushonomics," *Fortune*, November 4, 1991, pp. 105–114. The article gives Bush a "B" on "promoting research and high technology." The magazine's editors are not, however, ardent believers in industrial policy.

261

50. "White House Lists 22 Critical Technologies," *New York Times,* April 26, 1991. See also "Report of the National Critical Technologies Panel" (Washington, D.C.: The White House, March 1991).

51. "U.S. Technology Strategy Emerges," *Science,* April 5, 1991, pp. 20–24. See also, "Technology Official Quits at Pentagon," *New York Times,* May 10, 1990, p. D-1, which discusses the resignation of Michael Sekora, director of Project Socrates, a Defense Intelligence Agency program to build "the world's most accurate data base of many of the world's most advanced technologies to help planners assess the status of American high-technology efforts compared with those of foreign competitors." According to the article, Sekora had "become frustrated by the Bush Administration's refusal to support plans to assist the nation's high-technology industries."

52. "White House, Reversing Policy Under Pressure, Begins to Pick High-Tech Winners and Losers" *Wall Street Journal,* May 13, 1991, p. A16.

53. "Legislative and Policy Update," Council on Competitiveness, Washington, D.C.: July 29, 1991, p. 1.

54. John Young, "Technology and Competitiveness: A Key to the Economic Future of the United States," *Science,* July 15, 1988, p. 314.

55. "Report of the National Critical Technologies Panel," op. cit. For comparison see, for instance, *Gaining New Ground,* op. cit. pp. 22–28 and Appendix II (pp. 65–67), which gives lists developed by the U.S. Department of Commerce, Japan's Ministry of International Trade and Industry (MITI), and the Commission of the European Communities.

56. W. W. Rostow, *How It All Began: Origins of the Modern Economy* (New York: McGraw-Hill, 1975), pp. 191–192.

57. Stephen Cohen and John Zysman, *Manufacturing Matters* (New York: Basic Books, 1987), pp. 21–24. Much of the service sector in this country is directly linked to manufacturing. Cohen and Zysman cite a report from the Office of the U.S. Trade Representative, *Annual Report of the President of the United States on the Trade Agreements Program,* 1983: "25% of U.S. GNP originates in services used as inputs by goods-producing industries—more than the value added to GNP by the manufacturing sector" (p. 25).

58. "Dying Breed: No Glamour, No Glory, Being a Manufacturer Today Can Take Guts," *Wall Street Journal,* June 3, 1991, pp. A1, A7.

59. Lester Thurow, "A Weakness in Process Technology," *Science,* December 18, 1987, p. 1661. See also "Dying Breed . . .," op. cit., p. A1.

60. James Womack et al., *The Machine That Changed the World* (New York: Rawson Associates, 1990), pp. 198–200.

61. Ibid., p. 200.

62. One of the most comprehensive and detailed discussions of what the government can and should do to promote manufacture is the 244-page report *Making Things Better* by the Congressional Office of Technology Assessment, op. cit. Typically, OTA reports are among the most thorough and dispassionate analyses written on a given subject, but do not receive widespread attention. Another valuable study is the October 1991 OTA report, *Competing Economies:*

America, Europe, and the Pacific Rim, op. cit. See also *Gaining New Ground,* op. cit.

63. "U.S. Technology Strategy Emerges," *Science,* April 5, 1991, p. 23 (sidebar "Sematech: Techno-Policy in Action").

64. Maryellen Kelley and Harvey Brooks, "From Breakthrough to Follow-Through," *Issues in Science and Technology,* Spring 1989, pp. 43–44.

65. *Making Things Better,* op. cit., p. 54.

66. For discussion of the importance to national competitiveness of diffusing new manufacturing technology, and of the greater efforts the Japanese, Germans, Italians, and other countries make in this area, see Cohen and Zysman, op. cit., pp. 153–177, 224–227; Stuart A. Rosenfeld, "Regional Development, European Style," *Issues in Science and Technology,* Winter 1989–90, pp. 63–70; and the special report on "Flexible Manufacturing Networks," *Entrepreneurial Economy,* July/August, 1987, pp. 2–18. For recent United States efforts, see "An Industrial Policy, Piece by Piece," *New York Times,* July 30, 1991, pp. D1, D2.

67. *Making Things Better,* op. cit., pp. 55–56.

68. Kelley and Brooks, op. cit., p. 45.

69. *Making Things Better,* op. cit., p. 56.

70. Michael Porter, *The Competitive Advantage of Nations* (New York: The Free Press, 1990), pp. 637–638

71. David Alan Aschauer, "Public Investment and Private Sector Growth" (Washington, D.C.: Economic Policy Institute, 1990), p. 1. The study also concludes that "the pay-off in GNP growth from an extra dollar of public capital is estimated to exceed that of private investment by a factor of between two and five" (p. 2) and that far from "crowding out" public investment, the improved business climate created by new infrastructure means that *"for every dollar increase in public investment, private investment rises by approximately 45 cents"* (p. 19; emphasis in original).

72. See, for instance, Robert Reich, *The Work of Nations* (New York: Alfred Knopf, 1991), Chapter 21, "The Decline of Public Investment." See also "U.S. Contractors Trail Japan in R&D," August 6, 1991, p. 2.

73. Paul A. Summerville, "Japan's New Investment Agenda," *New York Times,* August 11, 1991, p. F13.

74. Womack et al., op. cit., p. 254.

75. Quoted in Walter Massey, "Science Education in the United States: What the Scientific Community Can Do," *Science,* September 1, 1989, p. 917.

76. *Making Things Better,* op. cit., p. 13. United States spending for kindergarten through twelfth grade *per pupil* is fifth among sixteen industrialized nations.

77. Richard Rosecrance, op. cit.

78. See Reich, *The Work of Nations,* op. cit., pp. 258–259; "The Global Economy, Can You Compete?" a *Business Week* Special Report, December 17, 1990, pp. 78, 81, 88–89; and "A Competitiveness Assessment of the President's FY 1992 Budget (Washington, D.C.: Council on Competitiveness, 1991), p. 12.

79. Nan Stone, "Does Business Have Any Business in Education?" *Harvard Business Review,* March–April 1991, pp. 58–60.

80.   As cited in *Making Things Better*, op. cit., p. 119. The studies from the late 1980s compared "matched British and German manufacturing plants—in metalworking, kitchen cabinet manufacture, and garment making."

81.   Stephen Hamilton, *Apprenticeship for Adulthood* (New York: The Free Press, 1990), pp. 140–141. Hamilton is professor of human development and family studies at Cornell University. He proposes a three-level apprenticeship system because he believes that anything short of a comprehensive approach will fail: "Making a diverse system of apprenticeship available to all youth means creating a *system*, not just a program. A program, such as the Job Corps or cooperative education, may be part of a system, but a complete system offers an array of diverse opportunities—or programs—and it links them in a coherent whole. Youth then move through sequential stages in the system, selecting the programs that are most appropriate and participating as long as each meets their needs" (emphasis in original).

82.   "Oregon to Stress Job Training in Restructuring High School," *New York Times*, July 24, 1991, pp. A1, A18.

83.   Porter, op. cit., p. 629.

84.   The Secretary's Commission on Achieving Necessary Skills, *What Work Requires of Schools* (Washington, D.C.: U.S. Department of Labor, June 1991), p. 12. It is surprising that Robert Samuelson gives these lines "an A for mumbo jumbo," in his column; see "Job-Skills Gibberish," Washington Post Weekly, July 15–21, 1991, p. 30. The thirty-one-page commission report, though too short to explain its proposals in detail, explicitly links this recommendation for teaching "systems" thinking to the shift in manufacturing strategy from the "traditional model" of "mass production," "long production runs," and "centralized control," toward the "high performance model," of "flexible production," "customized production," and "decentralized control." See p. 3 of the report, and specific manufacturing examples on pp. 7–8, 28.

85.   Darman and Boskin quoted in Clyde Prestowitz, "More Trade Is Better Than Free Trade," *Technology Review*, April 1991, p. 26.

86.   Bergsten, op. cit., p. 97.

87.   Ibid., p. 98.

88.   Typically, as I discuss in the next chapter, the Japanese will agree only to those demands that will ultimately benefit them, such as demands that they spend more on infrastructure or on overseas development assistance.

89.   See July 18, 1991, press release, Office of U.S. Senator Boren, 453 Russell Building, Washington, D.C., 20510. The bill received initial funding of $10 million. The release notes that since the National Defense Education Act of 1958, the proportion of federal education funds going for international and foreign language studies has declined more than 90 percent. It further notes that 100 percent of graduating Japanese high school students are required to have at least two years of English, with most having six years, while less than one tenth of 1 percent of American high school students study Japanese. It is one more reason why the Japanese are so adept at commercializing our inventions, and competing in America, while United States companies are so poor at competing in Japan. See

also "Security Concerns Prompt U.S. to Offer Aid for Foreign Study," *New York Times National Edition,* December 25, 1991, p. 9.

90. Kennickell and Woodburn, op. cit., and Robert Reich, "Who Champions the Working Class?" op. cit.

91. Norman D. Levin, "Japan's Defense Policy: The Internal Debate," in Harry Kendall and Clara Joewono, eds., *Japan, Asean, and the United States* (Berkeley, Calif.: Institute of East Asian Studies, University of California, Berkeley, 1991), p. 84. See also Umemoto Tetsuya, "Comprehensive Security and the Evolution of the Japanese Security Posture," in Robert Scalapino et al., eds., *Asian Security Issues* (Berkeley, Calif.: Institute of East Asian Studies, University of California, Berkeley, 1988), pp. 32–38.

CHAPTER 3: JAPAN'S ECONOMIC SECURITY SYSTEM

1. Testimony of Kenneth Courtis before the Congressional Joint Economic Committee, May 8, 1992. Courtis, a Tokyo-based economist, is first vice president of the Deutsche Bank Capital Markets, Asia. See also "Leaders Come and Go, But the Japanese Boom Seems to Last Forever," *New York Times National Edition,* October 6, 1991, p. E3. Japan's economy is capable of remarkable growth. From 1985 to 1991, Japan grew by the equivalent of one France.

2. George Friedman and Meredith LeBard, *The Coming War with Japan* (New York: St. Martin's Press, 1991), pp. 7–8, 165.

3. James Womack et al., *The Machine That Changed the World* (New York: Rawson Associates, 1990), p. 92. Even in their transplant auto factories in the United States, the Japanese provide new production workers 370 hours of training.

4. For discussions of Japanese investment and achievements in technology, see, for instance, Francis Narin and J. Davidson Frame, "The Growth of Japanese Science and Technology," *Science,* August 11, 1989, pp. 600–605; "Japanese Technology," an *Economist* survey, December 2, 1989; and "In the Realm of Technology, Japan Seizes a Greater Role," *New York Times,* May 28, 1991, pp. C1, C8. For recent figures on Japanese investment in new plant and equipment, see "Cranking Up the Export Machine," *U.S. News & World Report,* November 18, 1991, p. 78, and "Why Japan's Surplus Is Rising," *Fortune,* December 30, 1991, p. 95. For comparisons of United States and Japanese business spending on research, see "Japan Seen Passing U.S. In Research by Industry," *New York Times National Edition,* February 25, 1992, pp. B5–B9. The study quoted in the text is a 1992 draft report by the Competitiveness Policy Council, an advisory body whose members are appointed by the White House and Congress.

5. Nobutoshi Akao, *Japan's Economic Security* (New York: The Royal Institute for International Affairs, 1983), p. 1; quoted in Friedman and LeBard, op. cit., p. 186. "The Yen Block," *The Economist,* July 15, 1989. Other similar comments: "Japan continues to be motivated largely by the conviction that so long as it is able to lead in the competition for export of manufactures its security can be preserved." Former Defense Secretary Harold Brown, "The United States and

265

Japan: High Tech Is Foreign Policy," *SAIS Review*, Summer/Fall 1989, p. 11. The Dutch journalist Wolferen writes: "All these Japanese institutions with international dealings [MITI, Ministry of Finance] are essentially in the business of national security." Karel von Wolferen, "The Japan Problem Revisited," *Foreign Affairs*, Vol. 69, No. 4 (Fall 1990), p. 48. Defense strategist Edward Luttwak writes: "In how many major countries does the Minister for Telecommunications, or Energy, or Trade outrank the Defense Minister? Only—appropriately enough— in Japan." Edward Luttwak, "From Geopolitics to Geo-Economics," *The National Interest*, Summer 1990, p. 19. Former trade negotiator Clyde Prestowitz and Carnegie Endowment analyst Selig Harrison write: "Increasingly in recent years, Japan has sought to redefine the meaning of security in economic and political rather than in military terms. 'Comprehensive security' is the new watchword." Selig S. Harrison and Clyde V. Prestowitz, Jr., "Pacific Agenda: Defense or Economics?" *Foreign Policy* Summer 1990, pp. 61–62.

6. J. W. M. Chapman et al., *Japan's Quest for Comprehensive Security* (New York: St. Martin's Press, 1982), p. 149.

7. For a recent analysis of MITI's role in Japanese industrial policy, with a case study on the development of the computer and supercomputer industry, see Office of Technology Assessment, *Competing Economies: America, Europe, and the Pacific Rim*, OTA-ITE-498 (Washington, D.C.: U.S. Government Printing Office, October 1991), pp. 239–291. See also "Why Japan Keeps on Winning," *Fortune*, July 15, 1991, pp. 76–85.

8. See Kevin Kearns, "Japan's Sleight of Hand in Trade," *New York Times*, April 7, 1991; "The Rising Sun Tries to Ration Its Rays," *The Washington Post National Weekly Edition*, April 8–14, 1991, p. 8; and "U.S. Is Asked to Review Japan Trade," *New York Times*, March 25, 1991, pp. D1–D2. In 1990, the United States had a combined surplus of $14 billion with Japan in the following products: cork, wood, cereals, meats, fish, ores and scrap metal, tobacco, fruits and vegetables, coal, and paper. From 1987 to 1990, the total *rise* in the surplus in these goods was $6 billion.

9. *Far Eastern Economic Review*, October 11, 1990, p. 72; "Why Japan Keeps on Winning," *Fortune*, July 15, 1991, pp. 76–85; and T. Boone Pickens, "Japan's Cartels Hold a Lot of Hostages," *Washington Post Weekly*, May 6–12, 1991, p. 24.

10. T. Boone Pickens, op. cit.

11. U.S. General Accounting Office, "International Trade" (Washington, D.C.: GAO/NSIAD-91-278, September 1991). The report notes: "None of the U.S. companies or government laboratories that we contacted cited problems obtaining advanced technologies from any foreign supplier other than the Japanese."

12. As quoted in "Honda, Is It an American Car?" *Business Week*, November 18, 1991, pp. 107–109. See also *New York Times*, June 14, 1991, p. D2.

13. Quoted in "U.S. Says Honda Skirted Customs Fees," *New York Times*, June 17, 1991, pp. D1, D6. See also "Honda, Is It an American Car?" op. cit., and "U.S. Tariffs Imposed on Hondas," *New York Times National Edition*, March 3, 1992, pp. C1, C2. Japanese overproduction and underpricing in the automobile industry is part of their overall strategy to destroy foreign competition and gain

market share. The Japanese can subsidize losses abroad with higher prices in their domestic market. Moreover, with more patient capital than their competitors, the Japanese can afford to take a longer term perspective to business strategy.

14. The ASEAN nations also include two other members, Brunei and Singapore, but Brunei is not considered in this analysis and Singapore is more commonly grouped with the Newly Industrializing Economies.

15. See "The Yen Block," *The Economist*, July 15, 1989 (a special survey); Mike M. Mochizuki, "Japan After the Cold War, *SAIS*, Summer/Fall, 1990, pp. 135–136; Susumu Awanohara, "Japan and East Asia: Towards a New Division of Labor," *Occasional Paper 1*, Honolulu: East-West Center, August 1989; Harry Kendall and Clara Joewono, eds., *Japan, Asean, and the United States* (Berkeley, Calif.: Institute of East Asian Studies, University of California, Berkeley, 1991); "Reluctant converts," "Leading Questions," "Yen's Use Devalued," "Japan's Financial Barriers," in *Far Eastern Economic Review*, October 11, 1990, pp. 72–78; and Michael Borrus and John Zysman, "The Highest Stakes: Industrial Competitiveness and National Security," BRIE Working Paper 39, April 1991, to appear as a chapter in Wayne Sanholtz et al., *The Highest Stakes: Technology, Economy and Security Policy* (New York: Oxford University Press, forthcoming), pp. 32–36. In these analyses, Japan's regional industrial policy is also labeled a "multi-layered chase process," a "Confucianist economic sphere," and the "yen block."

16. "The New East Asia Co-Prosperity Sphere," *Fortune*, July 1, 1991, p. 12.

17. Walter Russell Mead, "The Bush Administration and the New World Order," *World Policy Journal*, Summer 1991, p. 393.

18. "Where Tigers Breed" (A Survey of Asia's Emerging Economies), *The Economist*, November 16, 1991, p. 4; "Cranking Up the Export Machine," *U.S. News & World Report*, op. cit., p. 78; and "Sayonara, America," *Newsweek*, August 19, 1991, p. 32–33. *Newsweek* quotes Marcus Nolan, an economist at the University of Southern California, for the estimate of potential jobs lost.

19. Quoted in Awanahara, op. cit., pp. 3–4.

20. Quoted in Borrus and Zysman, op. cit., p. 33.

21. Although the issue of aid tied to trade is controversial in Washington, Congress has significantly raised the ceiling of U.S. AID's authority to extend tied-aid credits, so it is likely to rise in coming years. "Conditional Generosity," *Far Eastern Economic Review*, January 24, 1991, p. 45. On the other hand, overall U.S. aid to Asia has been declining recently. See "The Shrinking Pie," *Far Eastern Economic Review*, January 24, 1991, p. 46.

22. The first description is from David Arase, "U.S. and ASEAN Perceptions of Japan's Role in the Asian-Pacific Region," in Kendall and Joewono, op. cit., p. 270. The second is from "The Yen Block," op. cit., p. 12.

23. Quoted in Arase, op. ct., p. 270.

24. The description here follows "The Yen Block," op. cit. pp. 12–14 and Arase, op. cit., pp. 272–273.

25. Arase, op. cit., p. 273.

26. See Steven C.M. Wong, "Japan in Search of a Global Economic Role: Realism vs. Regimeism," in Kendall and Joewono, op. cit., pp. 296–297; and "The Yen Block," op. cit., p. 8.
27. "Japan in Asia: Part 7: Malaysia," *Far Eastern Economic Review*, March 28, 1991, pp. 50–54.
28. Ibid., p. 53.
29. Ibid., p. 52.
30. Paul Blustein and Stuart Auerbach, "Building Alliances, Bloc by Bloc," *Washington Post Weekly*, June 10–16, p. 20. The authors write: "Some observers see as a harbinger of the future the fact that Malaysia, which was once occupied by Japan, would ask Tokyo to lead a regional trade bloc."
31. "Japan in Asia: Part 3: Indonesia," *Far Eastern Economic Review*, September 27, 1990, pp. 56–61.
32. Ibid., p. 60.
33. See " 'Things Japanese' Permeate Thailand, Bringing a Bit of Concern with the Boom," *Wall Street Journal*, June 24, 1991, p. A8; Gerald L. Curtis, "America's Evolving Relationship with Japan and Its Implications for ASEAN," in Kendall and Joewono, op. cit., p. 156; and "Thailand's Economy Surges, and Country Is Feeling the Strain," *Wall Street Journal*, June 12, 1991, pp. A1, A10.
34. "Japanese Investment in Asia Declining, Allowing Region's Economies to Cool," *Wall Street Journal*, July 1, 1991, p. A30. The article discusses the slight decline in Japanese investment since the middle of 1990, but notes that it may be due to straining of the economies from the torrid pace of earlier investment. Also, the article notes that Japanese overseas investment may be declining as "companies may use retained earnings from their foreign plants or may borrow locally for expansion."
35. Khatharya Um, "Southeast Asia and Japan: Political, Economic, and Security Implications for the 1990s," in Kendall and Joewono, op. cit., p. 197; and "Behind Diplomatic Smiles," *U.S. News & World Report*, November 11, 1991, pp. 51–53.
36. "Japan in Asia: Part 6: Taiwan," *Far Eastern Economic Review*, February 21, 1991, pp. 40–43; Borrus and Zysman, op. cit., p. 32; and "Taiwan Manufacturers Hooked on Japan," *Wall Street Journal*, July 30, 1991, p. A2.
37. "Where Tigers Breed," op. cit., pp. 13, 14. See also "$300 Billion Project to Rebuild Taiwan Draws Eager Bidders," *New York Times*, October 27, 1991, pp. 1, 10. The article notes that the Taiwanese plan "also includes money to improve manufacturing processes" and to "enhance research and development in many industries." See also Awanahara, op. cit., p. 9.
38. "Japan in Asia: Part 5: Korea," *Far Eastern Economic Review*, January 31, 1991, pp. 38–42.
39. As the *Far Eastern Economic Review* concluded in its 1990 focus story on South Korea: "Planners worry that it is harder to buy, borrow, beg or steal technology. South Korea has thrived by using imported technologies." "Away from Wigs Towards Hi-tech," *Far Eastern Economic Review*, June 28, 1990, pp. 42–45. For a lengthier analysis of Korea's dependence on borrowed technology,

see Alice H. Amsden, "Asia's Next Giant," *Technology Review,"* May/June 1989, pp. 46–53.

40.   Quoted in "Japan in Asia: Part 5: Korea," op. cit., p. 42. The article quotes a Samsung executive commenting on this national inferiority complex: "Koreans are always optimistic . . . but not with Japan."

41.   Walter Russell Mead details many of these problems in "The Bush Administration and the New World Order," op. cit. He writes: "For one thing, the hemispheric bloc is getting a late start. The EC [European Community] has grown out of half a century of European experience with steadily deepening economic ties, while East Asian economic integration reflects decades of patient and often coordinated Japanese public and private policy. The Western hemisphere, by contrast, benefits from no such history." In addition, the Western Hemisphere is a debtor bloc, and therefore must import capital. Mead cites a variety of other problems: a steadily weakening dollar leading to slow growth, a shortage of consumers, and a shortage of producers.

CHAPTER 4: ACHIEVING ENERGY SECURITY WHILE SAVING MONEY

1.   Amory Lovins, *Soft Energy Paths: Toward a Durable Peace* (New York; Harper and Row, 1979), p. 39.

2.   *Wall Street Journal,* August 17, 1990, p. 1. Much of Carter's legacy comes from a 1977 speech on energy, a speech that offered no sugar-coating to the American people: "Our decision about energy will test the character of the American people and the ability of the President and the Congress to govern this Nation. This difficult effort will be the 'moral equivalent of war,' except that we will be uniting our efforts to build and not to destroy." Carter linked change, which is inevitable, with sacrifice, which is not: "I'm sure that each of you will find something you don't like about the specifics of our proposal. It will demand that we make sacrifices and changes in every life. To some degree, the sacrifices will be painful—but so is any meaningful sacrifice. This will lead to some higher costs and to some greater inconveniences for everyone. But the sacrifices can be gradual, realistic, and they are necessary. Above all, they will be fair. No one will be asked to bear an unfair burden."

3.   U.S. Department of Energy, *National Energy Strategy* (Washington, D.C.: U.S. Government Printing Office, February 1991), pp. 118–129.

4.   Robert K. Kaufmann and Cutler J. Cleveland, "Policies to Increase U.S. Oil Production: Likely to Fail, Damage the Economy, and Damage the Environment," *Annual Review of Energy and the Environment,* 1991. See, also, "Departing Drillers, Weary of 'Dry Holes' in U.S., Independents Search for Oil Abroad," *Wall Street Journal,* April 20, 1992, pp. A1–A6.

5.   Department of Energy, *Interim Report, National Energy Strategy: A Compilation of Public Comments.* DOE/S-0066P, April 1990, p. 4; quoted in Alliance to Save Energy et al., *America's Energy Choices* (Cambridge, Mass.: Union of

Concerned Scientists, 1991), pp. 25–26. According to the DOE summary of the public hearings: "People in all parts of the country expressed concern about what energy production and consumption are doing to our air, water, and land. We heard concern about acid rain, urban air pollution, oil spills, the safety of nuclear power plants, our ability to harmlessly dispose of radioactive wastes, and possible global climate change resulting from the use of fossil fuels. Many were concerned about the need to develop advanced technology to convert and control energy in an environmentally sound way."

6. Robert Watson, *Looking for Oil in All the Wrong Places* (Washington, D.C.: Natural Resources Defense Council, February 1991), p. 1. Adding to the world's reliance on Middle East oil is the decline in production by the former Soviet Union, which in 1990 was a net exporter of three million barrels a day, but which could become a net importer by the end of the decade.

7. Hanns Maull, "Energy and Resources: The Strategic Dimensions," *Survival*, Vol. XXXI, No. 6 (November/December 1989), p. 502. James Schlesinger said in 1987: "I believe the United States should be worried. Its role in the world is unique. Unlike Germany, Japan, or France, all of which, incidentally, worry a great deal about oil dependency, the United States is the great stabilizing power in the free world. Other nations can be oil dependent. If, however, the United States is to sustain its role in the world and to maintain the necessary freedom of action in foreign policy matters, it cannot afford to become excessively dependent on oil imports, particularly from the most volatile regions of the world." James Schlesinger, "Oil and National Security: An American Dilemma," in Edward Fried and Nanette Blandin, eds., *Oil and America's Security* (Washington, D.C.: Brookings Institution, 1988), p. 11. For a presentation of the minority view, that dependence on imported oil is only of "minor importance," see M. A. Adelman, "Oil Fallacies," *Foreign Policy*, Winter 1991.

8. U.S. Department of Energy, *National Energy Strategy*, op. cit., p. 3.

9. Amory Lovins, *Soft Energy Paths*, op. cit., p. 39.

10. This definition borrows from Daniel Yergin, "Energy Security in the 1990s," *Foreign Affairs*, Vol. 67, No. 1 (Fall 1988), p. 111, who offered the following definition: "The objective of energy security is to assure adequate, reliable supplies of energy at reasonable prices and in ways that do not jeopardize major national values and objectives."

11. Ralph Cavanagh et al., "National Energy Policy," *World Policy Journal*, Vol. VI., No. 2 (Spring 1989), pp. 254–255.

12. These projections and others are cited in the California Energy Commission's *1990 Energy Efficiency Report* (Sacramento, Calif.: October 1990), p. C5.

13. Bodlund et al., "The Challenge of Choices: Technology Options for the Swedish Electricity Sector," in Johansson, Bodlund, and Williams, eds., *Electricity* (Sweden: Lund University Press, 1989), pp. 883–947. This book contains chapters detailing similar energy savings potential in other countries.

14. Fickett, Gellings, and Lovins, "Efficient Use of Electricity," *Scientific American*, September 1990. Arnold Fickett and Clark Gellings are, respectively, vice president and director of EPRI's customer systems division. Amory Lovins is

RMI's research director, The article is a consensus document; the only point of disagreement among the authors is the extent and cost of the possible electricity savings. This remarkable jointly authored article would be comparable to Ralph Nader and Lee Iaccoca coauthoring an article on auto safety.

15. "Energy and the Environment," *The Economist*, August 31, 1991, p. 13; and "Conservation Power: The Payoff in Energy Efficiency," *Business Week*, September 16, 1991, pp. 86-92.

16. For an excellent discussion of why efficiency measures have not been more widely implemented in one specific setting, see "Constraints on Increased Federal Energy Efficiency (or . . . If There's Such Great Potential, Why Is It Not Being Captured?)," Chapter 6 in Office of Technology Assessment, *Energy Efficiency in the Federal Government: Government by Good Example?* OTA-E-492 (Washington, D.C.: U.S. Government Printing Office, May 1991). See also the discussion in "Energy and the Environment," op. cit., pp. 13-19.

17. *National Energy Strategy*, op. cit., p. 37.

18. Fickett et al., op. cit., p. 67.

19. OTA, *Energy Efficiency in the Federal Government*, op. cit., p. 31, 75-79. The utility, San Diego Gas and Electric, covered 75 percent of the retrofit cost, which decreased the payback time from one year to three months. The retrofit was profitable for both the U.S. Postal Service and the utility. The OTA report detailed five other highly economical energy retrofits at federal facilities.

20. "EPA Urging Electricity Efficiency," *New York Times*, January 16, 1991. The DOE's Energy Information Administration (EIA) reported in March 1992 that for commercial lighting electricity, cost-effective savings of 72 percent to 80 percent were now possible. See Energy Information Administration, *Lighting in Commercial Buildings* (Washington, D.C.: EIA, March 1992). The EPA discussed those findings in an April 1992 meeting at Rocky Mountain Institute, in Snowmass, Colorado.

21. Fickett et al., op. cit., p. 73.

22. "Conservation Power," op. cit., p. 88. A variety of case studies involving companies involved in manufacturing, R&D, and the like, were documented in "Energy Management Case Studies," a September 26, 1991, paper presented by Jim Rogers of EUA Cogenex Corporation (an energy services company) at the September 1991 Competitek Forum in Snowmass Village, Colorado. A typical example: A $62,000 upgrade of motors in one manufacturing facility whose cost was covered by a utility rebate resulted in annual savings of more than 600,000 kilowatt-hours and $50,000.

23. Rick Bevington and Arthur H. Rosenfeld, "Energy for Buildings and Homes," in Ged Davis et al., *Energy for Planet Earth* (New York: W. H. Freeman & Co., 1991), p. 34.

24. Amulya Reddy and Jose Goldemberg, "Energy for the Developing World," and William Chandler et al., "Energy for the Soviet Union, Eastern Europe and China," in Ged Davis et al., op. cit.

25. Reducing electricity use would have only a small effect on oil use because less than 10 percent of the nation's electricity is generated by burning petroleum.

26. Office of Technology Assessment, *U.S. Oil Import Vulnerability* (Washington, D.C.: U.S. Government Printing Office, October 1991), p. 17; and Christopher Flavin, "Detroit: America's Best Source of Oil," *New York Times*, August 26, 1990.

27. *The Safe Road to Fuel Economy*, (Washington, D.C.: Center for Auto Safety and MCR Technology, April 1991), p. i.

28. Ibid., pp. 2–3. While lowered highway speed limits helped reduce the traffic fatality rate in the mid-1970s, the steady decline in the fatality rate that occurred throughout the 1980s came from technological improvements.

29. Paper presented by Arthur H. Rosenfeld at the September 1991 Competitek Forum in Snowmass Village, Colorado.

30. General Accounting Office, "Highway Safety," Washington, D.C.: GAO/PEMD-92-1, October 1991, p. 2.

31. *The Safe Road to Fuel Economy*, op. cit., p. 6.

32. Office of Technology Assessment, *Improving Automobile Fuel Economy: New Standards, New Approaches*, OTA-E-504 (Washington, D.C.: U.S. Government Printing Office, October 1991), p. 12; and General Accounting Office, "Highway Safety," op. cit., p.2.

33. OTA, *Improving Automobile Fuel Economy*, op. cit., p. 12.

34. "A Fuel-Efficient Grab for Power," *New York Times National Edition*, September 20, 1991, pp. C1, C6. See also "Fuel Efficiency: New Japan Coup?" *New York Times*, July 31, 1991, pp. D1, D7.

35. Robert Ervin and Kan Chen, "Toward Motoring Smart," *Issues in Science and Technology*, Winter 1988–89, pp. 92–97. Bleviss and Walzer, "Energy for Motor Vehicles," in Ged Davis et al., op. cit. The LCP 2000 also accelerates from 0 to 60 in eleven seconds, faster than the average car.

36. Lovins and Lovins, "Make Fuel Efficiency Our Gulf Strategy," *New York Times*, December 3, 1990. See also Jonathan Koomey and Arthur H. Rosenfeld, "Revenue-Neutral Incentives for Efficiency and Environmental Quality," *Contemporary Policy Issues*, July 1990, pp. 142–156. They add: "Under this version of the proposal, efficient cars would receive a rebate proportional to U.S.-made content. This would help protect U.S. jobs and motivate foreign manufacturers to move to the United States, as many have already done" (p. 151).

37. See, for instance, Harold Hubbard, "The Real Cost of Energy," *Scientific American*, April 1991, pp. 36–42, and "Societal Costs of Energy: A Roundtable" (Boulder, Colo.: American Solar Energy Society, March 1989).

38. Theodore H. Moran, "International Economics and National Security," *Foreign Affairs*, Vol. 69, No. 5 (Winter 1990/91), p. 85. Moran adds, "For those concerned about a 'level playing field' for U.S. competitiveness, an energy tax of up to $2–$3 per gallon of gasoline would simply match the burden borne by Asian and European firms."

39. Marc Ledbetter and Marc Ross, "Supply Curves of Conserved Energy for Automobiles," prepared for Lawrence Berkeley Laboratory, Applied Science Division, Berkeley, California, March 1990; and National Academy of Sciences, *Policy Implications of Greenhouse Warming* (Washington, D.C.: National Academy

Press, 1991), p. 59. Similarly, "Energy and the Environment," op. cit., p. 13, cites a Canadian study finding that increasing the efficiency of gas furnaces would cost only $8 to $10 for every barrel of oil saved—under half the 1984 price of oil ($22 a barrel). For a different view, see S. J. Deitchman, *Beyond the Thaw* (Boulder, Colo.: Westview Press, 1991), p. 125. Deitchman, a former Defense Department analyst, estimates a replacement cost of $22 to $28 per barrel, $5 to $10 per barrel *above* 1989 prices. Deitchman nevertheless believes the effort would be worth the cost because of the benefits to United States national security of eliminating dependence on Middle East oil, including the possibility of reducing defense spending.

40.   Idaho National Engineering Laboratory et al., *The Potential of Renewable Energy*, Interlaboratory White Paper, SERI/TP-260-3674, Golden, Colo., March 1990, pp. 8–9 and Appendix F; Weinberg and Williams, "Energy from the Sun," in Ged Davis et al., op. cit.; D. L. Elliott et al., *An Assessment of the Available Windy Land Area and Wind Energy Potential in the Contiguous United States*, prepared for the U.S. DOE (Richland, Wash.: Pacific Northwest Laboratory, August 1991); and Julie Ann Phillips, "Wind Power's Coming of Age," *Electricity Journal*, April 1992, pp. 22–32.

41.   Susan Williams et al., "Renewing Renewable Energy," *Issues in Science and Technology*, Spring 1990, p. 67.

42.   Richard Ottinger et al., *Environmental Costs of Electricity*, PACE University Law School Report to NYSERDA and USDOE (New York: Oceana Publications, 1990), and Olav Hohmeyer et al., *Social Costs of Energy Consumption* (Berlin: Springer-Verlag, 1988).

43.   Weinberg and Williams, op. cit., p. 112.

44.   Idaho National Engineering Laboratory et al., op. cit. The growth in renewable energy possible under the accelerated R&D scenario is achieved without any social pricing of fossil fuels. The study notes that with accelerated R&D for renewables *and* higher prices for nonrenewable energy sources (reflecting their environmental costs), renewables would make an even larger contribution to the United States energy mix in 2030.

45.   Lynd et al., "Fuel Ethanol from Cellulosic Biomass," *Science*, March 15, 1991, pp. 1318–1324.

46.   The statistics are from Christopher Flavin and Nicholas Lenssen, "Designing a Sustainable Energy System," in Lester Brown et al., *The State of the World 1991* (New York: W. W. Norton & Co., 1991), pp. 32–35; and Skip Laitner, Economic Research Associates, Eugene, Oregon, "Designing Energy Strategies to Incorporate External Costs into Public Policy: Where LES is More," paper presented to the National Regulatory Research Institutes' Annual Conference, Columbus, Ohio, September 1988, quoted in Michael Renner, *Jobs in a Sustainable Economy*, Worldwatch Paper No. 104 (Washington, D.C.: Worldwatch, September 1991), p. 25.

47.   Ajay K. Sanghi, "Economic Impacts in Bidding?" *Electricity Journal*, March 1991, p. 57, and *Jobs in a Sustainable Economy*, op. cit., pp. 26–27. See also Economic Research Associates, "The Impact of the Northwest Energy Code upon

273

the Idaho Economy," final report submitted to the Advisory Committee of the Association of Idaho Cities Economic Impact of Energy Project, September 30, 1990, and Steve Colt, University of Alaska, Anchorage, "Income and Employment Impacts of Alaska's Low-Income Weatherization Program," Institute of Social and Economic Research Working Paper 89.2, prepared for Second Annual Rural Energy Conference, Anchorage, October 12, 1989.

48. Flavin and Lenssen, "Designing A Sustainable Energy System," op. cit., pp. 32–35.

49. Council on Competitiveness, *Gaining New Ground: Technology Priorities for America's Future*, (Washington, D.C.: 1991), p. 14. The comparison year is 1988.

50. H. Richard Heede et al., "The Hidden Costs of Energy" (Washington, D.C.: Center for Renewable Resources, October 1985), pp. 9–10.

51. Jeffrey A. Dubin and Geoffrey S. Rothwell, "Subsidy to Nuclear Power Through Price-Anderson Liability Limit," *Contemporary Policy Issues*, July 1990, pp. 73–79.

52. Susan Williams et al., "Renewing Renewable Energy," op. cit., p. 68.

53. Olav Hohmeyer et al., *Social Costs of Energy Consumption*, op. cit., p. 103. Research done for the New York State Energy Research and Development Authority and the DOE put the environmental cost alone of nuclear power at 2.9 cents per kilowatt-hour. *Environmental Costs of Electricity*, op. cit.

54. See, for instance, National Academy of Sciences, *Policy Implications of Greenhouse Warming*, op. cit., p. 75.; "Time to Choose," *Time* cover story, April 29, 1991, pp. 52–61; and "Is Nuclear Winter Giving Way to Nuclear Spring?" *New York Times*, May 12, 1991, p. E4. Wolf Hafele, "Energy from Nuclear Power," *Scientific American*, September 1990, p. 105.

55. *National Energy Strategy*, op. cit., pp. 108–116.

56. "The Role of Federal Research and Development in Advancing Energy Efficiency," statement of Arthur H. Rosenfeld before the Subcommittee on Environment of the House Committee on Science, Space, and Technology, April 17, 1991. This testimony is an update of Howard Geller et al., "The Role of Federal Research and Development in Advancing Energy Efficiency: A $50 Billion Contribution to the U.S. Economy," *Annual Review of Energy*, Vol. 12 (1987), pp. 357–395. They wrote: "Even if it is assumed that these technologies eventually would have been developed commercially even without federal R & D support, say five years later, the net benefit of federal involvement would be roughly $50 billion. This still represents an extraordinary 3000-to-1 return to the taxpayer . . . and it ensures that the technology is manufactured in the United States" (p. 368).

57. The statistics cited are from the study "Energy Use in Federal Facilities" (Washington, D.C.: Alliance to Save Energy, January 1991).

58. Bevington and Rosenfeld, "Energy for Buildings and Homes," op. cit. In 1991, five engineering firms' conceptual designs found a cost-effective energy-saving potential of between 67 percent and 87 percent in a Pacific Gas and Electric Company research office that was already one third more efficient than typical American offices. So the potential exists for even greater savings by the

federal government. Amory B. Lovins and L. Hunter Lovins, "Least-Cost Climatic Stabilization," *Annual Review of Energy and the Environment,* 1991.

59.   It is striking that the two family case histories detailed in a 1991 *New York Times* article on low-income housing both concerned problems of paying for energy. According to the article, which opens by detailing the plight of the Coleman family of Charlotte, North Carolina: "In the past several years, the Colemans have been evicted twice and arrested once for pirating electricity from a neighbor's outdoor outlet. Mr. Coleman said he ran an extension cord to the outlet to plug in his alarm clock after his own electricity was shut off." The article ended with the story of Mary Patton and her two children: "Ms. Patton was still saving for her gas deposit when the fall's first freeze arrived; she and the two children spent the night huddled together beneath the family's electric blanket." "Poor Are Increasingly Facing a Tough Choice on Housing," *New York Times National Edition,* December 12, 1991, pp. A1, A13. Unfortunately, and (as I argue in the text) needlessly, the Colemans' story and the Pattons' story are repeated in hundreds of thousands of low-income households throughout the country.

60.   OTA, *Energy Efficiency in the Federal Government,* op. cit., pp. 39–46. About 20 percent of the HHS recipients live in HUD-assisted housing and receive subsidies from both. See also "Energy and the Poor, the Forgotten Crisis" (Washington, D.C.: National Consumer Law Center, May 1989), pp. 6–7.

61.   Dixon Bain et al., "Study of the Modernization Needs of the Public and Indian Housing Stock," HUD-1130-PDR (Washington, D.C.: HUD, March 1988).

62.   For a comprehensive set of market-oriented regulations to help the spread of energy efficiency and renewable energy, see Alliance to Save Energy et al., *America's Energy Choices,* op. cit., pp. 115–122.

63.   California Energy Commission, *1990 Energy Efficiency Report,* op. cit., p. 83.

64.   Eric Melvin, *Power in the Schools: How Your School Can Cut Energy Bills and Save Money for Education* (Chicago: Center for Neighborhood Technology, Winter 1990), p. 1.

65.   *Energy Management Financing for State Facilities and Public Schools* (Des Moines: Iowa Department of Natural Resources, 1988); and Melvin, op. cit., p.2.

66.   *School Services Program* brochure from the Commercial Buildings Group, Honeywell Inc., Minneapolis, Minn., 1990.

67.   "The Role of Federal Research and Development in Advancing Energy Efficiency," testimony of Arthur H. Rosenfeld, op. cit., pp. 10–21. See also H. Akbari et al., "The Impact of Summer Heat Islands on Cooling Energy Consumption and Global CO_2 Concentration," *Proceedings of ACEEE 1988 Summer Study on Energy Efficiency in Buildings,* Vol. 5 (Asiloma, Calif.: August 1988), pp. 11–23.

68.   "A Silent Cutback Victim: New York's Dying Trees," *New York Times National Edition,* August 27, 1991, pp. A1, A17.

69.   "The Role of Federal Research and Development in Advancing Energy Efficiency," op. cit.

70.   Kaufmann and Cleveland, op. cit., pp. 393–395. The authors note that while

the gap between output and investment in this sector disappeared in the late 1980s, "there is good reason to believe the gap would reappear if the US implements policies designed to increase effort by the domestic oil industry" (p. 394).

71.   In "Economic Impacts in Bidding?" op. cit., p. 58, Ajay Sanghi, chief of the Impact Analysis Unit at the New York State Energy Office, notes that the construction of a $4.2 billion nuclear power plant by the Carolina Power and Light Company raised costs of infrastructure projects in the Raleigh-Durham area.

72.   "The Role of Federal Research and Development in Advancing Energy Efficiency," testimony of Arthur H. Rosenfeld, op. cit., p. 9.

73.   H. Richard Heede et al., op. cit.

74.   Harold Hubbard, "The Real Cost of Energy," op. cit. Hubbard writes that "it has been estimated that if the U.S. produced all its own oil rather than importing it, the increased employment of U.S. workers would be worth $30 billion to the economy as a whole. Many economists, however, would dispute this conclusion, asserting that workers who lose energy-related jobs are absorbed into other sectors of the economy" (p. 38). It seems clear, however, that there must be some significant gain possible through spending money in America on energy-efficient products and biofuels rather than sending money overseas for imported oil (even if that gain is not equal to the full cost of the imported oil). This seems especially likely given that many of the new jobs created by efficiency and renewables would be in manufacturing, which tends to have much higher-paying jobs than other sectors of the economy.

The $15 to $54 billion given as the societal burden of the "military" represents a range of estimates for United States military spending to protect access to Persian Gulf oil. These estimates are from sources that are now several years out of date. The most recent and credible estimate I am aware of is that the Pentagon allocated $64.5 billion for the Persian Gulf in fiscal year 1990 (in 1992 dollars). William W. Kaufmann and John D. Steinbruner, *Decisions for Defense* (Washington, D.C.: Brookings Institution, September 1991), p. 8.

75.   California Energy Commission, *1990 Energy Efficiency Report*, op. cit., pp. 91, C6.

CHAPTER 5: ENVIRONMENTAL SECURITY AND THE INDUSTRIAL ECOSYSTEM

1.   An old parable, this telling comes from Peter Senge, *The Fifth Discipline* (New York: Doubleday, 1990), p. 22.

2.   Quoted in Cheryl Silver with Ruth DeFries (for the National Academy of Sciences), *One Earth, One Future: Our Changing Global Environment* (Washington, D.C.: National Academy Press, 1990), p. 60.

3.   Ibid., p. 103.

4.   Ibid., pp. 114–115. The concentration of CFCs will also increase after a ban because they will continue to escape from "existing reservoirs such as automobile air conditioners."

5. "Ozone Destruction Worsens," *Science,* April 12, 1991, p. 204. "The Vanishing Ozone," *Time* cover story, February 17, 1992, pp. 60–68.

6. Quoted in Stephen Schneider, "Cooling It," *World Monitor,* July 1990, p. 32.

7. Quoted in David Wirth, "Catastrophic Climate Change," in Klare and Thomas, eds., *World Security* (New York: St. Martin's Press, 1991), Chapter 17.

8. National Academy of Sciences, *Policy Implications of Greenhouse Warming* (Washington, D.C.: National Academy Press, 1991).

9. An excellent discussion of these interconnections can be found in "The Earth as a System," Chapters 2, 3, 4, and 5 of Silver and DeFries, op. cit.

10. Christopher Flavin and Nicholas Lenssen, "Designing a Sustainable Energy System," in Lester Brown et al., *The State of the World 1991* (New York: W. W. Norton & Co., 1991). For an alternate view, see Andrew Solow and James Broadus, "Global Warming: Quo Vadis?" *The Fletcher Forum,* Summer 1990, pp. 262–269. For a discussion of the limits of general-circulation models, see National Academy of Sciences (1991), op. cit., pp. 17–19.

11. Florentin Krause et al., *Energy Policy in the Greenhouse* (El Cerrito, Calif.: International Project for Sustainable Energy Paths, September 1989), p. I.1–15.

12. See Silver and DeFries, op. cit., pp. 90–96 and Jodi Jacobson, "Holding Back the Sea," *The Futurist,* September–October 1990, p. 23. Some 100,000 years ago, when the world was 1° C to 2° C warmer than today, the sea level was 5 to 7 meters higher.

13. National Academy of Sciences (1991), op. cit., p. 44.

14. U.S. Department of Energy, *National Energy Strategy* (Washington, D.C.: U.S. Government Printing Office, February 1991), pp. 172–185. The strategy does include a discussion and a chart that suggests the strategy will stabilize the United States output of gases that contribute to the greenhouse effect. This is, however, a projection, and not a commitment. Moreover, most of this achievement is due to projected higher energy costs and previous United States commitments to drastically reduce chlorofluorocarbon emissions, as well as planned reduction in some greenhouse gases that will result from enactment of the Clean Air Act and other previously decided pollution and efficiency measures. See also *Scientific American,* April 1991, p. 14.

15. "U.S. View Prevails at Climate Parley," *New York Times,* November 8, 1990.

16. President Bush quoted in "Bush shy about global warming talks despite Earth Day mood," *Aspen Times Daily,* April 23, 1992, p. 4.

17. One of the best discussions about global warming misconceptions is Stephen Schneider, *Global Warming* (New York: Vintage Books, 1990), Chapter 7, "Mediarology," pp. 191–237.

18. Lester Brown et al., *State of the World 1992* (New York: Norton, 1992), p. 180. "The Politics of Climate," *New Scientist,* October 27, 1990.

19. See, for instance, Peter Gleick, "The Implications of Global Climatic Changes for International Security," *Climate Change 15,* No. 1/2 (1989), pp. 309–325, and Neville Brown, "Climate, Ecology, and International Security," *Survival,* Vol. XXXI, No. 6 (November/December 1989), pp. 519–532. Brown cites the 1987 international study, *Our Common Future* (Oxford, U.K.: Oxford University

277

Press, 1987), requested by the UN Secretary General: "Environmental threats to security are now beginning to emerge on a global scale. The most worrisome of these stem from the possible consequences of global warming caused by the atmospheric build-up of carbon dioxide and other gases" (p. 522).

20. National Academy of Sciences (1991), op. cit., p. 22.

21. The Adaptation Panel of the National Academy of Sciences study on global warming concluded that mankind could probably adapt to global warming. They estimate a cost of perhaps $300 billion to $400 billion dollars, which could be spread over a century, and thus be no higher than $40 billion in a particularly bad year. In contrast, the Mitigation panel results showed that "the United States could reduce its greenhouse gas emissions by between 10 and 40 percent of the 1990 levels at low cost, or perhaps some net savings, if proper policies are implemented." Their best-case scenario is 60-percent reduction in United States carbon dioxide emissions at tremendous net *savings* (over $80 billion a year). The Synthesis Panel, which integrated the work of the Adaptation and Mitigation panels with other scientific research, recommended a variety of measures to spur energy efficiency and renewables. See National Academy of Sciences (1991), op. cit., Appendix A. I believe that the United States could come close to the high end of the Academy's mitigation estimates if the policies discussed in the previous chapter were put in place.

22. "Action Program to Arrest Global Warming," Decision made by the Council of Ministers for Global Environment Conservation, the Government of Japan, October 23, 1990, p. 14. See also "Can Japan Put the Brakes on Global Warming?" *Scientific American*, August 1991, p. 98. The article discusses Japan's plan to invest in environmental technologies, but quotes Richard J. Smith, a deputy assistant secretary of state, as calling for more study before acting: "Whenever the government favors a particular technology, it creates problems for the market to do its work. . . . That may strike some as too cautious, but it is not good to say ready, fire, aim."

23. Quoted in John E. Gray et al., "Global Climate Change: U.S.-Japan Cooperative Leadership for Environmental Protection," Occasional Paper (Washington, D.C.: Atlantic Council, November 1991), p. 68. This ninety-six-page paper makes clear the stark difference between Japan's can-do attitude concerning global warming versus America's "can-study" attitude of calling for more research.

24. Hanns Maull, "Energy and Resources: The Strategic Dimensions," *Survival*, Vol. XXXI, No. 6 (November/December, 1989), p. 500.

25. Richard Ullman, "Redefining Security," *International Security*, Vol. 8, No. 1 (Summer 1983), p. 144.

26. As noted in Chapter 1, a 1984 CIA study came to exactly that conclusion. Subsequently, a significant number of studies have expanded on this theme of the growing likelihood of resource-based conflict. See, for instance, Earthscan, *Environment and Conflict*, Earthscan briefing document 40 (Washington, D.C.: November 1984); Janet Welsh Brown, ed., *In the U.S. Interest: Resources, Growth, and Security in the Developing World* (Boulder, Colo.: Westview Press, 1990);

Norman Myers, "Environment and Security," *Foreign Policy*, Spring 1989, pp. 23–41; Mathews, "Redefining Security," op. cit.; Peter Gleick, "Environment and Security: The Clear Connections," *Bulletin of the Atomic Scientists*, April 1991, pp. 17–21. For a contrary position, see Daniel Deudney, "The Case Against Linking Environmental Degradation and National Security," *Millennium: Journal of International Studies*, Vol. 19, No. 3 (Winter 1990), pp. 461–476.
27.   Joyce Starr, "Water Wars," *Foreign Policy*, Winter 1991, p. 24, and Norman Myers, "Environment and Security," op. cit., p. 28.
28.   *World Resources 1990–91* (New York: World Resources Institute, in collaboration with U.N. Environment Programme and UN Development Programme, 1990), pp. 254–255.
29.   Myers, "Environment and Security," op. cit., pp. 30–32.
30.   "More Precious Than Oil, and Maybe as Volatile," *New York Times*, March 17, 1991, and Starr, op. cit. p. 12.
31.   Peter H. Gleick, "The Effects of Future Climatic Changes on International Water Resources: The Colorado River, the United States, and Mexico," *Policy Sciences*, Vol. 21 (1988), pp. 23–39. Gleick notes that in the 1940s, when the United States and Mexico were negotiating a treaty on water rights, both sides used strong rhetoric. Mexican officials described access to the Colorado River as "a national interest superior to any other," and Californians serving on the treaty committee warned that the treaty would "strike a deadly blow at the country's *national security* by taking water away from southern California's coastal plain—the nation's front on the Pacific" (emphasis added). Since the federal government is obliged to supply a quantity of Colorado water to Mexico, permanent reductions in the river's flow due to climate change could create bilateral problems. See also Gleick (1989), op. cit.
32.   See, for instance, Marc Reisner, "The Next Water War: Cities Versus Agriculture," *Issues in Science and Technology*, Winter 1988/89, pp. 98–102, and Sandra Postel, "California's Liquid Deficit," *New York Times*, February 27, 1991. A significant amount of subsidized water goes to irrigate crops that Agriculture Department programs pay farmers not to grow.
33.   Silver and DeFries, op. cit., p. 121.
34.   Myers, op. cit., pp. 35–38; *Wall Street Journal*, May 8, 1991; and *New York Times*, May 12, 1991.
35.   Paul R. Ehrlich and Edward O. Wilson, "Biodiversity Studies: Science and Policy," *Science*, Vol. 253 (August 16, 1991), p. 760.
36.   Edward O. Wilson, "Threats to Biodiversity," *Scientific American*, September 1989, pp. 108–116, and Mathews, "Redefining Security," op. cit., p. 165.
37.   Mathews, "Redefining Security," op. cit., p. 166. See also, "Tropical Forests Found More Valuable for Medicine Than Other Uses," *New York Times National Edition*, April 28, 1992, p. B8.
38.   *The Economist*, May 11, 1991, p. 25; "How Most of the Public Forests Are Sold to Loggers at a Loss," *New York Times National Edition*, November 3, 1991, pp. E2, E3. The forestry service uses a number of questionable accounting practices to show a profit on timber sales, including, in one instance, amortizing the

cost of a road with a 25-year lifetime over 1,800 years!; "Sawdust and Mirrors," *U.S. News & World Report,* July 1, 1991, pp. 55–57; and John Baden, "Spare That Tree!" *Forbes,* December 9, 1991. According to Baden: "In 1990 the Caribou National Forest in southeastern Idaho spent over $300,000 arranging timber sales and over $100,000 building roads to the timber sites—all of the money came out of taxpayers' pockets. The Caribou forest's managers collected $814,000 from timber purchasers. But of this amount, only $757 made it back to the U.S. Treasury; the rest was kept within the Forest Service's budget" (p. 230).

39.   *World Resources 1990–91,* op. cit., pp. 254–255; "Too Much life on Earth?" *New Scientist,* May 19, 1990, p. 28; and Mathews, "Redefining Security," op. cit., p. 163.

40.   *World Resources 1990–91,* op. cit., pp. 254–255.

41.   Michael Renner, "Assessing the Military's War on the Environment," Chapter 8 in Lester Brown et al. (1991), op. cit., p. 148; Robert Alvarez and Arjun Makhijani, "Hidden Legacy of the Arms Race: Radioactive Waste," *Technology Review,* August/September 1988, p. 47; and William Lanouette, "Savannah River's Halo Fades," *Bulletin of the Atomic Scientists,* December 1990, p. 27.

42.   In this brief discussion, only the domestic effects of some United States military policies are being considered. It is worth noting that the former Soviet Union's bomb program created similar problems for itself.

43.   David Albright et al., "A Smaller, Safer Weapons Complex Through Arms Reductions," *Arms Control Today,* July/August 1991; and David Albright et al., "Turn Off Rocky Flats," *Bulletin of the Atomic Scientists,* June 1990.

44.   Congressional Budget Office, *The START Treaty and Beyond* (Washington, D.C.: CBO, October 1991), pp. 64–65.

45.   See *Partnership for Sustainable Development* (Washington, D.C.: Environmental and Energy Study Institute, May 1991); *America's Stake in the Developing World* (Washington, D.C.: Citizens Network, Spring 1989); and Myers, op. cit., p. 40.

46.   National Academy of Sciences (1991), op. cit., p. 81.

47.   Robert Repetto et al., *Wasting Assets* (Washington, D.C.: World Resources Institute, June 1989), p. 2.

48.   Herman E. Daly and John B. Cobb, Jr., *For the Common Good* (Boston: Beacon Press, 1989). See also Lester Brown et al. (1991), op. cit., p. 10.

49.   *New York Times,* February 6, 1991. Between 1979 and 1988, the percentage of Americans with asthma increased to 4 percent from 3 percent. Annual deaths climbed to 4,600 from 2,600 and hospitalization for children under the age of fifteen almost doubled. See also "Link Between Asthma and 'Safe' Ozone Levels Is Studied," *New York Times,* August 6, 1991. New studies are beginning to provide a direct link between pollution, such as ground-level ozone, and asthma.

50.   Robert A. Frosch and Nicholas E. Gallopoulos, "Strategies for Manufacturing," *Scientific American,* September 1989, pp. 144–152. A small, but growing body of literature on this subject is developing. See, for instance, Valjean McLenighan, *Sustainable Manufacturing* (Chicago: Center for Neighborhood

Technology, 1990); Michael Renner, *Jobs in a Sustainable Economy*, Worldwatch Paper No. 104 (Washington, D.C.: Worldwatch, September 1991); and the articles and studies cited below.

51. Ken Greiser, "The Greening of Industry," *Technology Review*, August/September 1991, p. 72. According to Greiser, the term "clean production" was "coined at a 1989 meeting of the United Nations Industry and Environment Program on low-waste and no-waste technology." Greiser also writes that the Commission of the European Communities defined "clean technology" in 1985 as "any technical measure taken . . . to reduce, or even eliminate at [the] source, the production of any nuisance, pollution, or waste and to help save raw materials, natural resources, and energy" (p. 70).

52. Frosch and Gallopoulos, op. cit., pp. 150–151; and Michael Porter, "America's Green Strategy," *Scientific American*, April 1991, p. 168.

53. Greiser, op. cit., p. 69.

54. "Why AT&T Is Dialing 1 800 Go Green," *Business Week* (special issue on "Quality"), October 25, 1991, p. 49; also, in the same issue, "Doing It for Mother Earth," pp. 44–49; "Some Companies Cut Pollution by Altering Production Methods," *Wall Street Journal*, December 24, 1990, pp. 1, 21; the Dow and Du Pont examples come from "Chemical Firms Find That It Pays to Reduce Pollution at Source," *Wall Street Journal*, June 11, 1991, pp. A1, A6.

55. As cited in George Heaton et al., *Transforming Technology*, Washington, D.C.: World Resources Institute, April 1991, p. 17.

56. Ibid., p. 8; and Greiser, op. cit., p. 70.

57. Michael Porter, *The Competitive Advantage of Nations* (New York: The Free Press, 1990), p. 648; and "Making Disposal Easier, by Design," *New York Times*, May 28, 1991, pp. D1, D3.

58. Keith Mason, "The Economic Impact [of the Clean Air Act]", *EPA Journal*, January/February 1991, p. 47.

59. Porter (1990), op. cit., p. 531; and Porter (1991), op. cit., p. 168. See also "California Cashes In on Cleaning Up," *The Economist*, November 16, 1991, p. 79. In the United States, California has many of the toughest environmental regulations, which is giving it a head start in the fast-growing domestic environmental services industry; California may already account for a quarter of this industry.

60. Mason, op. cit., p. 47. See also "For Each Dollar Spent on Clean Air Someone Stands to Make a Buck," *Wall Street Journal*, October 29, 1990, pp. A1, A7. Even if the jobs gained were at the expense of a comparable number of jobs lost, the nation would still gain, because it would have the environmental and health benefit from the reduced pollution. In most cases, however, the nation gets the benefit of increased jobs *and* a cleaner environment. See, for instance, Mason, op. cit., pp. 45–46.

61. "Energy and the Environment," *The Economist*, August 31, 1991, p. 12; and "Some Companies Cut Pollution by Altering Production Methods," op. cit., p. 1.

62. George Heaton et al., op. cit., p. 28. Both the steel and chemical industry examples come from Mason, op. cit., pp. 46–47. The lead phase-out numbers

come from William G. Rosenberg (assistant administrator for Air and Radiation, EPA), "Clean Air Act Amendments," letter to *Science*, March 29, 1991, pp. 1546–1547.

63. Office of Technology Assessment, *Making Things Better: Competing in Manufacturing*, OTA-ITE-443 (Washington, D.C.: U.S. Government Printing Office, February 1990), p. 179. See also "Some Companies Cut Pollution by Altering Production Methods," op. cit., p. 21.

64. Marc H. Ross and Robert H. Socolow, "Fulfilling the Promise of Environmental Technology," *Issues in Science and Technology*, Spring 1991, p. 64.

CHAPTER 6: THE OLD ORDER COLLAPSES AND THE OLD ORDER CONTINUES

1. "Excerpts From Pentagon's Plan: 'Prevent the Re-Emergence of a New Rival,' " *New York Times*, March 8, 1992, p. 14. This draft report of the Defense Planning Guidance for the Fiscal Years 1994–1999 continues: "Even in the highly unlikely event that some future leadership in the former Soviet Union adopted strategic aims of recovering the lost empire or otherwise threatened global interests, the loss of Warsaw Pact allies and the subsequent and continuing dissolution of military capability would make any hope of success require several years or more of strategic and doctrinal re-orientation and force regeneration and redeployment, which in turn could only happen after a lengthy political realignment and re-orientation to authoritarian and aggressive political and economic control. Furthermore, any such political upheaval in or among the states of the former U.S.S.R. would be much more likely to issue in internal or localized hostilities, rather than a concerted strategic effort to marshal capabilities for external expansionism—the ability to project power beyond their borders."

2. "To deter such surprise attacks we can reasonably rely both on our other strategic forces and on the range of operational uncertainties that the Soviets would have to consider in planning such aggression." "Report of the President's Commission on Strategic Forces," April 1983, p. 17.

3. Ibid., p. 5.

4. For all its flaws, there seems little doubt that the B-1 can serve adequately as a platform for delivering nuclear-tipped cruise missiles.

5. Quoted in R. Jeffrey Smith, "Perle Rules Out Warsaw Pact Attack," *Washington Post*, January 25, 1990.

6. William W. Kaufmann and John D. Steinbruner, *Decisions for Defense* (Washington, D.C.: Brookings Institution, September 1991). Kaufmann and Steinbruner project that under the Pentagon's 1991 five-year program of spending cuts, 1996 Pentagon spending for nuclear forces would be $43 billion and that the DOE's budget for the military applications of atomic energy will be another $12 billion, bringing the total to $55 billion. Moreover, if nuclear weapons command the same fraction of America's intelligence budget as they do of our military budget, that would add more than $5 billion to the total. Further, these figures are all in 1992 dollars. Spending on all nuclear-related programs in 1996, in

1996 dollars, may total $70 billion. Since September 1991, the President has proposed somewhat deeper cuts in nuclear forces. This *decrease* in spending would, however, be more than offset by the *increase* required to fund production and deployment of a limited strategic defense system, which Bush has also proposed. For a similar calculation, see Congressional Budget Office, *The START Treaty and Beyond* (Washington, D.C.: CBO, October 1991), pp. 57–75. The CBO estimate of Pentagon costs for nuclear forces under a START Treaty (and following Bush's September 27, 1991, proposals) is $49.1 billion a year (in 1992 dollars) from 1992 through 2006.

7. Kaufmann and Steinbruner, op. cit. Strategic nuclear deterrence, tactical nuclear deterrence, and the nonnuclear defense of northern Norway, central Europe, and the Atlantic Sea Lanes come to $179 billion. Adding in the Department of Energy's military nuclear program and only half of the spending on national intelligence and communications—brings the figure to the $200 billion range. Moreover, much of the spending on the nonnuclear defense of the Mediterranean and the Pacific Sea Lanes represents a response to the Soviet and Warsaw Pact threat. Adding in just half of the spending on those two areas would bring the figure to more than $210 billion. Some numbers could be argued differently—a higher fraction for intelligence devoted to Soviet threat or a lower fraction of DOE's military nuclear budget. But the $200 billion estimate is reasonable. To calculate the full yearly United States cold war spending figures, one would add many other components, including some fraction of our foreign military assistance (and foreign nonmilitary assistance), Voice of America broadcasts, and the like.

8. For the origins of this doctrine, see Michael T. Klare, "Behind Desert Storm, The New Military Paradigm," *Technology Review,* May/June 1991, pp. 28–36. See also "Strategy for a Solo Superpower," *Washington Post Weekly,* May 27–June 2, 1991, pp. 8–9; and Madeleine K. Albright and Allan E. Goodman, "US Foreign Policy After the Gulf Crisis," *Survival,* November/December 1990, pp. 533–541.

9. In a February 1990 speech before the Commonwealth Club in San Francisco, President Bush itemized the third world threat: "Now, let me tell you something about the strategy behind our 1991 defense budget. First, new threats are emerging beyond the traditional East-West antagonism of the last 45 years. These contingencies must loom larger in our defense planning. Remember the threats of Libyan and Iranian terrorism. And remember the liberation of Grenada and Panama.

"And remember the dedication of our American servicemen on duty in the Persian Gulf two years ago, safeguarding not only the flow of oil . . . to the industrial democracies, but an action also welcomed by many small nations over there who were afraid that the Iran-Iraq War would adversely affect their own freedom.

"And remember, too, that there are more than 15 countries in the world that will have developed ballistic missiles by the end of the decade—15 countries, many with chemical and biological weapons. Nuclear weapons capabilities are proliferating, much to my regret and the regret of everybody here. And inevitably, high-tech weapons will fall into the hands of those whose hatred of America and contempt for civilized norms is well known. We will continue to work hard to prevent this dangerous proliferation. But one thing is certain—we must be ready for its consequences. And we will be ready.

"Then there are narcogangsters that concern us all, already a threat to our national health and spirit. And now they are taking on the pretensions of a geopolitical force—whole new force to effect change, and they must be dealt with as such by our military in the air, on the land and on the seas. And clearly in the future, we will need to be able to thwart aggression, repel a missile or protect a sea lane or stop a drug lord.

"We will need forces adaptable to conditions everywhere. And we will need agility, readiness, sustainability. And we will need speed and stealth, and we will need leadership. And in short, we must continue to deter both a global war and limited conflicts in new conditions, and for this reason, we doubly need to continue the modernization of our forces."

More recently, a February 18, 1992, draft Pentagon report on post-cold war strategy stated: "While the U.S. cannot become the world's 'policeman,' by assuming responsibility for righting every wrong, we will retain the pre-eminent responsibility for addressing selectively those wrongs which threaten not only our interests, but those of our allies or friends, or which could seriously unsettle international relations. Various types of U.S. interests may be involved in such instances: *access to vital raw materials, primarily Persian Gulf oil; proliferation of weapons of mass destruction and ballistic missiles; threats to U.S. citizens from terrorism or regional or local conflict; and threats to U.S. society from narcotics trafficking*" (emphasis added); quoted in "Excerpts From Pentagon's Plan: 'Prevent the Re-Emergence of a New Rival,' " *New York Times,* op. cit.

10.   Samuel Huntington, "America's Changing Strategic Interests," *Survival,* Vol. XXXIII, No. 1. (January/February 1991), p. 14.

11.   Hearings on the Patriot missile's performance in the Gulf war, before the Legislation and National Security Subcommittee of the House Government Operations Committee, April 7, 1992.

12.   Theodore Postol, House Armed Services Committee testimony, April 16, 1991; and "Lessons of the Gulf War Experience with Patriot," *International Security,* Vol. 16, No. 3 (Winter 1991/92).

13.   Even if Patriots were perfectly effective at preventing ground damage, they would provide little hope of defending the United States from attack. As Congressman Charles Bennett has written: "To give some idea of the scope of the problem SDI faces with Patriot, consider that a battery of 32 Patriot missiles can defend an area of roughly 40 square miles. If this system were capable of shooting down long-range nuclear missiles, we would need over 90,000 batteries with almost 3 million Patriot missiles to defend the territory of the United States. At present, there are a total of 53 Patriot batteries in existence." Charles E. Bennett, "SDI Is No Patriot," *Washington Post,* February 5, 1991, p. A19.

14. Postol, op. cit., p. 10.

15. Quoted in Leslie H. Gelb, "Right Wing Myths," *New York Times*, January 27, 1991. Gelb notes that Major Keating added the word, "Absolutely," for emphasis.

16. See statement of Frank C. Conahan, Assistant Comptroller General, before the Legislation and National Security Subcommittee of the House Government Operations Committee, May 16, 1991.

17. Testimony of Steven A. Hildreth before the Legislation and National Security Subcommittee of the House Committee on Government Operations, October 1, 1991.

18. See for instance the testimony of Peter Zimmerman at the same October 1, 1991 hearings. Zimmerman, research professor of engineering and applied sciences at George Washington University, testified, "The difficulty of building successful missiles increases rapidly with the size and range of the rocket. . . . After a missile has been designed and built, at least five *successful* full-scale tests are necessary to give its constructors reasonable confidence that it will fly to its target and explode at the proper point in space. . . . [E]arly test versions of new missiles are as likely to loop the loop (as the [U.S.] Trident D-5 did) or to explode on the pad as they are to fly 'hot, straight, and true.' "

19. Leonard Spector and Jacqueline Smith, "Deadlock Damages Nonproliferation," *Bulletin of the Atomic Scientists*, December 1990, pp. 43–44.

20. Raphael F. Perl, "United States International Drug Policy: Recent Developments and Issues," *Journal of Interamerican Studies and World Affairs*, Vol. 32, No. 4 (Winter 1990), p. 135.

21. Waltraud Q. Morales, "The War on Drugs: A New U.S. National Security Doctrine?" *Third World Quarterly*, Vol. 11, No. 3 (July 1989), p. 155; and Michael T. Klare, "Fighting Drugs with the Military," *The Nation*, January 1, 1990, pp. 8–10. See also Bruce Bagley, "The New Hundred Years War? US National Security and the War on Drugs in Latin America," *Journal of Interamerican Studies and World Affairs*, Vol. 30, No. 1 (Spring 1988).

22. Bagley (1988), op. cit., p. 165; Perl, op. cit., p. 125; and "The Newest War," *Newsweek*, January 6, 1992, pp. 18–23.

23. From a February 1990 speech before the Commonwealth Club in San Francisco, cited above.

24. For instance, Frank C. Conahan, the assistant comptroller general, told Congress in October 1991, "U.S. counternarcotics programs in Peru have not been effective, and it is unlikely that they will be until Peru overcomes serious obstacles beyond U.S. control." Conahan said of counternarcotics aid to Colombia: "There is little assurance that the aid is being used effectively and as intended." See "The Drug War," statement of Frank C. Conahan before the Legislation and National Security Subcommittee, House Committee on Government Operations, October 23, 1991 (GAO/R-NSIAD-92-2). See also "Cocaine Manufacturing Is No Longer Just a Colombian Monopoly," *New York Times*, June 30, 1991, p. E5, and "The Newest War," op. cit.

25.   Juan G. Tokatlian, "National Security and Drugs: Their Impact on Colombian-U.S. Relations," *Journal of Interamerican Studies and World Affairs,* Vol. 30, No. 1 (Spring 1988), p. 134.

26.   Raphael Perl, discussing the use of United States military forces in antinarcotics operations in other countries, writes: "An increase in militarization of what is basically a domestic law enforcement problem raises the specter that U.S. aid designed to strengthen the armed forces in their counter-narcotics operations might (1) inadvertently foster abuses of human rights as soldiers are not trained to respect the rights of civilians, and/or (2) could strengthen the military at the expense of civilian government, thus undermining the authority of already beleaguered democratic governments and the very institutions which the U.S. would like to encourage" (op. cit., p. 129). See also Bruce M. Bagley, "Dateline Drug Wars: Colombia: The Wrong Strategy," *Foreign Policy,* Vol. 77 (Winter 1989/90), pp. 154–171.

27.   "The Newest War," op. cit. According to the article, of the nine hundred Bolivian soldiers now being trained by the United States, 85 percent are conscripts with one-year hitches. Many of those conscripts have relatives working in the drug trade who may hire them as security guards, "paying a premium for U.S. know-how." The article quotes one United States adviser: "With few exceptions, all we're doing is training the bad guys."

28.   Tokatlian (op. cit.) takes issue with the "war on drugs" formulation of United States policy, arguing, "The concept of war demands that the predominant instruments should be of a coercive-repressive nature. In this logic, there is no room for the suggestion that demand may be generating the supply. . . . [T]he objective is to enlist the world in a major effort to reduce that supply. The assumption is that a reduced supply would then have the effect of reducing consumption by individuals in the United States" (pp. 134–135). See also Michael Dziedzic, "The Transnational Drug Trade and Regional Security," *Survival,* Vol. 31, No. 6 (November/December, 1989), pp. 533–548.

29.   Theodore H. Moran, "International Economics and National Security," *Foreign Affairs,* Vol. 69, No. 5 (Winter 1990/91), p. 88.

30.   Peter Passell, "Coca Dreams, Cocaine Reality," *New York Times,* August 14, 1991, p. D2. The street price reflects the risk in transporting and selling the drug, not growing it. See also Peter Passell, "Cocaine Policy: Gauging Success," *New York Times,* June 6, 1990, p. D2.

31.   Perl, op. cit., p. 125. Turner quoted in "Cocaine Manufacturing . . . " *New York Times,* op. cit.

32.   It is worth noting that Saddam Hussein's invasion of Kuwait on August 2, 1990, did more than focus renewed attention on the region; press accounts suggest that it helped stave off deep cuts in defense spending during the negotiations leading up to the October budget summit that set domestic and defense spending limits through fiscal year 1996. "New Deployment in Gulf May Slow Drive for Deep Cuts in Military Budget," *New York Times,* August 12, 1990, p. 10; "Peace Dividend: Casualty in the Gulf?" *New York Times,* August 30, 1990, p. 14; "Pentagon Finds an Odd Ally in Iraq for Budget-Cutting Talks," *New York*

Times, October 12, 1990; "In the Debate on Defense, Some Givens Disappear," *New York Times*, August 4, 1991, pp. E1, E2; and "Senate Backs $291 Billion Pentagon Budget Bill," *New York Times*, August 4, 1991, p. 35, whose lead paragraph begins: "Adapting only slightly to improved United States-Soviet relations, the Senate voted late Friday for a $291 billion military budget bill for the next fiscal year that continues to increase the nation's strategic weaponry."

33. For a detailed discussion of America's role in assisting the Iraqi nuclear weapons program, see Gary Milhollin, "Building Saddam Hussein's Bomb," *New York Times Magazine*, March 8, 1992, pp. 30–36. Milhollin notes that in August 1989, the Pentagon and Department of Energy invited three Iraqis to a "detonation conference," where international experts explained to the Iraqis and others how to design the sophisticated high explosives needed to trigger a nuclear detonation. See also *Nightline*, July 12, 1991.

34. It is certainly wiser to overestimate one's enemies than underestimate them. That does not change the fact that we could have achieved the same outcome to the war with smaller forces.

35. Powell quote from an *Army Times* interview, April 8, 1991; North Korea's and Cuba's economic problems discussed in Bruce Stokes, "Millions on the Move," *National Journal*, November 23, 1991, pp. 2850–2854. The article's point is that it is North Korean and Cuban refugees—not soldiers—that the world is more likely to face; and the CBO study from CBO testimony before the House Armed Services Committee, March 19, 1991.

36. Kaufmann and Steinbruner estimate that the United States allocated $64.5 billion for the Persian Gulf in fiscal year 1990 (in 1992 dollars). *Decisions for Defense*, op. cit., p. 8. They estimate that Pentagon plans for 1996 still call for devoting $55 billion to the region.

37. Quoted in "Bush Says Iraqi Aggression Threatens 'Our Way of Life,' " *New York Times*, August 16, 1990, p. A14.

38. Earl C. Ravenal, *Designing Defense for a New World Order* (Washington, D.C.: Cato Institute, 1991), pp. 43–57.

39. General Accounting Office, "The War on Drugs," Washington, D.C.: GAO/NSIAD–91–233, July 1991, and "Shark May Have Been Caught, but a Lot of Barracudas Remain," *Washington Post Weekly*, August 5–11, 1991, p. 25. See also "Cocaine Is Again Surging Out of Panama," *New York Times*, August 13, 1991, pp. A1, A9. Average monthly cocaine seizures are up sixfold between 1989 and 1991. As the article's subhead explains: "Emboldened Traffickers Ship More to U.S. Now Than Under Noriega."

40. James Baker, testimony before the House Foreign Relations Committee, February 6, 1991.

CHAPTER 7: THE END OF MILITARY SECURITY

1. Norman Augustine, *Land Warfare*, 1971, as reprinted after declassification in *IEEE Transactions on Aerospace and Electronics Systems*, September 1986.

Norman Augustine and Kenneth Adelman, *The Defense Revolution* (San Francisco: Institute for Contemporary Studies, 1990), pp. 98—99. The projection assumes a steady rise in overall defense spending in the future, based on "a projection of the history of the defense budget over the past century." Aircraft cost data are derived from an examination of the historical record since the 1920s and 1930s (pp. 90—97). The authors note that similar observations apply to other items of high-tech military hardware. See also Norman Augustine, *Augustine's Laws* (New York: Viking, 1986), pp. 108—114. Augustine and Adelman write of the current trend: "As a historical note, we shall soon have gone full circle, back to days of Calvin Coolidge who, in a moment of pique over having to pay $25,000 for an entire squadron of eighteen aircraft, asked, 'Why can't we buy just one airplane and let the aviators take turns flying it?' " (p. 99).

2.   Spinney and Rogers quoted in *Budgets and Bullets: Improving Our Conventional Forces*, report of the Congressional Military Reform Caucus, October 1988.

3.   Ibid.

4.   FYDP originally stood for five-year defense program or plan.

5.   The five-year defense plans cited here are from Franklin Spinney, "A Defense Strategy That Works," *Proceedings*, January 1990. For a longer exposition of Spinney's analysis, see Franklin Spinney, *Defense Power Games* (Washington, D.C.: Fund for Constitutional Government, December 1990).

6.   Moreover, in March 1990, Senators Sam Nunn and John Warner charged that the Pentagon had not accounted for $100 billion of the cuts necessary to achieve this new FYDP. *Aviation Week and Space Technology*, March 5, 1990.

7.   Other weapons in development in the 1980s included the Navy's amphibious assault ship, antisubmarine warfare aircraft, and advanced tactical aircraft, and the Army's forward air defense system, advanced antitank weapons system, and Air Force's AMRAAM missile.

8.   Although it clearly shares the blame for the defense budget morass, Congress really plays only at the margin of the defense budget. For instance, even though the debate over the fiscal year 1992 defense bill took place during a period of stunning change in the Soviet Union, Congress provided funding equal to or greater than the Pentagon's request for 16 of the Pentagon's 25 most expensive weapons systems. Another 7 systems (including SDI, the C-17, and the Seawolf sub) had only *minor* cuts in the Pentagon request (under 15 percent). Only 2 programs, the Stealth bomber and the MX rail-garrison "received major hits." See "Congress Fully Funds Nearly 70% of DoD's Top 25 Programs," *Armed Forces Journal International*, December 1991, p. 8.

9.   There has been confusion about this figure. The baseline used at the budget summit for 1990—1997 was the 1990 defense budget plus inflation (zero real-growth). The difference between the summit baseline and the final budget is $410 billion for the seven-year period. However, the summit baseline did not accurately reflect what the Pentagon had been expecting to get. In its previous FYDP, the Pentagon had been anticipating 1.7 percent real growth during those

years, not zero real-growth, and as noted above, the Pentagon may have been as much as $100 billion short in making the cuts necessary to achieve that FYDP.

10.   The sources for the figures cited are the Defense Department's "FY 1992/ FY 1993 Budget Highlights Briefing for the HAC [House Appropriations Committee]," and "Analysis of the FY 1992–93 Defense Budget Request," Defense Budget Project, February 4, 1991. These documents indicate that the Pentagon's initial cuts came to only $213 billion.

11.   This 25-percent reduction in force size was often portrayed as a response made possible entirely by the collapse of the Warsaw Pact and the end of the cold war. In fact, the Pentagon was contemplating similar reductions as far back as mid-1988 because of the budget deficit. Internal Defense Department studies from 1988 had suggested that the Air Force might shrink to thirty-two wings, the Army to twelve or thirteen active divisions, and the Navy to five hundred ships. "A Shrinking Military," *Newsweek*, September 26, 1988, p. 7.

12.   Also terminated were the Navy's amphibious ship, anti-submarine warfare aircraft, and its stealthy advanced tactical aircraft, as well as the MX rail garrison (the V-22 Osprey was canceled in 1990).

13.   Current program terminations also included the MX missile and Trident submarine.

14.   As of mid-1991, the Pentagon was still over $300 billion short of achieving the budget summit agreement. The Defense Department has indicated that additional budget reductions are achieved by "management initiatives," which cut $72 billion through consolidation of services and other streamlining, and by the so-called "budget scrub," which eliminated $125 billion in unneeded funding through as yet unspecified means. In other words, over the next seven years, the Pentagon promises to find and eliminate $197 billion in waste and inefficiency, most of which has not yet been made public. The Pentagon's previous overoptimistic projections suggest caution in expecting such large savings. For instance, in 1989, the Defense Department met the necessary reductions of the final three years of the FYDP only by counting $15 billion in unitemized subtractions each year, the so-called "negative funding wedge." The Pentagon also achieved comparable savings by assuming the inflation rate would decline from 3.6 percent in 1990 to 1.7 percent in 1994.

15.   "Pentagon Scraps $57 Billion Order for Attack Plane," *New York Times*, p. A1.

16.   Some of the rise in unit cost is also due to the original underestimation of the cost. As Spinney told Congress in 1983, the Pentagon often projects declining unit costs for its weapons in spite of the historical record. For instance, while the Pentagon had estimated in 1977 that the average cost for its fighter aircraft would be $13.5 million in 1982, it turns out that the actual average was $27 million to $28 million, more than double.

17.   Testimony of Henry F. Cooper before the Legislation and National Security Subcommittee of the House Government Operations Committee, May 16, 1991. The $120 billion figure is in then-year dollars (not inflation-adjusted). The es-

timate for SDI funding over the next fifteen years in 1991 dollars is $100 billion. Similarly, in 1991 dollars, SDIO does not expect funding to exceed $7 billion a year in 1991 dollars.

18. The GAO reports that this level of funding is unprecedented, and so the SDI program cannot be compared to a single weapons system, such as the MX missile, but instead must be compared to the deployment of our entire strategic triad of bombers, submarines, and land-based missiles. In other words, each component of the current SDI plan, such as the Brilliant Pebbles, space-based sensors, or ground-based interceptors, should be considered the equivalent of a major strategic weapons system in terms of cost and complexity. The primary difference is that if one of those elements fails to perform adequately—if, say, the space-based sensors turn out to be the "B-1 Bomber" of the SDI program and end up with very limited capability—the entire defensive system will be compromised.

19. See CBO testimony before the House Armed Services Committee, March 19, 1991, p. 1, and Defense Budget Project, "Midyear Activities Report" (Washington, D.C.: June 1991), p. 2. The report states: "Our research suggests that current Defense Department plans will also require increased funding for weapons acquisition by the mid 1990s, unless funding allocations are made more wisely in the near term."

20. William W. Kaufmann and John D. Steinbruner, *Decisions for Defense* (Washington, D.C.: Brookings Institution, September 1991), p. 55. These numbers are all in 1992 dollars and only reflect Defense Department spending, not overall national defense spending, which includes military DOE funding. The spending assumes a full go-ahead with current SDI plans.

21. Quoted in "New Weapons Cuts May Prompt More, Democrats Assert," *New York Times National Edition*, September 30, 1991, pp. A1, A4.

22. CBO Testimony before the House Armed Services Committee, March 19, 1991, pp. 23–25.

23. U.S. Congress, Office of Technology Assessment, *Redesigning Defense*, OTA-ISC-500 (Washington, D.C.: U.S. Government Printing Office, July 1991), p. 30.

24. Air Force General John M. Loh described what happened in the 1970s: "The services sought to retain force structure, retain numbers of airplanes, retain numbers of tanks, retain numbers of ships, in the wishful hope that over time the ammunition and the spares and the support would catch up. They protected force structure at the expense of a robust capability to support it." Quoted in "Strategy for '90s: Reduce Size and Preserve Strength," *Washington Post*, December 9, 1991, pp. A1–A10.

25. According to the November 4, 1991, issue of *Aviation Week and Space Technology*, rumors that a Joint Chiefs of Staff (JCS) planning group is working on a plan for deeper Pentagon cuts "is causing a rush by the services to protect pet programs in case the JCS study becomes a fiscal reality." The article quotes one official as saying, "The idea is to get as [many programs as possible] under contract now before the roof caves in." Such thinking can only undermine the nation's military security.

26. Kaufmann and Steinbruner, op. cit., pp. 54–63. See also the statement of John D. Steinbruner before the Legislation and National Security Subcommittee of the House Government Operations Committee, November 6, 1991.
27. Ibid., p. 44.
28. *Defense News,* March 11, 1991, p. 46.
29. Kaufmann and Steinbruner, op. cit., p. 62.
30. Ibid., pp. 55–56.
31. Ibid., p. 53. "Air Force Aide Says McDonnell's C-17 May Be $900 Million over Its Budget," *Wall Street Journal,* March 8, 1991, p. A5C; and "U.S. Cites High Costs of McDonnell Project," *New York Times National Edition,* August 27, 1991, pp. C1, C4. The FBI taped a senior engineer at McDonnell Douglas saying that the C-17 is "not up to our basic general quality." "McDonnell's C-17 Transport, Beset by Problems With Quality Control, Is Drawing More Scrutiny," *Wall Street Journal,* December 24, 1991. For recent investigations into the cost-overruns and the allegations of misconduct, see *20/20,* ABC News, May 8, 1992; and the hearings on the C-17 before the Legislation and National Security Subcommittee of the House Government Operations Committee, May 13, 1992.
32. Kaufmann and Steinbruner, p. 67.
33. Testimony of Richard Cheney before the Senate Budget Committee, February 3, 1992.
34. See, for instance, "Gaining Control: Building a Comprehensive Arms Restraint System," Michael T. Klare, *Arms Control Today,* June 1991, pp. 9–13. That entire June issue contains useful articles on arms transfer issues raised by the Gulf War.
35. Kaufmann and Steinbruner, op. cit., pp. 67–76. In 2001, U.S. forces would consist of 3,000 nuclear weapons, 11 Army division (7 active), 17 Air Force wings (10 active), 6 carrier battle groups, and a 231-ship Navy. See also John D. Steinbruner, Statement to the Senate Budget Committee, February 5, 1992.
36. World Bank President Barber B. Conable said in 1989, "It is important to place military spending decisions on the same footing as other fiscal decisions, and to explore ways to bring military spending into better balance with development priorities." Quoted in Klare, op. cit., p. 12. Klare writes that the Bush administration is, unfortunately, "encouraging weapons imports by proposing to Congress that the U.S. Export-Import Bank guarantee loans for weapons purchases, potentially including purchases by Third World countries, for the first time since the 1970s" (p. 12).
37. John W. Sewell and Peter M. Storm, *United States Budget for a New World Order* (Washington, D.C.: Overseas Development Council, 1991). All foreign aid numbers used here are from this report. Other useful reports are *Partnership for Sustainable Development* (Washington, D.C.: Environmental and Energy Study Institute, May 1991); and Janet Welsh Brown, ed., *In the U.S. Interest* (Boulder, Colo.: Westview Press, 1990).
38. Sewell and Storm, op. cit., p. 13. Their citation for this estimate reads as follows: "The 1990 data revised by Stuart K. Tucker and based on his *Update: Costs to the United States of the Recession in Developing Countries,* ODC Working

Paper No. 10. (Washington, D.C.: Overseas Development Council, January 1986)."
39. Ibid., p. 24.
40. For a fuller discussion of such energy aid, see Amory Lovins and L. Hunter Lovins, "Least-Cost Climatic Stabilization," *Annual Review of Energy*, Vol. 16. 1991, pp. 498–507.
41. Al Gore, *Earth in the Balance* (Boston: Houghton Mifflin, 1992), pp. 328–329.
42. From the forward to Philip R. Thomas, *Competitiveness Through Total Cycle Time* (New York: McGraw-Hill, 1990). Bucy and Thomas use the phrase Total Cycle Time rather than fast-cycle time or flexible manufacturing.
43. See "Defense: The Real Debate," *Newsweek*, July 15, 1991, p. 37.

CHAPTER 8: CONCLUSION: THE END OF ISOLATIONISM

1. Quoted in Francis Fukuyama, "The End of History?" *National Interest*, Summer 1989, p. 17.

APPENDIX: PSEUDOSCIENCE AND SDI

1. "SDI Officials Reevaluating Costs, Technology Needed for Brilliant Pebble Interceptors," *Aviation Week and Space Technology*, April 17, 1989, p. 19.
2. On March 23, 1983, Air Force Major General Donald Lamberson, assistant for Directed Energy Weapons at the Pentagon, told the Senate Armed Services Committee that he could not recommend an acceleration of the space-based laser program on technical grounds "at this point in time." See also testimony of Major General Randolph, director of Space Systems Research and Development for the Air Force, before the House Appropriations Committee, from the same day (quoted later in the text).
3. See David Miller, "Conjectural Knowledge: Popper's Solution of the Problem of Induction," in Paul Levinson, ed., *In Pursuit of Truth* (Humanities Press: New Jersey, 1982), p. 23.
4. Karl Popper, *The Logic of Scientific Discovery* (*Logic der Forschung*) (New York: Basic Books, 1959), p. 16.
5. Dan Quayle, "Remarks to the Navy League of the United States," Washington, D.C., March 23, 1989.
6. Robert Cooper, testimony before the House Armed Services Committee, April 22, 1987.
7. These quotes are from 1982 Memoranda released in a 1987 letter to Senator Bennett Johnston from then SDI director Lt. Gen. James Abrahamson.
8. In 1981, the Defense Science Board, the senior scientific advisory group to the secretary of defense and the Joint Chiefs of Staff, concluded unanimously: "It is too soon to attempt to accelerate space-based laser development towards

integrated space demonstration for any mission, particularly ballistic missile defense."

9. Testimony of Major General Randolph, director of Space Systems Research and Development for the Air Force, before the House Appropriations Committee, March 23, 1983.

10. For a detailed history of the role Teller played, see William J. Broad, *Teller's War* (New York: Simon and Schuster, 1992). Interestingly, Teller scorned space-based interceptors, saying: "High Frontier can be done for $100 billion dollars, let us say. But the Soviets can get rid of High Frontier for $10 billion." Teller also said in 1983 congressional testimony: "I believe we should not deploy weapons in space. . . . To put objects into space is expensive. To destroy space objects is relatively easy." Matthew Bunn, *Foundation for the Future: The ABM Treaty and National Security* (Washington, D.C.: The Arms Control Association, 1990), p. 43.

11. December 28, 1984, letter to Ambassador Paul Nitze and then National Security Adviser Robert McFarlane; and "Livermore Scientists Protest 'Biased' Teller Investigation," *The Scientist*, March 20, 1989, p. 1.

12. A variety of useful histories of SDI exist. See, for instance, Strobe Talbot, *Master of the Game* (New York: Alfred A. Knopf, 1988), pp. 195–196; Hedrick Smith, *The Power Game* (New York: Random House, 1988), p. 616; Frank Greve, "Out of the Blue: How 'Star Wars' Was Proposed," *The Philadelphia Inquirer*, November 17, 1985, pp. 1F–5F; and Janne E. Nolan, *Guardians of the Arsenal* (New York: Basic Books, 1989), Chapters 1,4, and 5.

13. G. Allen Greb, "Science Advice to Presidents: From Test Bans to the Strategic Defense Initiative," Institute on Global Conflict and Cooperation Research Paper No. 3, University of California, San Diego, 1987, p. 12. Richard DeLauer, then undersecretary of defense for research and engineering, said he "had no major input" into the speech. Even then-National Security Adviser Robert McFarlane, one of the primary instigators of the speech, has since acknowledged that he knew a population shield was impossible, and viewed the proposal more as a "sting" operation that could lead to trading SDI for deep cuts in Soviet offensive forces.

14. The Keyworth quotes are from Greb, op. cit., pp. 1, 11–12.

15. "Pole: Academy's Scientists Overwhelmingly Oppose SDI," *Defense News*, November 3, 1986; "Physicists Negative on Star Wars," *Defense Week*, March 24, 1986; and Robert Cooper, testimony before the House Armed Services Committee, March 26, 1987. Cooper reported the results of his own informal "poll," telling Congress that after discussing the matter with ABM scientists and engineers around the country, he found that "the vast middle class of engineers working in strategic defense today" believe that a city defense against ballistic missiles would be possible if the Soviet Union agreed to reduce its strategic forces by a factor of fifty or more, to perhaps two hundred warheads, but that against today's threat (let alone a responsive Soviet threat), "they will say not in this century, probably not in the next century unless some major breakthrough occurs." Cooper specified he was talking about a "*true* breakthrough" (emphasis

his), not the "breakthroughs" that defense enthusiasts "tell you [about] almost every week."

16.   "Out of the Blue: How 'Star Wars' Was Proposed," op. cit., p. 3-F. In an interview, Keyworth described Teller as "my father."

17.   Quoted in Talbot, op. cit., pp. 195–196.

18.   This was said by Dr. Theodore Postol, former scientific adviser to the Chief of Naval Operations; quoted in Nolan, op. cit., p. 178.

19.   Memorandum for Undersecretary of Defense (Acquisition): Letter Report of the Defense Science Board Task Force Subgroup Strategic Air Defense–Strategic Defense Milestone Panel, 1987. See also *The Washington Post,* July 10, 1987, p. 21.

20.   Christopher Cunningham, "Kinetic Kill Vehicles," *Energy and Technology Review,* Lawrence Livermore National Laboratory, July 1987; Interview of Richard Wayne, director of Component and Systems Research, Sandia National Laboratory, *National Defense,* July/August 1987; and OTA, *SDI Technology, Survivability, and Software* (Washington, D.C.: U.S. Government Printing Office, May 1988).

21.   Confronted for the first time with a specific price tag, the joint chiefs "expressed . . . concern to the Secretary [of Defense] at some length when we saw the big bite [it] would take out of the strategic budget," in the words of vice chairman of the Joint Chiefs of Staff General Robert Herres at a joint hearing of the Senate Armed Services Committee and House Armed Services Committee, October 6, 1988.

22.   Matthew Bunn, *Foundation for the Future,* op. cit., p. 43.

23.   Smith, op. cit., p. 616.

24.   "Hicks Attacks SDI Critics," *Science,* April 25, 1986, p. 444.

25.   Quoted in Robert Scheer, " 'Star Wars': All-Out Push to Gain Funding," *Los Angeles Times,* December 29, 1985. Flashy, if misleading, demonstration projects were a key component of Abrahamson's strategy. As he told an industry audience: "Performance is the key to maintaining public support for the SDI. . . . We will not be able to do that without showing visual progress. We must get Congress to sit up and take notice." Quoted in Nolan, op. cit., p. 198.

26.   Scheer, op. cit.

27.   *Aviation Week and Space Technology,* June 30, 1986, p. 15.

28.   Joseph Nye, Jr., and James Schear, eds., *On the Defensive? The Future of SDI* (Lanham, MD: University Press of America for the Aspen Strategy Group, 1988), p. 3.

29.   Ashton Carter, "Directed Energy Missile Defense in Space," background paper for the OTA, Washington, D.C., April 1984; "Department of Defense Comments on Directed Energy Missile Defense in Space," May 8, 1984; and John Toomay, Letter to OTA Director John Gibbons, June 22, 1984.

30.   Discussion of delay and declassification of OTA report from OTA press conference, June 7, 1988. See also, "SDIO Response to the U.S. Congress, Office of Technology Assessment Report," June 7, 1988.

31.   See "Perspectives on the American Physical Society Report," Strategic

Defense Initiative Organization, May 1987. See also Defense Department Spokesman Robert Sim, Pentagon briefing, August 13, 1987.

32. According to one of General Abrahamson's former chief assistants at SDIO, Pete Worden, "Once the external affairs office was established for the SDIO, we couldn't carry on the battle [for Star Wars]. It was full of hacks. We needed to do something more than to pour oil on troubled waters. It was a theological argument, and we needed to get out there and convert the heathen." Religious conviction had replaced scientific open-mindedness. One staff member for the chairman of the Joint Chiefs of Staff described the SDIO as follows: "The whole program pits men of principle against men who are mouthpieces. A lieutenant colonel hands up his critique of a system, his supervisor sends it up the ranks, and before long the critic is branded a troublemaker. Whenever the SDIO wanted clearance on something, the timing would be reduced to twenty-four or forty-eight hours for a really complex subject—really outlandish. If they didn't like the answer, [the SDIO] would simply shop around for a contractor who would give them the answer they liked. We called it McThought." These quotes come from Nolan, op. cit., pp. 197, 200.

33. "Boosting Our Scientific Future," *New York Times*, May 21, 1989, and *Scientific American*, May 1989, p. 22.

34. David S. Broder, "Government Over Its Head," *Washington Post*, April 30, 1989, p. C7.

35. The mere fact that weapons can be built is no guarantee that they will work. In this sense, designing, building, and deploying a strategic defense is not like other engineering problems, such as designing a cost-effective solar power system, or putting a man on the moon. As then deputy director of the SDIO Louis Marquet said in 1987, "The problem that confronts us in solving the ballistic missile defense system has been likened to both the Manhattan Project and the Apollo Project. I do not believe that this is a particularly apt analogy—we did not have to worry about the moon moving out of its orbit to dodge us, hiding by some stealth technology, or shooting back as we approached." See Bunn, op. cit., p. 41.

36. While critical organizations such as the Union of Concerned Scientists or the Federation of American Scientists might have anywhere from one to a handful of analysts focusing on the SDI program, the SDIO and its military contractors had enormous staffs churning out favorable reports and dazzling graphics for public consumption. In the summer of 1989, for instance, the administration published a glossy, thirty-one-page public relations booklet extolling the imaginary weapons pictured orbiting high above the blue earth.

37. Colonel Boyd discusses this analogy in "Conceptual Spiral," unpublished lecture notes January 1991.

38. Bunn, op. cit., p. 39. Schlesinger was the source of the oft-quoted $1 trillion cost estimate for a comprehensive nationwide strategic defense, as he acknowledged in "Rhetoric and Realities in the Star Wars Debate," *International Security*, Summer 1985, p. 4. He also wrote in that article: "The historic judgment . . . in the mid-60s was that the cost ratio between defense and offense was on the

order of five to one. In other words, one's opponent could, by an investment of 20 percent of one's own investment in defense, create the offensive forces that would neutralize that investment in defense. . . . It is now hypothesized that these cost ratios have modestly improved since the 1960s, although that argument is somewhat flimsy. . . . Nonetheless, it is clear that the ratio is still strongly weighted against defense and will remain so" (pp. 7–8).

39. Congress had demonstrated some spine in the previous year. In 1988, Congress provided no after-inflation increase in SDI funding, and attempted (unsuccessfully) to direct SDI funding to the most promising long-term technologies.

40. Harold Brown, "Yes on Patriot, No on SDI," *Washington Post Weekly*, April 1–7, 1991, p. 29.

41. Henry Cooper, "Memorandum for Undersecretary of Defense for Acquisition," December 9, 1991.

42. Bunn, op. cit., pp. 32–33.

43. Ibid., p. 33. This conclusion was reached by JASON, a group of independent scientists periodically asked by the Pentagon to evaluate weapons systems. Existing technology is vulnerable to the so-called electromagnetic pulse (EMP), created by a nuclear detonation, which can disrupt, damage, or destroy electronics and other key components. The command, control, communications, and intelligence (C3I) necessary to run the system could fail in a nuclear environment, rendering the system useless. As the Pentagon's head of C3I said in 1988, "SDI command and control is a total and complete disaster. We spent $600 million and have nothing to show for it. We can't show, except for what I call view-graph engineering, how it is supposed to work even for Phase One [of a strategic defense system]." Another serious concern is whether the complex software needed for "battle management" would work the first time, which would also be its first realistic test in a nuclear environment. Based on an analysis of previous experience with large, complex software systems, the OTA concluded in 1988: "There would be a significant probability . . . that the first (and presumably only) time the [ABM] system were used in a real war, it would suffer a catastrophic failure." Both quotes are from *Strategic Defense, Strategic Choices,* staff report of the House Democratic Task Force on the Strategic Defense Initiative, May 1988, p. 23.

44. Ibid., p. 33. This conclusion was reached by Livermore scientists. Ground-based antisatellite weapons (ASATs) typically have at least a 10-to-1 cost advantage over satellite-based weapons, such as Brilliant Pebbles, because satellites in low earth orbit are only in range of Russian missiles one tenth of the time, so ASATs only have to destroy 10 percent of the satellites to punch a hole in the space-based defensive shield. Also, it is much cheaper to fire an ASAT from the ground for a short intercept mission than it is to put a satellite in orbit and keep it there for years.

45. David C. Wright and Lisbeth Gronlund, "Underflying Brilliant Pebbles," *Arms Control Today,* May 1991, p. 16.

46. Testimony before the Senate Government Affairs Committee, January 15, 1992.

47. In his September 27, 1991, address to the nation on national defense, President Bush announced some useful unilateral plans (such as eliminating ground-launched tactical missiles in Europe) that should make it easier for the former Soviet republics to give up their nuclear weapons. He also proposed working with them to reduce the likelihood of accidental and unauthorized launch. Unfortunately, an integral part of his plan is the deployment of United States defensive weapons.

48. The United States is permitted to put one hundred long-range ABM interceptors at Grand Forks, North Dakota. The system we built in the early 1970s at a cost of $7 billion was deactivated in 1976. As Harold Brown has written: "There is no reason to go beyond the research-and-technology development program permitted by the ABM Treaty, or even to deploy missile defenses at the single site it allows. Still less should we abandon or substantially modify that agreement, which remains an essential component of our security policy" ("Yes on Patriot, No on SDI," op. cit.).

49. Testimony of Henry F. Cooper before the Legislation and National Security Subcommittee of the House Government Operations Committee, May 16, 1991.

50. "Strategic Defense Initiative Program," Statement of Frank C. Conahan, assistant comptroller general before the Legislation and National Security Committee of the House Government Operations Committee, May 16, 1991.

National Security Bibliography

National Security: General and Historical

Allison, Graham, and Gregory Treverton, eds. *Rethinking America's Security.* New York: Norton, 1992.

Barnet, Richard J., et al. "American Priorities in a New World Era," *World Policy Journal,* Vol. VI, No. 2 (Spring 1989), pp. 203–237.

Berkowitz, Morton and P. G. Bock. "National Security," Vol. 11, in David L. Sills, ed., *International Encyclopedia of the Social Sciences.* New York: Macmillan, 1968, pp. 40–45.

Brodie, Bernard. *War and Politics.* New York: Macmillan, 1973.

Brown, Lester. *Redefining National Security.* Washington, D.C.: Worldwatch Paper No. 14, October 1977.

Buzan, Barry. *People, States, and Fear: The National Security Problem in International Relations.* Chapel Hill, N.C.: University of North Carolina Press, 1983.

Cleveland, Harlan, and Stuart Gerry Brown. "The Limits of Obsession: Fencing in the 'National Security' Claim." *Administrative Law Review,* Vol. 28, No. 3 (Summer 1976), pp. 327–346.

Daly, Herman E., and John B. Cobb, Jr. *For the Common Good.* Boston: Beacon Press, 1989.

Deitchman, Seymour. *After the Cold War: U.S. Security for the Future,* Occasional Paper. Washington, D.C.: Atlantic Council, August 1990.

———. *Beyond the Thaw: A New National Strategy.* Boulder, Colo.: Westview Press, 1991.

Hirschman, Albert O. *National Power and the Structure of Foreign Trade.* Berkeley, Calif.: University of California Press, 1945; expanded ed. 1980.

Jordan, Amos A., and William J. Taylor, Jr. *American National Security.* Baltimore: Johns Hopkins University Press, 1981.

Kinnard, Douglas. *President Eisenhower and Strategy Management.* Lexington, Ky.: University Press of Kentucky, 1977.

Lasswell, Harold D. *National Security and Individual Freedom.* New York: McGraw-Hill, 1950, pp. 50–75.

Leffler, Melvin P. (and John Gaddis, et al.), "The American Conception of National Security and the Beginnings of the Cold War, 1945–1948" (and Comments). *American Historical Review Forum,* Vol. 89, No. 2 (April 1984), pp. 346–399.

Maier, Charles. "Peace and Security Studies for the 1990s." Unpublished paper for MacArthur SSRC Fellowship Program, June 12, 1990.

May, Ernest. "National Security in American History," Chapter 3 of Graham Allison and Gregory Treverton, eds., *Rethinking America's Security.* New York: Norton, 1992, pp. 94–114.

Moss, Richard H., and Richard C. Rockwell. "Reconceptualizing Security: A Note About Research," in Sergio Aguayo Quezado and Bruce M. Bagley, eds., *Issues in Mexican National Security.* Mexico City: Siglo Veintiuno Editores, 1990.

Post, Robert. "National Security and the Amended Freedom of Information Act." *Yale Law Journal,* Vol. 85 (January 1976), pp. 401–422.

Romm, Joseph J. *Defining National Security,* Occasional Paper. New York: Council on Foreign Relations, 1992.

Schultze, Charles. "The Economic Content of National Security Policy." *Foreign Affairs,* April 1973, pp. 522–540.

Taylor, Maxwell D. "The Legitimate Claims of National Security." *Foreign Affairs,* Vol. 52, No. 3 (April 1974), pp. 577–594.

Ullman, Richard. "Redefining Security." *International Security,* Vol. 8, No. 1 (Summer 1983), pp. 129–153.

Wolfers, Arnold, ed. *Discord and Collaboration.* Baltimore: Johns Hopkins University Press, 1962, pp. 147–165.

Wolpin, Miles. *America Insecure: Arms Transfers, Global Interventionism, and the Erosion of National Security.* Jefferson, N.C.: McFarland & Co., 1991, pp. 1–7.

Yarmolinsky, Adam. *The Military Establishment.* New York: Harper and Row, 1971, pp. 93–95.

Yergin, Daniel. *Shattered Peace: The Origins of the Cold War and the National Security State.* Boston: Houghton Mifflin, 1977.

Economic Security

American Assembly. *Economic Security for Americans.* Ann Arbor, Mich.: University Microfilms International, 1954.

Barnet, Richard, et al. "American Priorities in a New World Era." *World Policy Journal,* Spring 1989, pp. 203–237.

Bergsten, C. Fred. "The World Economy After the Cold War." *Foreign Affairs,* Vol. 69, No. 3 (Summer 1990), pp. 96–112.

Best, Richard, Jr. "The U.S. Intelligence Community: A Role in Supporting Economic Competitiveness?" CRS Report for Congress (90-571 F), December 7, 1990.

Borrus, Michael, and John Zysman. "The Highest Stakes: Industrial Competitiveness and National Security," BRIE Working Paper 39, April 1991. To appear as a chapter in Wayne Sandholtz et al., *The Highest Stakes: Technology, Economy and Security Policy.* New York: Oxford University Press, 1992.

Brock, David. "The Theory and Practice of Japan-Bashing." *The National Interest,* Fall 1989.

Brown, Harold. "The United States and Japan: High Tech is Foreign Policy." *SAIS Review,* Summer/Fall 1989, pp. 1–18.

Chapman, J.W.M., et al. *Japan's Quest for Comprehensive Security.* New York: St. Martin's Press, 1982.

Cohen, Stephen S., and John Zysman. *Manufacturing Matters.* New York: Basic Books, 1987.

Council on Competitiveness. *Gaining New Ground: Technology Priorities for America's Future.* Washington, D.C.: 1991.

Dietrich, William S. *In the Shadow of the Rising Sun.* University Park, Pa.: Pennsylvania State University Press, 1991.

Friedman, George, and Meredith LeBard. *The Coming War with Japan.* New York: St. Martin's Press, 1991.

Harrison, Selig S., and Clyde V. Prestowitz, Jr. "Pacific Agenda: Defense or Economics?" *Foreign Policy,* Summer 1990, pp. 56–76.

Huntington, Samuel. "America's Changing Strategic Interests." *Survival,* Vol. XXXIII, No. 1 (January/February 1991), pp. 3–17.

———. "The U.S.—Decline or Renewal." *Foreign Affairs,* Vol. 67, No. 2 (Winter 1988/89), pp. 76–96.

Inman, B.R., and Daniel F. Burton, Jr. "Technology and Competitiveness: The New Policy Frontier." *Foreign Affairs,* Vol. 69, No. 2 (Spring 1990), pp. 116–134.

Kennedy, Paul. *The Rise and Fall of the Great Powers.* New York: Random House, 1987.

Kuttner, Robert. *The End of Laissez-Faire: National Purpose and the Global Economy After the Cold War.* New York: Alfred A. Knopf, 1991.

Lincoln, Edward J. *Japan's Unequal Trade.* Washington, D.C.: Brookings Institution, 1990.

Luttwak, Edward. "From Geopolitics to Geo-Economics." *The National Interest,* Summer 1990, pp. 17–23.

301

Moran, Theodore H. "International Economics and National Security." *Foreign Affairs*, Vol. 69, No. 5 (Winter 1990/91), pp. 74–90.

Nye, Joseph S., Jr. *Bound to Lead: The Changing Nature of American Power.* New York: Basic Books, 1990.

Prestowitz, Clyde V., Jr. *Trading Places: How We Allowed Japan to Take the Lead.* New York: Basic Books, 1988.

Schultze, Charles. "The Economic Content of National Security Policy." *Foreign Affairs*, Vol. 51, No. 3 (April 1973), pp. 522–540.

Shintaro, Ishihara. "Learning to Say No to America." *Japan Echo*, Vol. XVII, No. 1 (Spring 1990), pp. 29–35.

Sorensen, Theodore C. "Rethinking National Security." *Foreign Affairs*, Vol. 69, No. 3 (Summer 1990), pp. 1–18.

Stern, Paula, and Paul London. "A Reexamination of U.S. Trade Policy." *Washington Quarterly*, Autumn 1988.

Tetsuya, Umemoto. "Comprehensive Security and the Evolution of the Japanese Security Posture," in Robert Scalapino et al., eds., *Asian Security Issues.* Berkeley, Calif.: Institute of East Asian Studies, University of California, Berkeley, 1988, pp. 28–49.

Trezise, Philip. "Japan, the Enemy?" *Brookings Review*, Vol. 8, No. 1 (Winter 1989/90), pp. 3–13.

Tsurumi, Yoshi. "U.S.-Japanese Relations: From Brinkmanship to Statesmanship." *World Policy Journal*, Winter 1989–90, pp. 1–33.

Von Wolferen, Karel. "The Japan Problem Revisited." *Foreign Affairs*, Vol. 69, No. 4 (Fall 1990), pp. 42–55.

Energy Security

Adelman, M.A. "Oil Fallacies," *Foreign Policy*, Winter 1991, pp. 3–16.

Cavanagh, Ralph, et al. "National Energy Policy." *World Policy Journal*, Vol. VI., No. 2 (Spring 1989), pp. 239–264.

Davis, Ged, et al. *Energy for Planet Earth.* New York: W. H. Freeman & Co., 1991.

Department of Energy. *National Energy Strategy.* Washington, D.C.: U.S. Government Printing Office, February 1991.

Fried, Edward, and Nanette Blandin, eds. *Oil and America's Security.* Washington, D.C.: Brookings Insitution, 1988.

Hubbard, Harold. "The Real Cost of Energy." *Scientific American*, April 1991, pp. 36–42.

Kaufmann, Robert K., and Cutler J. Cleveland. "Policies to Increase U.S. Oil Production: Likely to Fail, Damage the Economy, and Damage the Environment." *Annual Review of Energy and the Environment*, Vol. 16 (1991), pp. 379–400.

Krapels, Edward. "Revitalizing U.S. Oil Security Policy." *SAIS Review*, Summer/Fall 1989, pp. 185–201.

Lovins, Amory B., and L. Hunter Lovins. "The Avoidable Oil Crisis." *Atlantic Monthly*, December 1987, pp. 22–25.

Lovins, Amory, et al. *Least-Cost Energy: Solving the CO₂ Problem*. Andover, Mass.: Brick House Publishing, 1981.

Maull, Hanns. "Energy and Resources: The Strategic Dimensions." *Survival*, Vol. XXXI, No. 6 (November/December 1989), pp. 500–518.

———. "Oil and Influence: The Oil Weapon Examined," in Gregory F. Treverton, ed., *Energy and Security*. London: International Institute for Strategic Studies, 1980, pp. 3–39.

Morse, Edward L. "The Coming Oil Revolution." *Foreign Affairs*, Vol. 69, No. 5 (Winter 1990/91), pp. 36–56.

Office of Technology Assessment. *U.S. Oil Import Vulnerability: The Technical Replacement Capability*. Washington, D.C.: U.S. Government Printing Office, October 1991.

Romm, Joseph. "Needed—A No-Regrets Energy Policy." *Bulletin of the Atomic Scientists*, July–August 1991, pp. 31–36.

Schlesinger, James R. "Oil and National Security: An American Dilemma," in Edward Fried and Nanette Blandin, eds., *Oil and America's Security*. Washington, D.C.: Brookings Institution, 1988.

Stelzer, Irwin. "OPEC Specter Looms Large," Issue Paper for the American Enterprise Institute. Washington, D.C.: 1990.

Toman, Michael A. "What Do We Know About Energy Security?" *Resources*, No. 101 (Fall 1990). Washington, D.C.: Resources for the Future, pp. 1–5.

Yergin, Daniel. "Energy Security in the 1990s." *Foreign Affairs*, Vol. 67, No. 1 (Fall 1988), pp. 110–132.

———. *The Prize*. New York: Simon and Schuster, 1991.

Environmental Security

Barnett, Harold J. "The Changing Relation of National Resources to National Security." *Economic Geography*, Vol. 34, No. 3 (July 1958), pp. 189–201.

Benedick, Richard, et al. *Greenhouse Warming: Negotiating a Global Regime*. Washington, D.C.: World Resources Institute, January 1991.

Brown, Janet Welsh, ed. *In the U.S. Interest: Resources, Growth, and Security in the Developing World*. Boulder, Colo.: Westview Press, 1990.

Brown, Lester. *Redefining National Security*. Washington, D.C.: Worldwatch Paper No. 14, October 1977.

Brown, Neville. "Climate, Ecology, and International Security." *Survival*, Vol. XXXI, No. 6 (November/December 1989), pp. 519–532.

Congressional Research Service Interdivisional Team, coordinated by Martin Lee. "Applying Defense Resources to Environmental Problems," CRS Issue Brief 90127. Washington, D.C.: CRS, February 5, 1991.

Congressional Research Service. "The Environment as a Foreign Policy Issue" (by Curt Tarnoff). Washington, D.C.: CRS, June 3, 1991.

Deudney, Daniel. "The Case Against Linking Environmental Degradation and National Security." *Millennium: Journal of International Studies*, Vol. 19, No. 3 (Winter 1990), pp. 461–476.

———. "Environment and Security: Muddled Thinking." *Bulletin of the Atomic Scientists*, April 1991, pp. 22–28.

Earthscan. *Environment and Conflict*, Earthscan Briefing Document 40. Washington, D.C.: November 1984.

Foster, Gregory, et al. "Global Demographic Trends to the Year 2010: Implications for U.S. Security." *Washington Quarterly*, Vol. 12, No. 2 (Spring 1989), pp. 5–24.

Gleick, Peter. "Environment and Security: The Clear Connections." *Bulletin of the Atomic Scientists*, April 1991, pp. 17–21.

———. "The Implications of Global Climatic Changes for International Security," *Climate Change* Vol. 15, No. 1/2 October (1989), pp. 309–325.

Glenn, John. "National Security: More Than Just Weapons Production," *Issues in Science and Technology*, Vol. V, No. 4 (Summer 1989), pp. 27–28.

Gore, Al. "SEI: A Strategic Environment Initiative," *SAIS Review*, Vol. 10, No. 1 (Winter/Spring 1990), pp. 59–71.

Harvey, Hal. "Natural Security." *Nuclear Times*, March/April 1988, pp. 24–26.

Hoagland, Sara, and Susan Conbere. *Environmental Stress and National Security*. College Park, Md.: Center for Global Change, University of Maryland, February 1991.

Homer-Dixon, Thomas. *Environmental Change and Violent Conflict*, Occasional Paper No. 4. Cambridge, Mass.: American Academy of Arts and Sciences, June 1990.

———. "On the Threshold: Environmental Changes as Causes of Acute Conflict," *International Security*, Vol. 16, No. 2 (Fall 1991), pp. 76–116.

Lipschutz, Ronnie, and John Holdren. "Crossing Borders: Resource Flows, the Global Environment, and International Security," Resources and Security Working Paper No. 1. Berkeley, Calif.: Pacific Institute for Studies in Development, Environment, and Security, March 1989.

Mathews, Jessica Tuchman. "The Environment and International Security," in Michael Klare and Daniel Thomas, eds., *World Security*. New York: St. Martin's Press, 1991, pp. 362–380.

———. "Redefining Security." *Foreign Affairs*, Vol. 68, No. 2 (Spring 1989), pp. 162–177.

National Academy of Sciences. *Policy Implications of Greenhouse Warming*. Washington, D.C.: National Academy Press, 1991.

Myers, Norman. "Environment and Security." *Foreign Policy*, Spring 1989, pp. 23–41.

Porter, Gareth. "Post-Cold War Global Environment and Security." *The Fletcher Forum*, Summer 1990, pp. 332–344.

Prins, Gwyn, and Robbie Stamp. *Top Guns and Toxic Whales: The Environment and Global Security*. London: Earthscan Publications, Ltd., 1991.

Renner, Michael. "Assessing the Military's War on the Environment," in Lester

Brown et al., *The State of the World 1991.* New York: W.W. Norton & Co., 1991, pp. 132–152.

———. *National Security: The Economic and Environmental Dimensions,* Worldwatch Paper No. 89. Washington, D.C.: Worldwatch Institute, May 1989.

Sarkesian, Sam. "The Demographic Component of Strategy." *Survival,* Vol. XXXI, No. 6 (November/December 1989), pp. 549–564.

Skolnikoff, Eugene B. "The Policy Gridlock on Global Warming." *Foreign Policy,* No. 77 (Summer 1990), pp. 77–93.

Starr, Joyce. "Water Wars." *Foreign Policy,* Winter 1991, pp. 17–36.

———, and Daniel Stoll. *U.S. Foreign Policy on Water Resources in the Middle East.* Washington, D.C.: CSIS, December 1987.

Westing, A. H., ed. *Cultural Norms, War and the Environment.* Oxford, U.K.: Oxford University Press, 1988.

———. "The Environmental Component of Comprehensive Security." *Bulletin of Peace Proposals,* Vol. 20, No. 3. (1989), pp. 129–134.

———, ed. *Global Resources and International Conflict: Environmental Factors in Strategic Policy and Action.* Oxford, U.K.: Oxford University Press, 1986.

Index

309

KC-135 refueling aircraft, 72
Keating, Peter M., 185
keiretsu (Japanese cartels), 69, 94, 103–105
Kennedy, Paul, 66
Keyworth, George, 232–233
Kim Il Sung, 192, 197, 209
Knox, Philander C., 40
Konheim, Bud, 30–31
Korean War, 17–18, 44, 205
Kraft General Foods Group, 125
Kuhn, Thomas, 35
Kuwait, 49–50, 160, 191, 192, 193–194

labor, 23–24
Lasswell, Harold, 53, 56–57, 68
Latin America, 41
Lawrence Berkeley Laboratory (LBL), 49, 128, 139, 144, 146
Lebanon, 191, 193
"Legitimate Claims of National Security, The" (Taylor), 47
Libya, 191, 193
Lippmann, Walter, 54, 177
living standard:
   in Asia, 109
   economic security and, 68, 71
   environmental security and, 12, 168–170, 221–222
   reduction of, 34, 48, 59–65
   stagnation of, 12, 13, 59, 219–220, 221
"Long-term Outlook for Energy Supply and Demand," 159
Los Angeles riots (1992), 56, 65, 90
Lovins, Amory, 115, 121
Low-Income Home Energy Assistance Program, 141

M-1 tank, 70
McDonnell Douglas, 73, 202
MacNeill, Jim, 152
Maenchen, George, 232
Mahathir bin Mohamed, 109, 110, 111
Maier, Charles, 54, 55
Malaysia, 105, 106, 109–111, 113
management, 63, 90, 92, 111
   labor vs., 23–24
Mansfield, Mike, 253
manufacturing:
   Asian, 106–107
   clean production in, 33, 170–176, 223, 281
   computer-assisted, 84–85, 91
   distribution system for, 103–105

economic security and, 68–69
employment in, 30–31, 57, 62, 82–84, 85, 88–94, 135
energy efficiency in, 121, 125, 130
fast-cycle, 16, 18–32, 57, 64, 85, 87, 91, 96, 100, 101, 103, 113, 170, 216, 217
flexible, 18, 21, 22, 25–26, 32, 34, 68, 76, 79, 84, 87, 88, 121, 130, 173, 216–217, 224, 225, 228
friction in, 29, 103
government support for, 12, 35, 81–87
inventory for, 29
Japanese, 16, 18–19, 26, 83, 99, 102, 103–105
just-in-time supply system for, 18–19, 87, 88, 103
lean production in, 95, 170, 173, 216
macro vs. micro level of, 31–32
mass production in, 25–26, 83, 95
national security and, 39–40
out-sourcing strategy in, 85–86
as percentage of GNP, 62, 258
productivity in, 62, 65, 79, 87, 91
research and development for, 12, 31–32
services vs., 84
technology for, 11, 61–62
weapons, 216–217
see also automobile industry; products
Manufacturing Matters (Cohen and Zysman), 82
Manufacturing Technology Centers (MTCs), 86, 92, 93, 96, 174
Manufacturing Technology Program, 217
Mao Tse-tung, 24
marijuana, 187, 189
Marines, U.S., 27, 28
market:
   automobile, 26, 30
   computer, 69, 73, 76
   government intervention in, 34–35, 175
   life-style segments for, 26
Marshall Plan, 43, 68, 225
Mathews, Jessica Tuchman, 52
Matsushita, 106
"Meaning of National Security Policy, The" (Lasswell), 53
merchant marine, 40
methane, 158
Mexico City, 163
Michigan Modernization Service, 86–87
Middle East Peace Account, 214
MiG-15 fighters, 17

316

317

Wass de Czege, Huba, 23, 26
water security, 12, 152, 157, 160–162,
    167, 173, 214, 222, 279
Watkins, James, 127
weatherization, 116, 136, 141–142, 149,
    216
Weinberger, Caspar, 237–238
White, Robert, 77
White House Science Council (WHSC),
    232, 233
Wilson, Woodrow, 40
wind energy, 33, 115, 118, 132–134, 136
windows, insulated, 127, 139, 140, 216
Winton, Hal, 23
Wolfers, Arnold, 53, 54
Woodruff, Roy, 232, 236
Woodward, C. Vann, 40, 75
workers:
    blue-collar, 90

lifetime employment for, 22
number of, 65
wages of, 13, 62, 256
white collar, 21, 63
see also training, worker
World Bank, 213
World Climate Conference (1990), 156
"World Economy After the Cold War, The"
    (Bergsten), 66–67
World War I, 26, 41
World War II, 42, 55, 113
Wright, Gavin, 75

Yale Law Journal, 53
Yamaha, 29
Yonas, Gerold, 234

Zimmerman, Peter, 285
Zysman, John, 82